THE
ST⚥NE
FRIGATE

KATE ARMSTRONG

THE
ST♀NE
FRIGATE

The Royal Military College's
First Female Cadet Speaks Out

DUNDURN
TORONTO

Cover image: RMC Archives
Printer: Webcom, a division of Marquis Book Printing Inc.

Library and Archives Canada Cataloguing in Publication

Armstrong, Kate, 1962-, author
    The stone frigate : the Royal Military College's first female cadet speaks out
/ Kate Armstrong.

Issued in print and electronic formats.
ISBN 978-1-4597-4405-9 (softcover).--ISBN 978-1-4597-4406-6 (PDF).--
ISBN 978-1-4597-4407-3 (EPUB)

    1. Armstrong, Kate, 1962-. 2. Royal Military College of Canada. 3. Women military cadets--Canada--Biography. 4. Women soldiers--Canada--Biography. 5. Women and the military--Canada. 6. Discrimination in the military--Canada. 7. Sexism in higher education--Canada. 8. Sex discrimination in higher education--Canada. I. Title.

U444.K5R1 2019   355.0071171372   C2018-906506-0
                                                 C2018-906507-9

1   2   3   4   5   23   22   21   20   19

Conseil des Arts
du Canada

Canada Council
for the Arts

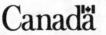

ONTARIO ARTS COUNCIL
CONSEIL DES ARTS DE L'ONTARIO
an Ontario government agency
un organisme du gouvernement de l'Ontario

We acknowledge the support of the **Canada Council for the Arts**, which last year invested $153 million to bring the arts to Canadians throughout the country, and the **Ontario Arts Council** for our publishing program. We also acknowledge the financial support of the Government of Ontario, through the **Ontario Book Publishing Tax Credit** and **Ontario Creates**, and the **Government of Canada**.

Nous remercions le **Conseil des arts du Canada** de son soutien. L'an dernier, le Conseil a investi 153 millions de dollars pour mettre de l'art dans la vie des Canadiennes et des Canadiens de tout le pays.

Care has been taken to trace the ownership of copyright material used in this book. The author and the publisher welcome any information enabling them to rectify any references or credits in subsequent editions.
— *J. Kirk Howard, President*

The publisher is not responsible for websites or their content unless they are owned by the publisher.

Printed and bound in Canada.

VISIT US AT

 dundurn.com | @dundurnpress | dundurnpress | dundurnpress

Dundurn
3 Church Street, Suite 500
Toronto, Ontario, Canada
M5E 1M2

For the First Thirty-Two Women

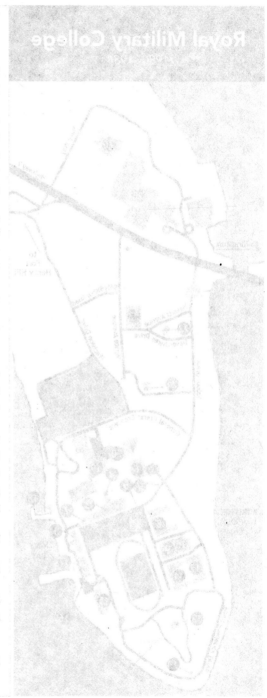

Royal Military College

PREFACE

A question I have been asked frequently during my adult life is why I ever wanted to go to the Royal Military College, or RMC. My answer has been correct to a point: I wanted to be an air force pilot and to pay my own way through university. But, of course, it was more complicated than that. The real answer is that I didn't actually set out to go there at all.

At sixteen years old, in 1978, I earned my glider pilot licence through the Royal Canadian Air Cadets, and from the moment my wings were pinned onto my uniform, I knew I wanted to become a professional military pilot. I had no idea that women weren't eligible to be pilots yet. In fact, I had no conception of the realities of military life whatsoever. I was not alone in this. Years later, few of us, male or female — even the ones who had grown up as army brats — had a clear sense of what was about to happen when we entered RMC.

I was one of thirty-two women surrounded by eight hundred male cadets. In my naïveté, I thought that we would be welcome, now that it was the law to include us. We were not welcome. In reality, the military solution to the quandary presented by the presence of women was to put an end to the farce before it picked up traction. If every female cadet quit or failed out, there could be no further question of our capability to meet the rigorous demands of military college life.

What happened to me happened because I was a woman, and not a quiet woman, not a compliant woman. I figured out quickly that they wanted me to quit. At the time, I didn't understand that knowing something intellectually didn't protect me from its emotional impact or that I was easy prey for doubt and for feeling less valuable than my male peers. It was as if I believed that the men knew more about me than I did and had more right to be there than I did.

And I was blind to the suffering of the other women. I didn't want to look. I heard the rumours from other squadrons: near-naked fourth years parading the recruit hallways wearing only jockstraps, piss being thrown on someone night after night for her comment made to the press, one woman being presented a dildo at a squadron party, a fourth year fondling a woman's breasts during intramural water polo and being treated with admiration rather than contempt, French Canadian women being inspected by bullying peers outside of their classroom each morning, and intelligent women being mocked for asking insightful questions in class.

Still, I was desperate to belong to the inner circle of male cadets. I was constantly trying to find out what it would take to fit in. Sometimes I achieved the blissful state of being one of the guys, a garden-variety peer. I basked in those moments, in our teasing, laughter, and roughhousing, enthusiastically joining in when they made fun of me or each other and eagerly roasting myself to show it was okay, so long as I was included.

In the years that followed, it was very difficult for me to overcome my loyalty to RMC and to my squadron. It took four years of breaking down my own resistance and self-doubt as I wrote, four years of overcoming my fear that I wasn't worthy to write my story and had no business telling it. Gradually, paragraph by paragraph, I learned to say things as clearly as I could.

This is a narrative constructed from memory. I have aspired to be rigorously honest, and all the people represented in this work are real, individual people, not composites. I have, however, changed names and identifying characteristics to provide them with as much anonymity as possible. I did not keep a diary during the years depicted in this memoir. Dialogue is as accurate as memory allows, though at times I have combined various conversations for the sake of readability and an economical telling of events. Naturally, there is much I have had to leave out.

My point of view is my own and of necessity, limited. I speak for myself, only about myself and those most directly involved in my experience. The process of transforming living people into players in a narrative was humbling and unavoidably reductive, and for that I'm sorry.

ROYAL MILITARY COLLEGE OF CANADA

Kingston, Ontario

August 1980

1

BRACE FOR SHOCK

Classical music blared in the hall with the tempo of a horse galloping across an open field, and Mr. Kendall was hollering over it. "Rise and shine, recruits! You have until the end of the wake-up song to make your beds and be standing in the hall dressed in PT gear!"

I flew out of bed and looked through the window into pitch black. *Morning already?* A backlit clock face shone from a tower across the parade square. It read 5:30 a.m. *It's 2:30 a.m. in Vancouver.* Nausea washed through me.

Meg jumped down and just missed landing on me. We pulled the bunk bed away from the wall and worked together to make the beds. I knew this song from somewhere, but I had no idea how long it would last. I threw on my physical training gear of pressed green shorts and a white T-shirt and rushed to the sink.

"Let's leave the bunks pulled out at night and push them back in the morning," I said through the foam of my toothpaste.

"Deal!" Meg said as she ploughed bobby pins into her bun.

"One minute!" Mr. Kendall, Three Section commander, our section, bellowed from the hall. We shoved the bed back against the wall. The music was reaching a crescendo and the yelling grew more intense.

We opened the door and tumbled out together. Meg stepped left and I stepped right in a moment that sealed our spots in the A Flight recruit hallway for the rest of the term. Twenty recruit bodies spilled out of doorways and stood at attention: four women and sixteen men.

Elated and nervous, I stared across at a room recently renovated in preparation for our arrival. On the door, the international symbol for women's washrooms facelessly stared back at me. Her head floated, detached, above her body. Her arms stretched out to her sides in surrender.

I could smell fresh paint.

The song ended. Mr. Kendall yelled, "It's showtime, folks!"

That was it! The song was from the opening scene of *All That Jazz* — the Alka-Seltzer, the cigarette in the shower, the eye drops, the Dexedrine.

"Fall in outside."

We crowded down the stairs into the cool, damp pre-dawn air to find Mr. Theroux, Two Section commander, already waiting on the parade square. His full lips and dark-circled eyes gave me the sense that it wasn't just recruits who were feeling tired this morning. "A Flight! A-ten-shun! Time to separate da boys from da men."

The fourth years wore navy-blue T-shirts with a huge white spider blazoned on the chest above the letters *SFMA* — Stone Frigate Military Academy. I vied for a spot in the middle of the pack. I despised morning runs.

"A Flight, repeat after me," commanded Mr. Kendall with a hint of playfulness. We mimicked him as he leaned his head back and yelled, "Yea stone, yea boat, yea, yea, stone boat!"

A responding cry from the seven recruit flights formed up across the parade square reverberated over us: "Stone boats don't float! Stone boats don't float!"

Mr. Kendall drew in a deep breath and shuddered in feigned enjoyment. I got it. Hudson Squadron stood alone in the cadet wing, as the undergraduate student body was known, in more ways than just our dorm being separate from everyone else's. We were special and we owned it. I could handle being universally despised by the rest of the cadet wing if there was pride in it.

The morning run pace was double time, only twice as fast as walking. I took heart. *I can do this!* I was an athlete. I had just made it through ten weeks of basic officer training and seventy morning runs. How hard could it be? Half these guys looked like scrawny teenage boys.

We ran platoon style down a little slope and out onto a gravel road along the water, passing between an old boathouse on the right with an eclectic flotilla secured to a concrete jetty and a modern academic complex on the left, which appeared to interconnect over a few acres of land. From there, we crossed an expansive undeveloped field and then took a right uphill on a long, winding road toward the Fort Henry National Historic Site and down a steep path along the backside of the fort to the St. Lawrence River. I caught my first glimpse of the Thousand Islands.

We had run about three kilometres when the path, now as narrow as a goat trail, turned up a steep hill. The Stone Frigate came into view across a small bay. The old, yellow limestone building stood alone, separated from the other cadet dorms by 200 metres of parade square. The sun rose in a splash of colour across the phallic-shaped peninsula of the RMC grounds jutting out between Navy Bay on this side and Kingston Harbour at the mouth of the Rideau Canal on the other.

"Break ranks for Heartbreak Hill!" ordered Mr. Kendall. We morphed into a single line. One of the guys stopped dead in his tracks and grabbed his side.

"Let's go!" Mr. Kendall screamed at him. "Are you a fucking pussy, Recruit Dahl?"

"No, Mr. Kendall!"

"You can't even keep up with the girls. Doesn't that make you a pussy, Dahl?"

"Yes, Mr. Kendall! I have a cramp."

"No one cares, Dahl! If you're looking for sympathy, you'll find it in the dictionary between shit and syphilis!"

"Yes, Mr. Kendall!" Dahl hollered. He was feigning an effort to run again as I shuffled past him on the path. He looked like he was going to cry, bending over now, clutching his side. He had an athletic build like Moose from the Archie comics. I left him behind.

"Passed by a girl, Dahl! Have you no shame?"

I cringed at being singled out by Mr. Kendall. I didn't like him broadcasting the fact that I was female. I wanted him — and the rest of A Flight — to see me as just another one of the guys.

Mr. Kendall remained behind with Dahl. We reformed ranks at the top of the hill and ran on without Dahl. When we reached the edge of the field, Mr. Theroux turned us around.

"Time to pick up da trash," Theroux said. "No one get left be'ind, if you know what I mean."

Loud and clear. If you drop out, the entire flight will suffer.

We ran back up the hill, scooped up Dahl, and turned back toward home. He winced with each stride but stayed in our ranks. I wanted to punch him. One stride at a time, I concentrated on controlled breathing, keeping cadence with the centipede of legs shuffling alongside me. The repeat of the hill was a killer. I felt shaky with exhaustion.

We arrived back at the Frigate just after 3:30 a.m. Vancouver time. At this hour the previous morning, before our long day of travel to RMC, I had still been asleep in my bunk, freshly graduated from basic officer training on the West Coast at Canadian Forces Base (CFB) Chilliwack. That night, when we had first stepped off the recruit buses from the Ottawa airport into the Kingston evening air, I was struck by an almost tropical humidity. In the distance, someone was playing a lament on the bagpipes and the notes squeezed in my chest. I was frightened. I didn't know how to be a cadet at military college or how I should act.

I had been assigned to One Squadron in the dreaded Stone Frigate and formed up at the stanchion holding a navy-blue burgee, a tiny triangular flag, with a white number one on it. The flight leader had told us to stand easy and look in his direction. He was formally dressed in a scarlet uniform. His red doeskin tunic fit like a second skin, a red sash crossed his chest from his right shoulder to his left hip, his sleeves were adorned with badges, and his gold-trimmed pillbox hat hung precariously off the right side of his head, held on by a thin black chinstrap. He was good-looking in a dark, brooding way, like a pirate.

"Welcome to the Royal Military College of Canada," he said. "I'm Fourth Year Donald Morgan, your recruit flight leader for One Squadron, known as Hudson Squadron. Do not speak unless I address you. Call me Mr. Morgan. Do not call me sir. We are all officer cadets here. First thing, grab your bags off the truck and get back here. STAT. Dismissed!"

We raced as a gang, alongside the other recruit flights, to the army truck full of luggage that had trailed our buses from Ottawa. I jostled for position at the ladder to get on the truck and help unload bags. A big guy shoved me aside and went up before me. I gained my balance and scrambled up behind him. I stood with the men, hurling luggage to the waiting arms below. I knew that first impressions were lasting impressions and if I could appear keen from the beginning, it would save me hassles later. Soon the truck was cleared, and I jumped down and found my bags. Then we were marched straight into the Frigate and assigned our roommates. Recruit term had officially begun.

For the next six weeks, we would have no control over whom we lived with or talked to, what we did, or where we went. Rumours had circulated at basic training about recruit-term hazing, physical exhaustion, lots of yelling, mind games, even death — at least one recruit had died running the obstacle course. Less than half of us would graduate.

I knew it was a game. They could haze me but they couldn't really harm me. They called it recruit training, though it wasn't really training but a test designed to crack us and expose our emotional underbellies, to see if we had the guts to be cadets at RMC and, later, officers in the military. I felt ready to face the big tests, physical and emotional, but as an eighteen-year-old girl, the concept of psychological warfare was lost on me.

That morning, after our run, Mr. Morgan met us in the recruit hallway. He was dressed in the dress of the day, the No. 5 uniform of navy-blue pants with red piping, a tricoloured belt, and a light-green short-sleeved shirt. He still wore his red sash, indicating his cadet rank of three barmen, from the night before. He gave us seven minutes to shower, dress, and be standing in the hall. The four women of A Flight — Meg Carter, Nanette Travers, Nancy Sloane, and me — stood smiling at each other in the women's shower room, introducing ourselves in whispers. We didn't have to say it. No men allowed. We could hear screaming from down the hall, coming from the men's shower room, as the fourth years lorded it over the guys. Being amongst the first women to enter RMC, we had no one above us to supervise showers.

Back in our room, I put on my work dress uniform, consisting of an oversized cyan-coloured heavy cotton shirt, forest-green trousers, black belt, and parade boots. We would not earn the right to wear first-year cadet uniforms until we passed recruit term in October. I ran my fingers through my damp brown pixie cut and tugged on my green beret to contain it. Meg fussed with bobby pins to resecure her bun. I was glad I had cut my hair off.

"One minute, A Flight!"

Mr. Jansen, One Section commander, was peacocking up and down the hall, screaming at the top of his lungs. "Move it, dogs!" Jansen was a wiry, slightly stooped cadet who looked much older than a fourth-year university student. When he strained to be loud, his voice cracked, breaking into a higher pitch like a teenage boy's.

"Five seconds!" There was a mad shuffle. Fitzroy rushed out and into his spot.

"Recruit Fitzroy. You're late," Mr. Kendall said. "What's the delay, Fitzroy? Recruit Holbrook was out here on time."

"I couldn't find my beret, Mr. Kendall."

"Why didn't you help him, Holbrook?"

"No excuse, Mr. Kendall!" Holbrook yelled. At basic training, we had quickly learned that no matter how genuine a request for an explanation seemed, it wasn't.

"So you biffed your bud. B-I-F-F. Biff. Buddy fuck. That's what we call it, Holbrook," said Mr. Kendall. He was mid-sized and pudgy. He looked unkempt, like he was dressed in someone else's uniform.

Mr. Morgan was back in charge. Everything about him was keen: his mannerisms, his calculated pace of speech, his deep nasal voice, his piercing green eyes. He seemed like one of those cadets who does everything right — perfect posture, expert marksmanship, academic excellence, ability to speak two languages, athletic prowess, boots polished to shine like a glassy body of calm water.

"Listen up, people. You need each other. You will *not* make it here on your own. Forget standing out or being a superstar. You're a team now. Without your flight mates, you're *nobody*. If you didn't already know it, everything here is a competition. Winning is all that matters."

I looked back at the floating head on the bathroom door. I noticed a spider walking along the top edge of the door moulding. Its body was rotund and its leg joints were visible from across the hall. I shuddered involuntarily and looked away.

Now Mr. Morgan was telling us that our mascot was a spider, and he was shouting our squadron cheer. "Yea stone, yea boat ..."

Then he told us the rules. No food, no booze, no cigarettes, no personal books or possessions, nothing in our rooms but uniforms, rifles, and issued kit of bedding, towels, and sports gear. One framed personal photo was permitted on our desk. No talking after lights out. Recruits slept with their doors open. "Use of fire escape stairs is a second-year privilege unless there is an actual fire. All movement within the hall will be done using proper drill: quick time during the day, slow time during the evenings. Keep right shoulders as close to the wall as possible. Stay out of our way. Make proper turns. No wheels. We're into angles around here.

"Circles are the indiscriminate method we use to steal your time. One circle equals a lap of the track. Circles are run at 22:00 hours nightly. Section commanders will keep your circle tallies. You will continue to run a maximum of eight circles per night until you have run them all. That's two extra miles a night, people. Do the math. On top of all the other shit coming your way, you do not want circles, people. Any questions?"

Cadet Section Commander, or CSC, Jansen snapped to attention, raising his right thigh while shooting his fist-clenched right arm out, both parallel to the ground. His foot slammed down loudly and his arm remained out. He looked like a competition diver taking the last bounce at the end of the board. He spoke loudly, staring straight ahead, exaggerating his pronunciation. "Excuse me, Mr. Morgan, 13117, CSC Jansen, P.D., One Squadron, A Flight, One Section reporting."

"Yes, Mr. Jansen?"

His right arm snapped back to his side and he remained at attention. "I am demonstrating *reporting* — the correct way for a recruit to initiate a conversation with a fourth-year cadet, Mr. Morgan." He spoke in a clipped monotone.

"Well done, Mr. Jansen. Nice demonstration. Show the recruits how to carry on, Mr. Jansen."

We're supposed to talk like robots?

"Aye aye, Mr. Morgan," he answered and executed a sharp about-turn and marched a few paces away. *Aye aye* is the naval way of saying more than yes; it means "Yes, I understand and yes, I will comply."

Immediately, Fitzroy executed the move. "Excuse me, Mr. Morgan, 14456, Recruit Fitzroy, G.A., One Squadron, A Flight ... Three Section reporting."

"Yes, Recruit Fitzroy?"

"I heard that circles are a form of discipline for recruits. Recruits can get circles for infractions of dress codes, inspections, college rules, and pretty much anything, Mr. Morgan," he said, imitating Mr. Jansen's cadence of speech.

"Are you trying to be brown, Fitzroy? I don't like brown-nosers."

"No, Mr. Morgan."

"What's the question? Are you pretending to ask a question, to tell me what you know? Don't waste my time. I don't give a shit what you know, Fitzroy! Take two circles."

First blood.

"Aye aye, Mr. Morgan."

"Carry on, Fitzroy."

"Aye aye, Mr. Morgan." Fitzroy did an about-turn and faced the wall.

"Are you an idiot, Fitzroy? Take two more circles and turn around. Jesus," Mr. Morgan said and jutted his chin at Mr. Kendall, who scowled, pulled out a pocket-sized notebook, and scribbled in it. "Recruit life is a game of time. You don't have enough. That's the game. When I say dismissed, go into your room, collect every time-keeping device in your possession, and bring them back into the hall. You have one minute. Dismissed!"

Meg and I squeezed through the door jamb in the same instant, dogged by a chorus of "Move it!" I found my folding travel alarm clock in my suitcase. Meg was rummaging in her luggage.

Mr. Kendall yelled out, "Thirty seconds, A Flight! I want to see pairs of recruits coming out those doors together like synchronized fucking swimmers."

I took off my watch and held it in my left hand with my alarm clock. I shook with adrenaline. Meg and I looked at each other. "Ready?" I asked.

She nodded. We timed our exit to re-enter the hallway together and snapped to attention. I peeked out of the corner of my eye and could see that most people were back in the hall.

"RECRUIT ARMSTRONG! Quit deking! Take two circles for lack of discipline," yelled Mr. Morgan. A deke was anything sneaky, like looking around or taking illegal shortcuts to avoid running the parade square. "When Mr. Theroux walks past you, drop your time-keeping devices into the box he's holding. You'll get them back for Thanksgiving weekend, which is the next time you will breathe free air off the college grounds. For the next six weeks, your time is ours. We'll keep it for you."

Theroux started his collection at the other end of the hall. My turn came last. I dropped my watch and my alarm clock into the overflowing shoebox. My mind flashed to a movie scene of criminals being dispossessed of their belongings.

Morgan walked to our end of the hall and stood right in front of me, mad-dogging me with a glare. "What's discipline, Recruit Holbrook?"

"Doing what we're told, Mr. Morgan!" Holbrook yelled out at Mr. Morgan's back.

"Wrong, Holbrook. Take two circles. Discipline means taking responsibility for our behaviour and the consequences." He turned away from me now and faced the length of the hall. "No inspection this morning. Today is room set-up day. Let's get to breakfast before all those greedy pigs across the wing eat our share of the food. Fall in outside."

The word *food* unlocked a cavern in me, and my stomach growled. I could have eaten a horse.

2

BREAKFAST

We marched across the square, arms swinging shoulder high, to a chorus of "Left. Right. Left. Right. Left-right-leeeeft." I had done it. I was on my way. I wasn't in trouble all the time like Fitzroy, and I was determined not to be. I straightened a bit taller and lifted my chin.

We dropped our hats near the door on a row of shelves labelled with tape that read "Frigate Recruits." One of my flight mates, Colbert, stood off to one side staring at me. He whispered in French to another. I smiled at him. He glared at me. I stared back in shock, certain that he must have been mistaken. He did not avert his gaze; instead, he raised his eyebrows in a challenge. I looked away and moved on.

A long line of skittish recruits weaved through the sea of solid oak tables. The twenty-foot-high ceilings were held up by a series of castle-like arched support beams at regular intervals. Ten feet up, the walls were adorned with a tidy row of military crests and memorabilia that encircled the massive dining room, which was built to accommodate eight hundred cadets eating at the same time.

"Don't look around, you pieces of shit!" yelled a cadet flight leader, or CFL, ahead of us. The baby-blue patch on his epaulettes meant he was a member of Frontenac Squadron.

"Eyes front, dog breath!" yelled a cadet section commander from Wolfe Squadron, who wore a grey shoulder patch. "What the fuck? Are you crying? Are you a faggot? The girls aren't even crying."

One of the first things I would learn was not to spend precious energy feeling sorry for anyone else. We were all in this together, but also alone. It was an easy trick for me, after my childhood. *If these guys think they're scary, obviously they've never met my mother.* I suppressed a smile and focused on a side table loaded with cold cereals, jugs of juice, and fruit.

Mr. Jansen's voice sounded in my ear. "Are you looking around, Recruit Armstrong? Do you see something funny? Take five circles. The cold table is off limits to recruits. Don't even fucking look at it!" Five circles were the maximum that could be handed out at once.

I noticed the raised shoulders and sweat-stained backs of the other recruit flights ahead of us. *Maybe being in the Frigate won't be worse than anywhere else.* I glimpsed the recruit handbook peeking out, like a miniature New Testament, from Holbrook's front pants pocket. I regretted I hadn't thought to bring mine.

The recruit handbook was full of college history, trivia, lessons in proper etiquette, and definitions that we were expected to memorize. It included not only every fact we'd have to know about RMC, but also the name of every member of the recruit flight staff from all eight squadrons. The recruit bible also contained the name of every fourth-year cadet holding a bar position of three or four bars. There was only one cadet with five bars: the cadet wing commander, or CWC, Mr. Dansen. I already knew his name but didn't know what he looked like. Recruits were expected to find these yelling lunatics, memorize their faces, and greet them by name during any encounters.

Eventually, I had a warm plate in my hand and the choice of scrambled eggs, hard-boiled eggs, pancakes, French toast, hot syrup, limp bacon, greasy sausage, unbuttered toast, and congealed oatmeal. Dishes of light brown sugar and sliced almonds were resting next to large bowls filled with peanut butter and jam.

Four women in white aprons and hairnets, armed with serving utensils, were dishing out portions. *This is just a job for them. They get to go home after work.* I caught a whiff of coffee — I'd acquired a taste for it at basic training.

"May I have scrambled eggs and sausage, please?" I said, looking around for a coffee urn. The woman served my eggs without speaking, shot me a quick smile, and handed my plate back.

"Here you go, honey," she said, leaning closer and winking at me. "Good luck."

"Don't fucking talk to the recruits, Sheila," yelled a yellow patch.

The recruit tables were crammed together by squadron, with five recruits per side bookended by a fourth year at each end as "the parents." The tables were set with flatware, paper napkins, one glass per person, and two jugs of milk. No coffee.

I strove for a seat close to the middle but was edged out by Holbrook and ended up right next to Mr. Theroux. We set down our plates and waited.

"Sit," Theroux said. We dragged out the heavy wooden chairs with a loud rumble and sat. Despite being ravenous, I didn't dare make the first move to start eating. "Say grace, Recruit Pitt."

"Aye aye, Mr. Theroux," Pitt said. We all bowed our heads. The *amen* triggered a flash of hands grabbing knives and forks.

"Whoa. 'Old on," Theroux said and slammed his hand on the table. My hand froze with a forkful of eggs halfway to my mouth. I swallowed the anticipatory saliva, put down the fork, and looked at Mr. Theroux. "Recruit eat da square meals. All h'eyes on me."

He demonstrated the technique: sitting on the front three inches of his chair, back impeccably straight, chin tucked, fork in his right hand, he pronged some eggs and loaded more eggs on with the knife in his left hand, lifted the fork at ninety degrees to mouth level, brought the eggs straight across to his mouth, put the eggs in his mouth, reversed the square journey, and placed both utensils on the outside rim of his plate to form the top two sides of a triangle. The utensils never touched the table. His hands went to his lap as he sat up straight without looking around and chewed. The circular motion of his large lips looked comical, and a shock of thick brown hair flopped down from the crown of his head into his eyes.

Three squares a day.

Maxwell sat across from me and we locked eyes. He had a Stan Laurel quality to him — straight man to Hardy's antics, goofy grin, drooping head, looking sort of tired, but never missing a beat. A smile broke out between us. Food kept falling off my fork from the top of the square on the way to my mouth.

"Somet'ing funny, Recruit Armstrong?"

"No, Mr. Theroux."

"Put your utensils down while speaking during da meal. Take t'ree circle."

I balanced my utensils across the top of my plate as demonstrated and put my hands in my lap. "Yes, Mr. Theroux."

"It's 'aye aye' in da Frigate. Take two circle."

"Aye aye, Mr. Theroux."

Then Mr. Theroux handed me two empty milk pitchers, explaining that whoever took the last glass had to fill both. By the time I had done that, my eggs were cold. I managed a few more square bites of sausage before Mr. Theroux laid his utensils together on his plate at the five-o'clock position to signal that he was done eating. He exchanged a nod with Mr. Jansen at the other end of the table. "Time's up. Breakfast is over. Take your dish to da kitchen and fall h'in outside. You 'ave two minute."

My heart sank. I had eaten barely half my meal. As we rose, Mr. Jansen called out, "Question of the day: Who are the Old Eighteen?"

No one spoke. I thought someone was going to get fingered, but Mr. Jansen said, "Be prepared to answer this question before lights out tonight."

3

THE STONE BOAT

The previous night, fresh off the bus in the dark, I had stood at the focal point of the college, on the parade square, walled in on three sides by floodlit buildings. I felt anxious, like I was supposed to be somewhere else and I was late. I couldn't believe that I had been chosen to be a student here.

The other recruits and I faced the Mackenzie Building, stage lit in all its glory, proudly framing one long side of the square. It was a three-storey grey limestone building with a green oxidized copper roof, a clock tower, and creeping ivy growing up its walls — my exact notion of a private boys' school in England. At our backs, the pavement gave way to a formal sports field with a large oval track and a scoreboard in red and white, the college's colours. The Stone Frigate stood alone on our right, bookending the east side of the square opposite a maze of interconnected buildings on the west side: the facades of the Fort LaSalle Dormitory, the Yeo Hall dining facility, and the Fort Haldimand Dormitory, which started at the square and continued along the entire length of the sports field. A paved driveway with street lights fronted the massive dorm complex and ended at a large stone wall, above which the red roof of the Fort Frederick Martello Tower was visible. The entire grounds were on a peninsula surrounded by water.

When I'd been at basic training, the most harrowing conversations on life at RMC were about squadron assignment: which squadrons were good and which ones were bad. I'd consistently heard, "Whatever happens, pray you don't end up in the Stone Frigate." The trouble was, no one could give a straight answer on what the reasons were. It was just known. The fear mostly seemed to revolve around living in the building itself. The Frigate was a magnificent limestone building erected as a warehouse for the navy during the War of 1812 and was literally surrounded by a moat. It served as a dormitory for cadets assigned to One Squadron, who called it "the boat" and were fiercely proud of living there. They were rumoured to be a strange group of misfits living an existence outside the mainstream of college life. The Frigateers. It didn't take long to figure out that an invisible line was drawn across the parade square that everyone else regarded as tangible. On one side of the line was the cadet wing and on the other side was *over there* in the Stone Frigate: the squadron building in which I had just been assigned to live for the next four years.

The place was infested with huge spiders. An annual tradition was to catch one and train it for Halloween-night spider races. I was terrified of spiders — a fear second only to my fear of ancient, potentially haunted buildings.

When RMC first opened in 1876, the Stone Frigate housed the cadets, and all the activities of the entire university took place in this single building, which led to our squadron nickname of Stone Frigate Military Academy, or SFMA. For a hundred years, drill had been held on this very parade square. In the early years, the college had a stable because back then every cadet had a horse. The newer cadet dorms, for the other seven squadrons, were not built until decades later.

The buildings edging the square had been watching over the evolution of college life since the late 1800s. The night we arrived, they witnessed the birth of a new era. Women had joined the ranks as recruits.

The Vancouver recruiting centre staff had pitched RMC as an Ivy League–style university where the Canadian Establishment — the Eatons, Labatts, Molsons, Bishops, and Pearsons — had sent their sons for generations. It was true that some cadets came to RMC from all-boys' schools like Upper Canada College, Ashbury College, and Eton College. Of course, there were also some boys who had been admitted not because they were good at anything in particular, but because their fathers were connected to the school. But in general, I discovered RMC to be a university populated by a microcosm of Canadian society at large, with cadets coming from high schools in their hometowns and from every type of family in the social strata, their selection driven by provincial quotas and stringent qualifying requirements. An emotional microcosm existed amongst these men, as well; the contingent most outspoken against female cadets were tough-talking, mean-spirited men with loyal civilian girlfriends who saw us as a threat. On the other end of the spectrum were the more benign cadets, kind and friendly but not willing to enter the fray and put themselves at risk of being seen as contrary to outspoken opinion against us. The social construct was wholly unnatural — nearly eight hundred men, eighteen to twenty-two years old, all living together for four years in the dorms on campus. There were no children, no pets, and barely any women. Adult interactions were rare.

The only emissaries from the outside world were the occasional freshwater gulls taking respite on the college yardarm along the edge of the parade square, oblivious to the meaning of the frantic rushing and constant drilling and yelling and activity taking place below their perch.

But I'd learn all this later. That first evening, all I saw was a majestic university. When I had been asked to make a split-second decision about whether to attend RMC or not, my head said it was a chance to do something important for equality of women. My instinct told me it was nuts to put myself through it. I told myself it *should* be right for me, and I *should* commit. I told myself that, as a middle-class nobody, I *should* jump at the chance to rub shoulders with Canada's elite, to make history, and to get away from my mother, all in a single blind leap. I promised myself I could quit if I hated it. In the first moments, I trembled as we marched with our luggage toward the spotlighted walls of the Frigate. A big silver bell hung in a black frame next to the large navy-blue double doors and some kind of heritage plaque was mounted on the outer wall. A creepy stained glass window set above the double doors depicted a bulbous, leggy spider with the number one behind it. When we had first crossed the entrance ramp, I had glanced down into the moat and was relieved to see there was no water, just floodlights spaced out along a grassy bottom.

This morning, we marched from breakfast straight to the college supply building to be issued our Canadian Forces FN rifles. I had my first good look at the Frigate. The parade square was so large it seemed to form its own horizon culminating at the light-yellow limestone building, which looked less ominous in the daylight. Almost pretty, with its clean lines and symmetry.

Back from supply, I was struck by the musty old-building smell in the foyer. We clipped single file up the grand spiral staircase curving in front of us, with its thick wooden railings and faded yellow plaster walls. The stairs formed a precarious-looking fan up to the third floor.

On the second floor, we marched onto a worn cornflower-blue carpet in another foyer. Two hallways extended in opposite directions, one with red carpet and the other with green. Port and starboard, like red and green running lights on a ship. The recruit hallway was on the left with the red carpet. The Stone Frigate was modelled after a ship — albeit a creepy, rundown ship in need of a new coat of paint and fresh carpet.

My new home.

Meg and I shared the first room on the left in the recruit hallway. We dismantled our weapons, chained them onto the custom rifle racks, and placed the magazines and breechblocks into our shared gash drawer. *Now I'm a girl with a rifle locked up in her bedroom.* I hid the gash drawer key in a stack of my panties in the dresser.

Our room was not much larger than a walk-in closet. It had institutional lime-green walls and we were forced to turn sideways to pass each other between the bunk bed and the sink. The bay window had an alcove large enough to sit in and heavy green curtains that closed it off from the room.

I plunked down on the lower bunk, shaking the red metal frame, and yanked off my beret. I ruffled my hair and pushed the heels of my palms against my burning eyes. My stomach made loud grumbling noises and I felt shaky.

Meg grabbed a chair from the built-in desk and sat down with an air of confidence. She was lean and long-legged — we had similar builds, except at five nine, I was a few inches taller than she was. Plus Meg had the litheness of a dancer. At basic training, I had seen her bend in half, hug her chest to her thighs, and slide her legs into side splits until her chest rested on the ground with her arms stretched overhead. I could barely touch my toes. She slipped her beret off and set it gently on the desk so that it held its shape. Her brown bun was still perfect. No pins showing. We had been told to memorize vital statistics about our roommates — and to expect quizzes later.

"How can you still look so good after the day we're having?" I asked.

She smiled. "Good one," she said. "Okay. I'll start. I'm Margaret Carter, no middle name. I'm eighteen." She rolled off all her vital stats including place and date of birth, that she was the youngest of four siblings, the places she'd lived, and the name of her all-girls' private school in Victoria. She finished by saying her dad was a commander in the navy, her mom didn't work, and she was studying engineering.

"Holy crap. I hope I can remember all that for the quiz. All right. Kathryn Anne Armstrong. I'm eighteen. Born in Flin Flon, Manitoba," I said.

Meg laughed. "Is that really a place?"

"For real. My dad's a manager at Eaton's. My mom's a secretary for the federal government. I grew up in small towns all over British Columbia and graduated from high school in Abbotsford. I'm the youngest of five kids; my sister is oldest, with three brothers between us." I told her the rest and ended by saying I had wanted to be a pilot ever since I had earned my glider pilot licence in air cadets when I was sixteen. When I had applied for military service, I was shocked to discover that women were ineligible to be pilots.

"You came here to get into pilot? What are you now?"

"I'm a logistics officer, the only job available to me as a woman studying commerce." I deflected by asking Meg another question about herself. "What classification are you?" I liked her. I wanted her to like me. I knew that if she wanted to know, I would blurt out my whole life story. I wanted a fresh start in a new place with new people. I didn't want Meg or anyone else to know what I had left behind back home.

"AERE. Aerospace engineer," she said. My eyebrows shot up at that.

Mr. Kendall's voice sounded in the hall. "Three Section get your asses into Holbrook and Fitzroy's room, STAT!"

Their room was the closest to us across the hall, next to the women's washroom. Meg and I converged with Maxwell and Becker at the door and entered one by one. It was instantly obvious why Mr. Kendall had chosen to meet there. All seven of us were able to form a comfortable circle — the room was huge compared to ours and had a view across Navy Bay onto the Fort Henry barracks.

"Relax, recruits. This is section commander time. Let's get to know each other. You'll go first, Combat," he said, gesturing toward Becker. "State your name, where you're from, something interesting you're known for, and what you're doing here, in that order. Go."

My mind went blank. *What's interesting about me?* I started to panic.

"Aye aye, Mr. Kendall. My name is Trevor Becker —"

"Don't look at me, idiot. I already know everything about your sorry ass. Tell them."

How could he possibly know everything about us? We just got here last night.

"I'm Becker. I grew up as an army brat, so I'm not from anywhere. My parents live in Ottawa right now."

Mr. Kendall interrupted again. "And your dad's a major general and an ex-cadet of RMC. Isn't that right, Becker?"

"Aye aye, Mr. Kendall." Becker blushed. I'm not sure he wanted us to know that. My panic flared anew. I didn't want Mr. Kendall to talk about my family.

"I'm known for wanting to grow up and kill people for a living. I'm taking military strategic studies and will be an infantry officer."

Becker was the most nondescript of all of us. Plain features, sandy-brown hair, medium height, and medium build. He didn't look particularly strong or fit my stereotype of a future killing machine.

Kendall grunted. "How do you feel about being a recruit in the first class with women?"

Shit. He's not going there, is he? I wasn't sure I wanted to know Becker's opinion.

"I'm good with it. So long as they keep 'em outta the combat arms."

"Moving on. Holbrook, sound off."

Holbrook was efficient and rattled off his answers in succession. "Richie Holbrook. Most recently, I'm from Brussels, Belgium, but I mostly grew up in Rome. My dad's a diplomat. I'm known for being able to do an infinite number of chin-ups. My degree program is political science. I'm going to be a pilot and I'm extremely funny."

"That's fucking hilarious, Holbrook. You are funny. But I'd say you're going to be more famous around here for needing to shave twice a day, Stubble Boy."

Stubble Boy? From where I stood, Holbrook's face had a slight shadow but nothing serious. His standout feature was piercing blue eyes, ringed with thick black lashes that were incongruously feminine compared to his barrel-chested body and gorilla-like arms.

"Carter, sound off."

Meg shifted from foot to foot. "Aye aye, Mr. Kendall. I'm Margaret Carter from Victoria, B.C. I'm known for being flexible. My degree program is mechanical engineering and I'm going to be an AERE officer."

I glanced around seeking signs that the guys were impressed. No one showed any.

"Whoa, whoa, whoa. What do you mean flexible? Are you talking temperament or in the physical sense?" he asked.

"Physical, Mr. Kendall, like doing the splits both ways."

The guys perked up at this news. I instantly saw a flash of regret cross Meg's face. Kendall must have seen it, too. He sprung into damage control.

"Okay, Cartwheel. Maxwell, sound off."

"Nigel Maxwell. I'm from Ottawa. I'm known for being cool." He calmly struck a silent Fonzie-style pose. "I'm studying electrical engineering and will be a communications engineer in the signal corps, and I like having women in our class."

At breakfast, I had liked him instantly — his blond hair, icy blue eyes, and long face came together to form a friendly countenance with just a hint of seriousness. He had thrown down his opinion on our side. I suppressed a smile of relief at having at least one ally.

"Of course you do, Fonzie. Always good with the women. Fitzroy, you're next."

"I'm Grant Fitzroy from outside of Shelburne, Nova Scotia. I'm known for being top of my class since kindergarten and being willing to go the extra mile. My degree program is political science and I'm going to be a naval officer."

"No shit, Sherlock. You probably had to walk to school the extra mile with no shoes in wintertime. Top of the class out of how many, Fitzroy? Two?"

"Seven."

"Welcome to the big leagues, Valedictorian. Okay, Armstrong. Hit it."

My turn. *I'm here because I wanted to put five thousand kilometres between me and my mother and I don't want to owe my parents another thing for the rest of my life.* "Kate Armstrong from Abbotsford, B.C. I'm known for being a basketball jock and a glider pilot. My degree program is commerce. I'm going to be a logistics officer and I'm funnier than Holbrook."

Everybody laughed.

"Dream on, Army," Holbrook jibed and just like that, my hated nickname from high school had entered the conversation. I stayed quiet and hoped it wouldn't stick. I would much rather have worn one of Mr. Kendall's inventions.

"Okay, enough fun for today," Mr. Kendall said. He paced back and forth for a moment rubbing his eyes. "So, Three Section, here's what we got: Combat, Stubble Boy, Cartwheel, Fonzie, Valedictorian, and Army. This is gonna be entertaining. Let's get back to work."

In the end, I didn't see the point of the nicknaming session because we rarely used them. Mostly, we called each other by our last names, even when we were alone.

We spent the rest of the morning receiving a demonstration of intricate kit layout requirements both for day-to-day living and for formal inspections. After lunch, we were sent to organize our rooms. Our door was closed and the quiet was a huge relief. Meg and I took turns reciting the names of the Old Eighteen listed in our recruit bible as we worked. We measured and double-checked every single item in our kit according to the layout specifications given to us. Meg's uniforms faced left, mine faced right inside the closet; hangers were spaced exactly half an inch apart; shoes and boots faced toes out with one inch between pairs; drawer contents were folded to specification and in the correct place. Even my panties were refolded into three-inch-by-three-inch stacking squares.

"Are you scared?" I asked, watching Meg holding a ruler over her underwear on her desk, adding pair after pair to the growing stack.

"Crapless."

"Me too," I said. I suddenly wanted to go home. "Do you mind if I stand on your bed?"

"Why?" she asked. I pointed to a bulbous spider high in the corner above our bunks. Meg shrugged. "It's not hurting anyone, but go ahead as long as you don't leave any marks on the wall."

Armed with a wad of tissues from my purse, I crawled up onto Meg's bed, took a deep breath, and got ready to make a quick stab at it. I gasped, lunged, and ground it against the wall in a sickening crunch. I quick-marched across the hall and flushed the wadded tissue down the toilet. Back in our room, I noticed Meg's ruler hovered frozen over the same pair of underwear.

They confiscated everything that wasn't military issue and we made an attic run to deliver our duffle bags and stuffed personal suitcases filled with "contraband," including my Levi's jeans, Sperry Top-Sider shoes, pink Lacoste sweater, Vuarnet sunglasses, beloved yellow Walkman, and favourite cassettes. Up on the third floor, we pulled a hidden set of stairs down from the ceiling using a rope and formed a fire-brigade chain to pass the bags along, one to the next, all the way up into the attic. My spot in the chain was inside the attic, and I realized it was better to see the attic than not to see the attic. I saw for myself that there was nothing to fear.

4

PANIC

Before going for dinner, the fourth years seemed rested and re-energized.

"I need a volunteer," Mr. Morgan said.

No one stepped forward. I fought my impulse to step up. I wanted to make an impression. At basic training, we had learned the rule: never volunteer.

"Good. No volunteers. I like it," Mr. Morgan said. "Recruit Holbrook!"

"Aye aye, Mr. Morgan!"

"You're my volunteer. Who are the Old Eighteen? You speak for A Flight, Holbrook."

"Aye aye, Mr. Morgan. The Old Eighteen were the members of the first class to attend the Royal Military College in 1876."

"Very good, you idiot! I want names!"

I was glad that it wasn't me on the firing line.

"Wurtele, Freer, Wise, Davis," and he rattled off a few more names, then paused. I held my breath. Holbrook stuttered and then finished the list.

"Close but no cigar, Holbrook. A Flight, take two circles each. Recruit Armstrong. What's the problem with the list?"

Why does he always pick on Three Section? Richie's pause had helped me.

"Davis. The second Davis was missing, Mr. Morgan."

"Right. Take it from the top."

In my mind's eye, I could see names written on the page in my recruit handbook. My chest tightened and my voice felt far away.

"Wurtele, Freer, Wise, Davis, Reed, Denison, Irving, Davis," and I finished the list. The fourth years started to clap, a slow, sarcastic clapping.

"Good job, A Flight. As a reward, you can have dinner after all."

After dinner, we sat in the hall in PT gear, working on our boots together. Earlier in the day, we'd learned how to shine our boot-laces using melted shoe polish soaked into the fabric.

"Tell the recruits the surprise, Mr. Kendall," Mr. Morgan said.

"The surprise is that we are going to help you learn how to panic. You people don't know how to panic. We were talking it over this afternoon and realized it's our fault. We haven't really given you enough chance to practice," Kendall said. "That's not really fair, is it, A Flight?"

"No, Mr. Kendall!"

"You have three minutes to put away your polishing kit, change back into work dress, and be back in the hall with your weapons. Go!"

Meg and I banged heads in the doorway as we reeled into our room. I went straight for the gash drawer key, unlocked the drawer, and grabbed out the breechblocks and magazines. Meg unlocked the weapons. We assembled our weapons and changed into our work dress uniforms. We folded and put away our PT gear, looked at each other, and stepped out in the hall at the same moment. The smell of hot tin and burnt wax lingered in the air.

"You're late, people!" Mr. Morgan yelled. "Get down and give me twenty!" We laid our rifles down, dropped to the floor, and cranked out twenty push-ups. I strained for the last three, being careful not to scuff the toes of my boots, cheating by not dropping all the way to the floor.

"Secure your weapons and change back into your PT gear, and let's take it from the top. Don't think you can get tricky. You must learn to work together, help each other. Be smart. Be efficient. Go!"

In and out. We did the drill so many times that I didn't know if we were coming or going. I started to feel like one of Dr. Seuss's Sneetches. Mr. Morgan was our Sylvester McMonkey McBean sending us around and around and around in a mass of confusion.

You can't teach a Sneetch.

Eventually, we were standing in the hall in our PT gear, pouring sweat and panting. My arms shook involuntarily from adrenaline and round after round of push-ups.

"Would you like to sit down, recruits?"

"YES, Mr. Morgan!" This yes had oomph.

"Sit."

Before the word was out of his mouth, a general collapse happened down the hall. We literally threw ourselves to the ground.

"On your feet. Up!" We bounded back into place. "Too slow!" he said. This was another game we had learned at basic. The game was to spring to your feet fast enough not to hear *too slow*. We went through several rounds that left us gasping on our feet.

"Good panicking, recruits," Mr. Morgan said. I hated him and, in the same instant, I was pleased to be praised. I wanted to do whatever it took to get more, to earn his respect. "Enough fun for tonight. Fall in outside for circle parade."

We rushed outside onto the parade square ready to run off our first circles. An unknown fourth-year cadet waited for us dressed in the cadet No. 5 uniform and a red sash like Mr. Morgan's.

"A Flight!" he bellowed. We all braced at attention. He stood with his arms across his chest and feet wide apart in a stance that seemed to invite a fight.

"My name is CSTO Davis Jamieson. I am your cadet squadron training officer. My job is implementation and maintenance of all things military. I am the watcher from the shadows. I see all. I'm gonna be your worst nightmare."

He lectured us on proper circle protocol. Circles, he kept saying, weren't a punishment but a correction. I hated all this running, especially in my "cripplers" — the nickname for military-issue canvas high-top running shoes with flat rubber soles.

"Take three, Armstrong," said Mr. Jamieson, as he looked me up and down on inspection. "You have creases on the front of your sleeves and shorts, and there is a twist in the loop of your left shoelace."

No one else had been given circles. The creases in my clothes were from being alive in them through panic drills. I had no idea what he saw wrong with my shoelace but didn't dare move to look. *How can he even see me in this light?* I rolled my eyes at the unfairness of it all.

"Armstrong, you will cease all inappropriate facial contortions. You are a military machine. You are not paid to feel. What is your problem?"

My lips trembled. I pressed them together and swallowed. "No excuse, Mr. Jamieson."

"Drop down and give me twenty!"

I plunged to the ground and assumed the high plank of push-up position. I pumped off the first five easy ones, yelling out the count at the peak. My pace slowed as I did another one, trying hard not to sag. My arms were so tired from panic drills that I could barely go down at all. I definitely wasn't going all the way to the bottom. At fifteen, Mr. Jamieson placed his foot on the middle of my back to resist my upward return.

"Louder, Recruit Armstrong. I can't hear you!"

I pushed up against the pressure of his foot like my life depended on it.

"Yes, Armstrong! Yes!"

I was a one-woman show being humiliated in front of my classmates, and I hated him for it. My mind flashed back to when I was twelve years old and my mother had humiliated me in front of my friends in Williams Lake. She had screamed at me from across the playground, storming toward me with a switch in her hand and eyes on fire with hatred. I sat frozen on my swing and braced for impact. She grabbed my arm and yanked me to my feet and whipped at my bare legs. I rallied into action to get away from her. My friends sat immobile on their swings and stared at their feet. The shame of it fired anew in me. I hauled in a lungful of air, compacted it into a burning coal of rage, and exploded off the last four push-ups.

Mr. Jamieson nonchalantly removed his foot and stepped back. "On your feet, Armstrong. Your miserable cheating carcass is making us late for circle parade."

From that moment on, I became the object of Mr. Jamieson's special attention. His voice would haunt my steps from great distances whenever he saw me marching outside between buildings. He would yell, "Armmstroooong! Get your aaaarms up!"

As we approached the gravel oval track, recruits from other squadrons, clad in white shirts and green shorts, were making their way to the form-up area. It would be our first chance to join in with classmates from across the square. We halted shy of the track and waited. *Now I have another three kilometres to run.*

"Class of 1984!" a voice roared from the hazy dark. The track was not lit. We relied on the weak light from nearby dorm buildings. "I am the cadet wing training officer. My name is CWTO

Helstone. All those with eight circles, fall in!" He said the letters of his bar position as "C-dub-T-O."

Three Section was well represented: Fitzroy, Maxwell, Holbrook, and I made crisp right turns, raised our forearms parallel to the ground with closed fists, ran over to the track, and formed up in three ranks with the eight-circle runners from other squadrons.

Mr. Helstone stood right in front of me. His epaulettes had a four-bar pin next to the epaulette patches for Wing Headquarters — a square formed by two triangles, one red and one white. A strand of white spittle danced at the corner of his mouth. I lowered my eyes. Within moments, two hundred recruits had formed up into one big mass, three bodies wide, with the eight-circle runners leading the pack and one-circle runners at the end.

"Circle parade, right turn! By the left, DOUBLE TIME!"

On the furthest curve of the track, away from our guards, whispers of greeting buzzed through the ranks and then quieted as we rounded the homestretch of the first circle.

Mr. Helstone yelled out, "All those with one circle fall out. The rest of you little pukes, shut the fuck up! One more sound and you're all taking home eight fresh ones."

No one spoke again. After all eight rounds were done, Mr. Jamieson marched us back to the Frigate, repeatedly yelling at us, "A Flight, get your arms up!"

When we got back to our hallway, the recruit flight staff were waiting for us, and they were smiling. I instantly felt uncomfortable.

"Welcome back, recruits. Fifteen minutes until lights out, people! Change into your housecoats and flip-flops for shower parade. You have two minutes."

I followed Meg into our room. She stopped short just inside the door and I banged into her back.

"Oh my god."

"Oh my god." I echoed her when I looked up and saw what she'd seen.

Our room had been tossed. Everything we had spent the entire day preparing with such care was destroyed. The contents of our closet were balled up in the bay window, piles of clothes and bedding were a jumbled heap on my bunk, and everything from the drawers was strewn on Meg's mattress, my panties and socks mixed in with hers. Even the pillows had been pulled from their cases. Our footwear was a tangled mess under my desk. Our toiletries were strewn in the sink. I was gobsmacked — putting everything right was going to take more energy and more patience than I had the power to muster.

I came out of the shock first. "Come on, let's go! You find the housecoats. I'm on the flip-flops," I cried.

Meg moved into action. She frantically sifted through our things. I burrowed under my desk for the flip-flops and pulled out our precious boots at the same time. The toes of all four boots and our newly polished laces were gashed.

"Fuckers!"

Back from showers, I took the uniforms and drawers. Meg took the beds. By the time lights out was called, everything was back in its place. Our boots were a mess, our uniforms were wrinkled, and the spacing between items and the measurements of our folded clothing were approximate. Our entire day's work was lost.

I sat on my bunk feeling strange and hollow, unable to cry. I had never been so exhausted in my life. I swayed between confusion and exhilaration and astonishment that my life had been so wholly, instantly redirected. I was far from everything that I knew in the world — my boyfriend, Gary; my friends; my family; my dog, Trixie; the smell of cedar trees; the mountains; even recognizable food and my own clothes.

I slow-marched straight across to the women's bathroom, toes pointed and the balls of my feet skimming the floor without touching, like a zombie bride floating up the aisle.

The moment the door closed behind me, I felt calmer. There were two stalls in the first room and a second door on the back wall. After I peed, I pushed through the other door into the shower room, where there were two curtained stalls and a large, deep soaker bathtub next to the bay window. I sat on the edge of the tub, ran my hand along the cool surface of the ceramic, and smiled.

"One minute to da light out!" yelled Theroux.

I slow-marched back to the room, slid into bed, and let out a sigh. I whispered to Meg in the bunk above me, "Don't you have to pee?"

"I went. Where were you?"

"Checking out the tub."

We kept our doors open at night. The fourth years yelled, "Good night, A Flight!" one at a time.

We responded like kids on *The Waltons*. "Good night, Mr. Morgan; Jansen; Theroux; Kendall."

The hall lights went out. In the moment of quiet, I could hear a strange noise coming from across the parade square, infrequent bursts of a long hum that sounded like the transporter charging on *Star Trek*.

The hiss of a speaker, the sound of the needle catching on record vinyl down the hall, and an achingly beautiful French ballad ended our day. The words made no sense, but that didn't stop my tears. I imagined the lyrics telling the tale of a mother who loved her daughter and was lamenting her fate, feeling sorry that she hadn't rescued her.

As I lay on my bunk, I was totally wiped out, yes — but also, I realized, relieved to be away from home. I was terrified with the alienation from all things familiar but, oddly, the fear was coupled with exhilaration. Here, the violence was implied; no one could actually touch me. Here, I didn't have to pretend that what was happening wasn't really happening. My mother couldn't open my door without knocking, come into my room uninvited, call me names and blame me for her unhappiness, punish me for what *he* had done to *me*. I was out of her reach. She couldn't even phone me.

5

PICKLES

As a child, I was always a bit of a daredevil. If I felt unhappy or scared, I raced toward whatever I thought would make me feel better. Most often, I thought getting attention would be the thing to do it. I had a history of jumping — leaping headfirst — into the next thing without thinking of the consequences, so long as wherever I went someone would see what I was doing and approve, or disapprove, or whatever. But see me. "Kodak courage," we had called it.

When I was five, in 1967, our family lived in Kelowna. A November storm dumped several feet of snow. My youngest brother, Craig, who was eight, and I dragged the toboggan to a small hill behind our house. We fought over who would sit in the front and steer. He won, and at the bottom of the first run our sled struck a snow-covered combine blade that sliced open the right side of his face. My parents rushed him to Children's Hospital in Vancouver. They expected to bring home a dead boy, but he lived. My sister, Ellen, was nineteen and had moved away to attend secretarial school in Calgary. So, off and on over the next six months while Craig was in Vancouver, I was left in the care of my fifteen- and thirteen-year-old brothers, Robert and Peter.

In the fallout of the crash, I tried to be a good girl and not cause any trouble. No one asked me if I was okay or talked to me about the accident. Since I hadn't been physically hurt, it was like I wasn't even there. It became *Craig's accident*.

During their first trip to Vancouver, my parents were gone for weeks and I was sent to stay with friends of the family, which scared me, but I didn't let anyone know. Craig had brain surgery and skull reconstruction. My parents sat at his bedside night and day. At home, my fifteen-year-old brother, Robert, was in charge of the house, and eventually I moved back home with him and Peter. The neighbourhood ladies and friends of the family took turns bringing us meals and helped clean up before my mom came home. Mostly, she stayed in Vancouver while my dad returned to work at Eaton's and travelled back and forth frequently to the hospital. Robert paid lots of attention to me and played games with me and read to me before bed and cuddled me when I cried. I missed my mom and dad. I wanted so much to be loved and held and stroked. I ached for it. Even though I used to fight almost constantly with Craig before the accident, I missed him, too, and didn't want anything bad to happen to him. We used to bathe together, but now Robert sat on the floor beside the tub watching over me while I had my bath alone before bed. I was scared to go to sleep and every night had to look under my bed and in my closet and sleep with the door open and the light on in the hall. I had bad dreams about the hole in Craig's face with his eyeball hanging out, just like on the day of the accident. Whenever I woke up screaming, Robert would come, rub my back, and rock me to sleep, lying beside me on top of the covers.

In January, Robert turned sixteen. One night during my bath, a few months into our new family reality, he quietly asked, "Do you want to play a secret game?"

"Yes," I whispered.

"No one can know. It will be our secret game."

"Okay."

"Are you good at secrets?"

"I think so."

"Do you promise to keep it secret?"

"Yes! I promise."

He laid out a fresh towel beside the tub and told me to lie on it. I got out of the bath and lay down on it and he told me to spread out like a starfish. He told me to close my eyes and when he lay on me to close my legs together as tight as I could. I closed my eyes and heard him unzip his pants and then I heard the sucking sound of lotion. I wanted to look but I didn't. When he floated down on top of me, I felt his shirt on my bare skin but hardly any weight on me. I felt his swollen thing pressing on me between my legs, hot and slippery.

"Close your legs now," he whispered. "Don't make any noise."

My hands clenched the towel and I closed my legs on his penis with all my might. He rubbed it up and down against me between my thighs. I heard his breathing get raspy and he grunted. Hastily, he jumped up and I opened my eyes. His pants were down and he had a hand towel covering him.

"Back in the tub," he said gently. I was confused and a bit scared.

I got back in the tub. He took my hand and leaned close to me. "That's our secret game. It shows you that I'm the one who really loves you. That you're special to me."

From then on, whenever Robert whispered, "Let's do it," I knew what he wanted. By the time my parents finally brought my youngest brother home, I had started wetting the bed almost every night.

"You know this is making a lot of extra work for me," Mom would say when I woke her up to help me change my nightie and my sheets. "I have my hands full taking care of your brother. I need you to be a big girl now."

"I'm sorry. I can't help it. I don't mean to do it."

"It must be the pickles you ate tonight before bedtime. No more pickles for you. I think you're allergic," she muttered as she spread a clean sheet across my bed.

I stopped eating pickles at night, but I kept wetting the bed until I was twelve years old.

6

MADNESS

Recruit term was another kind of living hell. We never had a moment alone. We marched everywhere. We did daily drill, which was marching for the sake of improving our marching. We were startled awake each morning at 05:30 hours by the first hiss of the speakers, to commence seventeen and a half hours of insanity followed by a bedtime song. Our wake-up song, Vivaldi's Concerto in G Major, played for two minutes and fifty-three seconds — the time allotted to do ablutions, make beds, get dressed in PT gear, and be in the hall ready for a five-kilometre run. Post-run we had a seven-minute shower parade.

07:00 hours: March to breakfast.
08:00 hours: Room inspection. Military skills training.
12:00 hours: March to lunch. Drill practice (more marching). Emily Post–style etiquette training. College history training (memorize the recruit bible).
18:00 hours: March to dinner.
19:00 hours: Section commander time.
22:00 hours: Circle parade or time for personal keening — pressing, polishing, and cleaning for inspections — for those without circles.

23:00 hours: Lights-out song, in French; to this day I don't know the name of it. Repeat the cycle daily until the start of classes in September.

Every moment was packed with the frenzied energy of being assessed, which, for me, inevitably ended in earning more circles. If by some miracle I managed to find some spare time, I'd use it to catch up on other duties I had been assigned. The big challenge was keeping pace. Economy of effort and optimization of time infected all decisions of the day. During shower times, I'd be frantically practising my chin-ups on the overhead bar of the shower stall. Even mealtimes became strategic. Never take the last glass of milk from the jug. Eat calorie-dense, square-meal-friendly foods: sausages, savoury meatloaf, scallop potatoes, and most disgusting, Hawaiian ham, a thick slab of ham garnished with a pineapple ring and a maraschino cherry that left a disconcerting green spot on the meat beneath it.

Morning inspection included our uniforms, rifles, kit layout, closets, drawers, beds, and even our cleaning materials. Every square surface of the room had to be immaculate. There could be no signs of dust or hair or dirt even in obscure places.

During endless hours standing outside our room awaiting inspection, I stared ahead at the stylized woman on the bathroom door, her head floating above her body. When I closed my eyes, her afterimage glowed on my eyelids.

What is she trying to tell me?

It's simple enough to stand still, but being motionless in one position for an hour was excruciating. I started out supertight and keen in the resting position called *stand at ease*. Chin in, eyes straight ahead, left arm at my side with my hand in the fist for attention, right hand jutting my weapon out at the extension. I quickly understood. This was going to hurt.

In time, I learned how to ease my lower back, how to keep my feet from falling asleep, how to make indiscernible movements to keep my circulation flowing. The art of tiny movements of toes in boots, knees bending and straightening, butt contracting and relaxing, hands soundlessly tapping, and slow, deep breathing. I learned to hide in plain view by imagining the boundaries of my physical self as a shield to conceal the squishy vulnerability I felt inside and to let my mind wander to happy thoughts in the peace of waiting our turn.

Normally our room was last to be inspected. Mr. Morgan was almost always in a foul mood by the time he reached us. We snapped to attention when he and Mr. Kendall approached us. Mr. Kendall held a notebook at the ready to jot down our corrections.

"Fraust," Morgan said, holding up a minuscule scrap of lint in my line of sight.

They made up a word for lint?

"Take three circles, Recruit Armstrong." He inspected me carefully, looking me up and down, front and back. He snatched my rifle from my hand, cracked the breech, and peered inside the muzzle. "Too much oil. Take three circles."

Morgan turned his attention to Meg and grabbed at her epaulette. "Irish pennant," he said as he held a stray thread under her nose. "Take one circle, Miss Carter." He peered into the open breech of her weapon. "Too dry. Take one circle."

The moment Morgan and Kendall entered our room, sounds of destruction echoed into the hall, reminding me of my mother in a rage. My body froze at attention and tensed in anticipation of an attack.

After a particularly bad inspection, Mr. Morgan stormed down the length of the hallway and hollered at us more than normal. "Are we going backwards, people? Your rooms are a disgrace. I'm disappointed."

I was surprised to feel a pang of shame. Letting him down felt worse than being reamed out by him. Whatever was going to satisfy their standards was going to take some superhuman efforts on our part.

"You've earned a round of wall sits! Look this way, recruits, for a demonstration," said Morgan.

Mr. Jansen grabbed Becker's rifle, backed up to the wall, and slid into a squat with his legs bent at a ninety-degree angle while holding the weapon in both hands, straight armed at chest level.

"Here's how it works. You assume the position, and as soon as you can tell us the meaning of every part of the college cheer, you'll be dismissed. Sound fair?" asked Morgan.

"Yes, Mr. Morgan!"

"Don't biff your buds! Assume the position!"

I pushed hard against the wall to keep as much weight as possible from my legs and raised my rifle parallel to the ground. My arms burned immediately. I heard Meg groan softly.

"Let's do this," said Mr. Morgan.

"GIMME A BEER!" blasted Mr. Jansen.

We roared in sync, "BEER ESSES EMMA. TDV! WHO CAN STOP OLD RMC? SHRAPNEL. CORDITE. NCT! RMC!"

Mr. Morgan started at the other end of the hall and asked, "Dahl, what does 'Beer Esses Emma' mean?"

"It stands for the initials BSM which meant 'battery sergeant major' in early days of the college, Mr. Morgan!"

Morgan's voice moved closer. "Tate, what is 'TDV'? Don't fuck this up, Tate."

"Truth, duty, valour! The college motto, Mr. Morgan."

My arms quivered in an uncontrollable tremor.

"Sloane, what is 'Shrapnel'?"

"Tribute to the wars fought by cadets," she called out.

"Holbrook, 'Cordite'!"

"The steel boat built by cadets and named *Cordite* after the smokeless propellant!"

"Yes, Holbrook!"

Mr. Morgan stood in front of me.

"Armstrong, what is 'NCT'?" he smirked at me. I was visibly shaking now, and a knot of shame caught in my throat.

"No cunt tonight, Mr. Morgan." I spoke directly in his face. *Fuckyoufuckyoufuckyou.*

"What? Louder, Recruit Armstrong!" he yelled back.

"NO CUNT TONIGHT!" I screamed.

"Good! Did you hear that, boys? Recruit Armstrong says no cunt tonight," he boomed. "Better luck next time. Release!"

As we collapsed to the ground, I yelled, "Fat chance!" Everyone was laughing, except me. I was shaking and furious.

That night, during our lights-out song, I stared up at the underside of Meg's mattress; slats of wood and sagging wire bedsprings held it in place. As quietly as I could manage, I whispered to Meg, "What is the purpose of all this?"

Meg leaned over the side of her bunk, and in the near-complete darkness I couldn't discern her features. "To break us," she said softly.

"To what end?"

"To build us back up again."

"As what?" I asked.

"Good cadets?"

"Does the process make sense to you?"

"Not really." Meg tipped back into her bed and I could no longer see her.

"What if we do all this and end up becoming someone we

don't want to be. I don't want to become some kind of cadet robot — a *cadot*."

A stillness hung in the air. Out on the square beyond our window the unnatural quiet was broken every so often by that strange, distant intermittent hum that continued to mystify me.

Meg's whisper cut the silence. "It's amazing to me that you still believe you have any choice in the matter."

I heard Meg's breathing change. She was asleep. For some reason, I lived in terror of losing myself altogether, though I had no idea who I was in the first place.

A sense of superstition grew amongst us that we could help our chances of surviving by observing the rites and rituals and protocols. We keened our rooms and our uniforms. We studied the question of the day. We kept our weapons clean. We paid attention. We swung our arms high. We made our best effort. We didn't volunteer or take unnecessary chances or try to stand out above our flight mates. We helped each other.

The concept of individuality had been quashed in the opening speech and was reiterated several times a day. Do what you're told and work as a team doing it. Eventually we mimicked our recruit staff's way of talking and walking, even when alone with each other. The indoctrination process infested our language, our mannerisms, and our sense of humour, morphing some into unrecognizable versions of their earlier selves.

My efforts only got me so far. I didn't have enough hours in my day to get it all done. The hour of circle parade was the time allocated for personal keening. I was running eight circles a night.

Recruits were not allowed in the halls after lights out except to visit the bathroom. The only loophole: sleepwalking. We were told, "Sleepwalking cadets will not be woken up, as this is medically counter-indicated, *but* sleepwalking cadets will do proper drill in the halls."

That's when I discovered the Apache alarm clock — two large glasses of water at bedtime to wake me in the middle of the night. My childhood fear of wetting the bed was my ally now.

Around three o'clock every morning, anyone looking into the hall would have seen me slow-march sleepwalking to the ironing room, arms straight out, iron in one hand and uniform in the other, glazed eyes staring ahead.

The ironing "board" was a rock-hard, fabric-covered table that took up half the ironing room. It was like a waist-high mattress on huge wooden legs. The padded canvas cover was stained with watermarks where irons had tipped over and left rust-rimmed blotches. The air was close, with a smell like starched wet wool. I ironed with the light on and the door closed, all the while worried sick about the start of classes and adding homework to this routine.

7

ACADEMICS

We went straight to the Old Gym for our textbooks, and when we got back, I marched down the hall at the specified quick-time pace, executed a crisp left turn, and halted in front of Mr. Kendall's door. I knocked three times, as instructed.

"Enter."

I opened the door, took one step forward into his room, and snapped to attention. This was my first time in a nonrecruit room. The decorative throw pillows and duvet cover, plants, and a collage of photo frames around his desk surprised me. The air carried a faint trace of incense. A khaki-coloured poster with the burgundy silhouette headshot of a long-haired guy in a beret with a communist star was the only wall art. Mr. Kendall was seated at his desk, flipping through a pile of papers.

"Excuse me, Mr. Kendall, 14390, Recruit Armstrong, K.A., One Squadron, A Flight, Three Section reporting," I said to his back.

"Yes, Miss Armstrong?" he said, turning halfway in his chair toward me.

"Mr. Kendall, there's been some kind of mistake. I've been given first-year engineering books but my degree program is commerce."

"Everyone here studies engineering in first year, Miss Armstrong. You switch to non-engineering-degree program curricula in second year," he said.

I was dumbstruck. I had come prepared for a different answer, feeling resolute that it was a simple mistake, but now my head swam with anxiety.

"So, you're the first," he said, turning back to shuffle the papers on his desk into a stack.

"I beg your pardon, Mr. Kendall?"

"First. First woman in history to be assigned a cadet college number at RMC." He looked up at me. "College numbers are assigned alphabetically. *Armstrong.* That makes you first."

"Very well, Mr. Kendall," I said uncertainly. Our eyes locked.

"You say that now," he replied with a grin. "Anything else?"

My throat clenched into a burning lump. *Don't cry. Don't cry. Don't cry.* "No, Mr. Kendall," I replied. "Permission to carry on?"

"Carry on, Miss Armstrong."

I returned to our room parched and sweating. I had taken commerce prerequisites in high school: law, economics, statistics. I had only Physics 12, Chemistry 11, no biology, and poor math preparation. My high school didn't even offer calculus. I went straight for the sink. The tap flowed glorious cold water. I gulped at the stream.

"Do you know the guys piss in the sinks?" Meg said as she shelved her last textbook. I stood straight up and water splashed down my sweaty work dress shirt. "Dahl told me. They're furthest from the men's washroom. He said they just piss in their sink. Everyone does it."

"We don't though. Right?" I looked at her.

Meg burst out laughing. "God. *No!*"

"Good," I said, bending over the sink again.

One night, the ironing room door flew open during my sleep-walking session and Holbrook smirked at me from the doorway. I jumped back and yelped.

"I love how easy it is to get you," he said. "I'm usually here earlier. I nearly slept through." He laid his pants out on the other half of the table. I noticed my pant legs were longer than his.

Unexpectedly, the door flew open again and banged against the wall. Mr. Kendall stood there wearing an ankle-length kaftan covered in a motif of pastel-coloured peace signs and flowers. Richie and I switched to living-dead mannerisms, staring straight ahead and continuing to iron. Kendall laughed and closed the door.

"This place is fucking nuts," Richie whispered.

"No kidding. What the hell was he wearing?" I asked.

"Have you seen the poster of Che Guevara in his room?"

"The guy in the beret?"

"'The guy in the beret.' You crack me up, Armstrong. Che's only the most famous communist guerrilla fighter ever. He fought for Castro and got killed in Bolivia or somewhere."

"How the hell would I know that? I'm from Abbotsford."

"Oh, there's a good defence."

We ironed in silence for a moment.

"How are we going to survive if we keep getting so many circles?" I asked. Richie was holding a close second to my tally.

"Beats me. Every day, I just keep going, getting as much done as I can. The hole keeps getting deeper," he said.

"I get them everywhere. *Everywhere*. Inspection. Meals. Even on fucking circle parade itself." I paused. "Do you ever regret coming here?"

"Every two minutes."

"I feel sick just thinking about the start of engineering classes."

I secured the iron cord around the handle in exact loops with the plug trapped in a specific fashion, held out the hot iron at ninety degrees, and slow-marched back to the recruit hallway. I slid down the hall ruminating on the ridiculousness of my situation. My problem was quitting. No matter how insane or hard things got, I had never quit anything. Besides, if I quit, it wasn't just *me* quitting. It was a *woman* who couldn't cut it. The translation: *women* can't cut it.

On Labour Day weekend, the entire cadet wing returned from summer training and triggered the start of college life in earnest. On Sunday night as I was heading out for circle parade, I stepped into the hall and saw two second-year cadets standing there with a coffee urn and a tray full of food. Mr. Kendall walked up to them and pointed toward our tiny utility room next to the fire escape doors.

"A Flight, kye has arrived," he announced. "As the cadet wing returns, so doth the cadet wing traditions. All those with circles, fall in outside. The rest of you, come on down to the utility room for kye!"

After circle parade, I asked Meg, "What's kye?"

"Are you sure you want to know?" Meg replied. She told me that each night at 10:00 p.m., an evening snack called kye was served. Milk, hot chocolate, toast, peanut butter, and jam, and apparently pastries and cookies were sometimes included on special occasions.

My stomach rumbled.

With the start of classes, squadron duties were activated and rotation between English week and French week commenced, alternating languages for all announcements and college business.

Alphabetical order put me on squadron runner duty first of all the recruits. The job turned out to be easy enough: run across the square four times a day to pick up mail for the squadron, deliver the mail, ring the Frigate bell at precisely noon every day, call out announcements at 22:00 hours in the language of the week on each hallway, update the days-to-grad count for the fourth-year class, spend the evening in the orderly room answering the phone, and make sure the squadron first-aid box was stocked with condoms — free condoms for male cadets to use during trips to town.

On Monday, September 1, I stood at the head of the hall on the third floor, terrified, and made the first set of announcements for the year from the script:

> *Attention! Attention! Attention! All personnel on board, let it be known that: tomorrow evening at 18:30 hours there will be a sports fair for recruits and cadets to sign up for varsity teams. There are 257 days until graduation. Thank you.*

Six hallways. Six repetitions. Five hallways full of curious male cadet faces leaning out their doorways to check out the new female recruit. The humiliation was worth the silver lining payoff of being excused circle parade and having my first chance to get some kye.

At breakfast the next morning, the dining hall was crowded with a sea of staring eyes. A quiet fell over the room as our recruit flight lined up for food. Some of the cadets put down their utensils or held them slackly; their audible comments trailed in our wake.

"Oh, look. That one's a hottie."

"I'd like to get myself a piece of that."

"Heellllo, sweetheart."

"She's gonna need a permanent mattress on her back for the amount of action she's gonna get around here."

"You can have the short redhead. I want the tall one with the brown hair."

"Who said admitting girls was a bad idea? One look at her rack and I'm warming up to it."

My head trembled with the effort of not turning to see the faces attached to these voices. I fought the urge to fold my arms across my chest and hide my breasts as shame swept through me. The act of eating while being watched felt surprisingly vulnerable, and being forced to eat square meals embarrassed me.

A class curriculum was posted on our door — the first-year cadets had all the same classes together — next to our individual *disposition indicators*, which we were to use to indicate where we were. The choices were in class, at sports, at library, across the wing, at the mess. A paperclip slid up and down the list. Most of those choices were not available to the first years until after recruit term, but the list gave a glimpse of hope for the promise of another life starting soon.

On the first morning of classes, I grabbed my notebook in my left hand and slid my marker to "in class." Meg and I clipped down the stairs together, and as her left foot hit the main-floor landing, her right arm flew up to shoulder height. She marched out to the white line on the parade square and I was right behind, in sync with her.

"Recruits, halt!" blared an unfamiliar voice from behind us. We halted side by side. A second-year cadet swooped around in front of us, much too close for comfort.

"I'm Second Year Arsenault. Do you know why I have stopped you?" He addressed the question to me. He had pretty-boy prep looks and a slight French Canadian accent.

"No, Mr. Arsenault," we answered as our flight mates streamed past us.

"Do you think you're fucking cheerleaders? Carry your books at your side, not squeezed to your chest like some schoolgirls! I'm reporting you to Mr. Morgan for two circles each. Do you understand?"

"Yes, Mr. Arsenault," we said. We dropped our left arms to our sides and squeezed the books tight to our hips.

"Carry on, recruits!" he spat out and marched away.

We executed the required about-turns and marched in a semicircle back toward the white line marking the edge of the parade square. In perfect synchronicity, we halted, looked right, looked forward, looked left, looked forward, and then raised our books to our bodies for running and crooked our right arms at a ninety-degree angle. This was proper running-the-square protocol.

"Who the fuck was that? Don't tell me that anyone and everyone can stop us," I whispered through barely moving lips after we set off.

"It looks that way!" Meg kept staring straight ahead as we ran at full speed.

"What a sadistic asshole. It's like he's already forgotten what a drag it is to be a recruit," I moaned.

The classroom was buzzing with more than two hundred recruits settling into university-style desks. I saw an open seat next to one of my guy friends from basic training, now a recruit in Seven Squadron, and went over to join him. I was looking forward to talking to someone else besides another A Flight member for a few hours.

"This seat's taken," he said, placing his hand on the empty chair. He turned his back to me. Flummoxed, I scanned the room. I sought refuge in Holbrook's and Fitzroy's watching eyes. They glanced uncomfortably at each other and looked away. I spotted an open seat and rushed over to sit next to Meg.

The moment I was settled quietly into my seat, I struggled to stay awake. Chronic exhaustion had settled into my bones. Now that I was away from the constant panic and adrenaline, my hundred-pound eyelids wanted to close. I resisted, but my head bobbed down as I drifted to sleep and snapped back up in the microsleeping display known at the college as *depth-finders*.

At the first break, I walked over to join the Seven Squadron guys' group in the hall, determined to ask what was wrong, but they closed ranks to shut me out.

"What did I do?" I asked their backs. They just ignored me, and that cut me deeper than open cruelty.

Heidi Gottlieb, another friend from basic and one of their flight mates, whistled at me from several feet away and motioned for me to come over to her. "Don't waste your breath," she said, nodding in their direction. "The senior cadets have gotten to them."

"What do you mean? We were all good friends at basic," I said. A sense of panic gripped me by the throat, and deep down I felt the shame of trying to force my way into a place where I wasn't wanted.

"Not anymore. We're the enemy now. We're *ruining* RMC for them."

Study hours were my crash landing — nothing except home-work was permitted from 19:00 to 22:00 hours. Meg and I shared comfortable silences, respecting each other's need for privacy and study time. I had the first module of calculus to get started on, physics chapters to read, and chemistry questions to answer. Every other moment of our days was crammed, so this was our only chance to do homework. We had two hours each of drill and PT class weekly, as well as one hour daily of French language immersion. I continued to get circles every day for minor infractions. My rejection by the guys and fighting to stay awake in class had crowded out my ability to pay attention and absorb the material. A sort of academic entropy had seized my mind. I had no momentum. I couldn't calm my thoughts and concentrate. I would continually catch myself reading material without a clue of the context and give my head a shake. At times, I'd have to turn back two or three pages before I found a section that I understood well enough to begin making progress on my lesson in good faith.

One day, after calculus class, one of the guys from Four Squadron walked up to me and stuck out his hand. "Brad Boulter," he said. Brad was an unassuming, stocky character with a hiccup laugh that seemed to come easily to him.

"Hi?" His friendliness made me uneasy. I had already learned not to trust myself when it came to reading the intentions of male cadets, even my peers.

"Look," he said. "I've overheard you talking with Meg about being in first-year engineering. I want to help you with calculus."

"What do you mean?"

"I mean I am bored shitless. The curriculum is stuff I covered in grade thirteen in Ontario and it bored me then. My degree program is honours math and physics. If you need help, I'm offering."

"I need help," I said. We shook hands on it.

Our first PT class was a fitness-level assessment that would be repeated in November and April. This was one challenge that did not give me anxiety. The PT test was a five-event test consisting of doing the maximum number of chin-ups possible, a timed agility run, timed sit-ups, a standing broad jump, and a mile-and-a-half run that had to be completed in twelve minutes.

I excelled in every category until we hit the chin-up bar. I pulled up on the first chin-up with no problem and dropped down to straight arms. On the second pull-up, I could not raise my chin closer than halfway to the bar. I hung in mid-air, straining to canter my elbows the rest of the way, but it was like being paralyzed. I gritted my teeth and focused all my energy to my arms. Nothing. I simply could not do it. I dropped to the floor, defeated.

"I don't know what's wrong," I said to the PT instructor.

"Don't worry, it's been happening to all the gals. You'll need to train," he said. "If you can get three, you'll qualify for the crossed-clubs fitness badge."

I hung my head, flung myself down, and took my seat with the rest of A Flight. Holbrook jumped up and cranked off twenty chin-ups before the instructor ordered him down.

"You've exceeded the necessary number of chin-ups, Recruit Holbrook," he said.

I felt hot breath against my neck and heard the whisper: "That's because he's not a girl." I turned and glared into Colbert's face. His head was broader at the top and narrowed down into a weak chin.

8

LCWB

Thursday night, I ran over to the SAM Centre, a massive sports complex across the highway from the main college grounds, named after Sir Archibald Macdonell from the class of 1886, for varsity-team basketball tryouts. It was nuts to contemplate adding anything more to my schedule, but basketball had always been a refuge for me during high school — it was the thing that had sustained me. At practice or playing in a game, I was somebody. I belonged and was valued on the team. *If I had gone to Simon Fraser University, I'd be in varsity-team tryouts now.* For a split second, I felt that without basketball, I didn't want to stay at RMC.

"You want to try out for the guys' basketball team?" Coach Jeff Winter asked me. No other women had shown up for basketball. I looked over at Mr. Samson, a fourth year from Eight Squadron and the team captain. He was nodding encouragement.

"Have you ever played with guys before?"

"Yes, Coach." I had played with my high-school boyfriend, Gary, and his friends in pickup games; they were varsity-team superstars. I didn't admit that their aggressive, faster play scared the crap out of me. "I was a high-school varsity all-star and MVP."

"Let's give it a shot," Coach said.

I played hard, scored a few baskets, and tried not to show fear when the guys fought me for a rebound. After practice, Coach said that I had made the team, for practices only. I couldn't play in the Ontario University Athletics Association as a girl on a guys' team.

I ran back to the college grounds with Kurt Samson and two guys from the Frigate, Second Year Jerry Stawski and Third Year Kevin Blackwood.

"How's recruit term going?" Kurt asked.

"Fine, Mr. Samson. I'm finding it hard, but hope basketball will cheer me up."

"Yeah. I heard you're getting a lot of circles," Blackwood snorted.

"You did?" I couldn't believe he knew or cared.

"Recruit watching is a source of entertainment for us," Blackwood said.

"Yeah, for people without a life," Jerry retorted and gave Blackwood a shove with his elbow. They kibitzed the rest of the way. Kurt and I stayed silent.

Kurt said goodbye when we reached the bronze statue of a cadet wearing the dress scarlet uniform with a sword at his hip, nicknamed Brucie the Fag Cadet because of his effeminate posture. Something about him reminded me of my oldest brother, Robert. It happened sometimes. More often than I'd like. I tried to push the thought of him away.

I halted at the edge of the square as was mandatory for recruits, and the others ran ahead without me. Suddenly I was having a flashback of Robert. I didn't want to, but I found myself remembering. Our family had just moved to Fort St. John, into a new house with a finished basement. I was seven years old. Usually, Robert and I had to be home alone for him to play his game, but sometimes he'd call me downstairs while everyone else was upstairs. Those times were always the scariest. If we got caught, I'd be in big trouble, he said. I would listen to the TV sounds coming from the living room and for any sign of footsteps on the stairs. His favourite place to do it was in the downstairs bathroom because the door locked.

"Have you had any blood down there?"

"No," I answered, wondering why he asked me that so often.

"Kiss it," he said. I said no. I always said no — I didn't want to kiss him where his pee came out.

Then he would hold out the tub of Vaseline and I would take a scoop and spread it around the head of his penis. There was barely room for us on the tiny bathroom floor now that I was getting so tall. He rubbed Vaseline on me, too. I would lie still and he would penetrate me. It didn't hurt so much anymore, but I still didn't like the feeling of it. I would stare at the holes in the ceiling tiles, looking for happy faces and recognizable shapes. He never took long.

"I'm going to pee in you now," he would say and then shudder, and it was over. I was always glad when he was done and I could get away.

After he left the room, I would wipe myself with toilet paper, flush it, and hang up the towel to make sure everything looked normal. I knew I had to be careful; I had to do a good job. If there were any signs and we got caught, he wouldn't be able to treat me special anymore. He was always paying attention to me, taking me aside, asking about my day and what I liked, listening to my stories. He would whisper in my ear, saying that he loved me, that he was the only one who looked out for me, his lips brushing against my ear, his hands pulling me down onto his lap in front of everyone, and grinding his groin up into me. Only letting go when I looked into his eyes, when I smiled.

I didn't understand yet what was happening to me or what was being robbed from me. The most terrifying moment was going back into the living room, feeling sure that we had been caught this time, but we never were. No one ever paid any attention.

The white line on the parade square at the Frigate shocked me back into the present. No one would ever know. Robert had been gone for a long time. I didn't have to think about him anymore.

"Wake up, wake up," someone whispered, shaking my shoulder.

"What the fuck?" I lunged upright in bed. *I'm going to kill this person.*

Two men were standing by our bed, and one of them was shaking Meg above me.

"Shhhhhhhhhhh. Be quiet. We're second years. Get dressed in PT gear and sweaters. Take the fire escape and wait down by the boathouse. Don't say anything."

"What is going on?" I whispered. *This better be for real. If I don't see any of our flight mates on the way there, I'm going to scream bloody murder.*

"You'll see. Don't worry."

I looked out at the clock tower. Midnight. We had only been asleep for an hour. We dressed silently, snuck down the hall, and tiptoed out onto the fire escape stairs.

My eyes adjusted to the dark and I saw a crowd gathered at the boathouse. Arsenault was waiting in front of the group and I felt a wave of disgust. I didn't want to go anywhere if he was going to be there.

"We're still missing two people," Arsenault said in a normal talking voice. Just then, Leigh and Dahl came out the door and down the stairs. "Jesus. Let's go, you slackers. You're fucking lucky we didn't leave without you."

We set out and ambled down the road in a gaggle, following the route of our morning run up Fort Henry Hill. I walked next to Jerry Stawski, from basketball, as he loped along like a jester from Monty Python, talking incessantly. I kept well away from Arsenault.

"We have a surprise for you. It's Frigate tradition for the second years to take the first years out on the first Friday after the start of classes," said Jerry.

When we got to the top of the hill, I saw a cooler overflowing with ice and beer on a picnic table, with bags of chips scattered next to it. The second years stepped back and gestured for us to dig in.

I pulled a beer from the ice and a second year flipped off the top for me. I took a long, greedy chug and sidled up to Jerry and one of his second-year buds.

"So, what's your impression so far?" Jerry asked.

"You have no idea what a miracle it is to see bags of chips and take a sip of cold beer. Thank you, I'm blown away," I said.

"I meant RMC," he laughed.

"Oh. It's hard. And lately I've been more and more freaked out about the obstacle course."

His bud spoke up and stuck out his hand. "Bobbie Babineaux. Yeah. The only thing standing between you and the end of recruit term is our obstacle course."

I tried to wow him with the firm handshake I'd practised in etiquette class. "Kate Armstrong. What do you mean 'our' obstacle course?"

"The LCWB builds the recruit obstacle course. It's only five miles long and full of countless heinously evil obstacles. No reason to be freaked out."

"What's LCWB?"

"Last class with balls," Bobbie puffed his chest and pumped his elbows out to the side.

"Oh wow, good one. Did you make that up?" I asked dryly.

"Nope. We got it from West Point. The LCWB graduated from there in 1979, before the first women graduated this spring," Bobbie said with a sly grin.

Holbrook and Maxwell walked over to join us.

"LCWB. Last class with balls," I said, thumbing in Bobbie's direction. Richie and Nigel raised their eyebrows. I turned back to Bobbie. "Let's hope you don't fail and end up in our class. Sounds like it could be painful."

Jerry shot Bobbie a grin. Richie and Nigel laughed. The beer was delicious, and I felt bold. I swaggered toward the cooler for more. I may not have had balls, but I wasn't going to let that stop me from anything.

Colbert stood near the table with Arsenault. Colbert snarled at me as usual. "Not as painful as having women here."

"What's your fucking problem? I haven't done anything to you. Why are you being such a jerk?"

"Because of you girls, there's no more recruit boxing."

"You look like a real boxer." I looked up and down his frame: skinny as a heroin addict and head shaped like an alien.

"Come on, Kate. Forget about it." Jerry grabbed my arm from behind and pulled me away.

When we were out of earshot, I asked him, "Did you box?"

"Yeah, recruit boxing was a tradition."

"For what?"

"For tradition's sake?" He shrugged. "Boxing was a nightmare. I got pounded. They matched us by weight. I had never been in a fight in my life and ended up boxing against a rugby player. It's a right of passage to be considered a real man around here. The guys in your class won't get that."

Then he gave me some advice. "One suggestion. Steer clear of the French guys. Some of them are bitter because they did a prep year at CMR in Saint-Jean and then found out they have to do recruit term all over again when they got here. It's the same every year." CMR referred to the Collège militaire royal, the French feeder college to RMC in Saint-Jean-sur-Richelieu, Quebec.

"That sucks. One of the things I was looking forward to the most about RMC was making friends with French Canadians."

"Good luck with that," Jerry said with a smile.

9

SHOULD I STAY OR SHOULD I GO?

By the third week of classes, the atmosphere made it clear that even within our own year the women were outsiders. There was a core group of male cadets who did not hide their deep resentment toward us: ignoring us like we weren't there; making snide comments; telling obscene stories; and finding ways to harass, ostracize, and ridicule. I had known there would be guys who wanted me to fail. To cry. To quit. To rant. But I hadn't expected that treatment to come from some of my own classmates. We'd been friends at basic training. I was fighting for my future, just like they were. It wasn't their right to rob it from me. Their mean-spiritedness reminded me of my mother. She loved to put me down in similar ways.

I had to succeed. I had no other plan for myself. I couldn't go back home.

"Outta my seat, sweat," said one of the guys. I stared at him in disbelief. By now we had established a fairly regular pattern of who sat where, and I was in *my* seat.

"Fuck off," I said. "I'm not moving."

"Whooooaaaaa," some of the guys nearby groaned at me. I stared straight ahead, flustered but unbudging.

Separately, their behaviour would not have been overly distressing. I could accept that assholes existed. But collectively their treatment stacked up enough to erode my sense of confidence and forced me to face the reality that some of them truly wanted me gone — and were willing to help me along if I needed encouragement to leave. It was nothing personal. They wanted all the women to fail.

At that moment, Mary Tyler of Six Squadron waddled across my line of sight, chest lifted and head held high. Her obesity sickened me. She was already on remedial PT and had been warned to get in shape or be kicked out. I lashed out in my mind against her. *How did she ever get accepted here?* I had heard her dad was a general and that she had been instrumental in the fight to get woman accepted to RMC in the first place. But it didn't change the fact that she dragged down the impression of the rest of us girls, like Meg and me, who worked hard to prove we could be as tough as the guys. To prove we belonged here. I felt myself hardening against her, and against any woman giving an impression of weakness that reflected on the rest of us.

One day, during a break, a group of guys broke out in raucous laughter. When I approached them, the laughter stopped short and they wedged closely together. I wouldn't have been able to squeeze in even if I'd tried. Seeing the guys chum around together made me feel strange inside, but I couldn't pinpoint the actual emotion. It was a mixture of feeling insignificant, unwanted, and jealous, all at the same time.

I walked past, pretending not to notice, and went straight into the women's washroom. In that private space, I literally looked myself up and down in the mirror, trying to discover if there was something about me that was making them laugh.

What was wrong with me? I couldn't see it. I'd been found wanting when I so badly wanted to fit in, to be part of the fun and jokes, not the target of them.

In response, I did what had come naturally to me in high school. I played the clown. I made jokes. Pretended they weren't getting to me. I hit my stride and discovered a knack for drawing a laugh. It became like a drug to me. I needed my fix to survive this place. In my worst moments, my skill could be dark. I would lash out with humour and cut them with my words.

Back on the recruit hallway, Mr. Theroux called out, "Mail call!"

Please, God, let me have a letter.

"Fitzroy. Armstrong. Holbrook. Dahl. Carter. Carter. Travers. Maxwell. Carter. Your mommies love you. The rest of you, you've already been forgotten by your families."

I instantly recognized the handwriting on my letter. It was from Gary, my boyfriend back home, who had rarely entered my thoughts these past weeks. Straight away I could picture his easy smile and habit of casually hanging his arm over the steering wheel as he drove his beloved car, a burgundy 1969 Cougar with flame decals on the hood, and his blond hair, longer than mine now, standing straight up from his head like wheat stubble.

Mr. Morgan spoke from the end of the hall. "Okay, A Flight, listen up. We've been thinking that your mommies and daddies might want to hear from you. We bought some postcards for you. Pick one that you like and pass the stack along."

The postcards were identical. Each bore a view of RMC taken from Fort Henry Hill. The Stone Frigate was front and centre across Navy Bay. In the background, Kingston City Hall and the docked Wolfe Island ferry were visible across the water on the other side of the college peninsula.

"Damn it, Holbrook," Mr. Morgan said. "You'd better not be writing already! Take three circles."

Richie looked up and froze. He had written a line. Mr. Kendall walked over, tore the postcard from his hand, ripped it in half, and threw him a blank one.

Mr. Morgan continued. "You will write what I tell you to write, when I tell you to write it, and only what I tell you to write. 'Dear Mom and Dad.' Stop. Don't be an idiot. Decide now who is going to receive it and address your postcard appropriately. Mom, dad, guardian, but *no* girlfriends or buddies. This is a family postcard."

Mr. Morgan spoke slowly, one line at a time, until we got through the text. "'It's hard to believe I have been here nearly a month and haven't made time to write. I really miss you, even though life in the Stone Frigate makes me happy beyond my wildest dreams. Our senior cadets are the best, paying such care and attention to every little detail of our lives, and they are SO fun. They laugh all the time. I'm eating well and getting in great shape. The biggest surprise is how much sleep we get around here. Wish you were here. Write soon. Please send care packages. Love, X.' When I say *X,* sign your fucking name, people. Address the postcard and pass them back up here to Mr. Theroux."

Back in our room, I hid my unread letter in our underwear drawer. After lights out, I snuck across the hall into the women's bathroom and sat on the toilet, raised my unopened letter to my face, and breathed in deep. Old Spice.

The letter was only one page long, and my heart sank at how little he had written. The handwriting was pinched and messy. "I hope you're enjoying your new life," it began. Gary told me about his progress on his plumbing apprenticeship at the British Columbia Institute of Technology and a bit about hanging out with the guys to shoot hoops and kill time on weekends. My mind flashed to our gang of friends meeting under the causeway by the Fraser River on Friday nights for music from car stereos, a bonfire, and drinks. I craved a sip of fizzy cool rye and 7 Up. A little farther on, he got to the point: "You're married to the Army now." Gary was dumping me. I doubled over and stifled a cry in my terry housecoat.

The life I used to know is carrying on without me.

I felt the same sick feeling I'd had after Gary came back from the grade-twelve guy's basketball trip to California and broke up with me for refusing to have sex with him. I was only in grade eleven. I couldn't know for absolute certain, but I was sure he had cheated on me.

I reacted instantly with an intense need to be found attractive by someone. In the coming days, I began to flirt relentlessly with my favourite fourth year, Mr. Theroux, which was no easy feat while under constant scrutiny. He picked up the thread of my attention and our short-lived dalliance culminated with a kiss in his room one night after lights out that was interrupted by yelling in the hall.

"Armstrong is out of bed! She's off the hallway!"

A mad search was underway as I stood shaking behind Mr. Theroux's open door. He set out to help them look for me and led them down the fire escape stairs and I slinked back to bed undetected. I had never been more terrified since arriving at RMC. Later, I said that I had been sitting on the back steps of the Frigate stealing a moment alone from all the madness. That lapse in reason cost me a pretty penny in circles and I smartened up. We stopped flirting and never spoke of it again. Meg never let on that she ever doubted my story.

One evening, recruits were granted a five-minute phone call home. The fourth years called it a privilege. The heavy black receiver was still warm when I picked it up and dialed.

"Hello?" my mother's voice sounded hesitant. The operator asked if she would accept long-distance charges from Miss Kate Armstrong in Kingston, Ontario. I swallowed hard. I was afraid I might cry.

"Yes, of course we'll accept," she said, as though the operator should have known already. "Gordie! It's Kate on the line from camp."

"Mom, it's not camp. It's RMC," I said. The tingle in my sinuses disappeared.

I heard the second receiver rattle when Dad picked it up.

"Hi, Dad!" I said.

"Hey, girl! How's life in Kingston?"

"Okay. It's really hard. They never let up. We made a joke about the recruiting commercial: 'There's no life — like it.' I'm tired and pissed off a lot and it's fun at the same time. It's hard to explain. How's everything at home?"

"We're all good. Everyone is doing well. Nothing much has changed here," Mom answered. "We got your postcard. The grounds sure are beautiful."

"I can't wait for you to see them. That postcard was a joke, dictated by the fourth years and mailed for us. We all sent home the exact same one."

"I thought things sounded a bit rosy compared to your other letters," said Dad. "By the way, your friends come by to visit me in the store all the time and ask how you're doing. Gary was in the other day —"

Mom cut in. "He really looked terrible and smelled like pepperoni. I don't know how you ever dated him."

"Mom —"

She was talking over me again. "Anyhow, he was crying and telling your dad that he regrets breaking up with you. He cried right in the store. Can you believe it? How did he break up with you when you can't even receive phone calls?"

For her, it was all about the logistics. I didn't expect her to ask how I felt, because she never did.

"I got a letter," I said. There was no way I was talking to her about this. "It's okay. I get it. Hey, thanks for sending the leftover grocery money. What I would really love is a care package with food and goodies, if you get a chance. We share the treats with each other."

"Just like camp," Mom said.

"Gary said he's been running to get fit and win you back at Christmas," Dad said.

"I am sure you can find a much nicer young man at RMC," Mom piped up. "I told one of the ladies at work that you're going to university in Kingston. She said to make sure you get yourself invited to an RMC ball. When I told her that you're a *cadet* at RMC, she thought you were lucky to be right there and able to meet a really nice eligible bachelor for sure."

"The last thing I want right now is a boyfriend," I said hotly, thinking of my treatment by my classmates. "Especially an RMC cadet. I barely have enough time to sleep, much less date. Did you get my letter about having to study first-year engineering?"

"You'll do fine. You've always been smart in school," Dad said.

"I can't concentrate. I keep reading the same lines over and over in my textbooks, but nothing goes in," I said, checking over my shoulder to make sure I was alone. "Listen, I really don't know if I want to do this. I'm in way over my head in classes. Being with so few women is really hard — much harder than I expected. Some of the guys really hate us."

There was silence on the line. I didn't even know I was thinking it until the words flew out of my mouth. "I'm thinking of quitting," I said.

"I think you should," Mom said eagerly. "I never liked this idea in the first place. You can come home, live here, and go to

Simon Fraser University. We'll help you," she added, her voice firm, as if the decision were already made.

"Actually, now that I've said it out loud, it feels too soon to quit. I'll at least make it through recruit term and see if life gets better. We have an awesome flight. I like lots of my classmates. If I quit, they'll say women can't cut it at the college," I said, back-pedalling as fast as I could. I could picture her wilting smile.

"Why do you even bother asking when you never listen?" she asked.

"Well, give it your best shot. If you don't make it, you'll always know you tried hard," Dad said reassuringly.

"I know, Dad," I said. "I will." I felt a tap on my shoulder and turned with a start. Colbert was holding up a finger for the one-minute warning. I scowled at him.

"I have to go. My turn is over."

"You just called. That can't be right. Tell them to wait," Mom argued.

"I can't, Mom. I gotta go. Don't worry about me. I have friends here. I'm doing well. The food is good. Take care of yourselves. Say hi to everyone for me."

I made my way back through the gunroom, the navy term for a junior officers' lounge on a ship. Our gunroom was in the basement. It was basically the squadron rumpus room, furnished with an old TV and some dilapidated couches and chairs. The ceiling was networked with a series of plumbing pipes painted baby blue. Recruits were forbidden in the gunroom without permission, but we had been allowed to pass through to use the phones.

My feet barely touched the stairs on the way up. I looked around at the yellow-beige paint, the huge spiders out of reach adorning the fixtures, the worn grey-specked linoleum on the stairs, and I felt proud.

I'm going to do this. I laughed out loud in relief as I made my way across the blue carpet of the second-floor foyer.

And then I heard a voice fill the stairwell. "Recruit halt!" Footsteps bounded up the stairs, two steps at a time.

I halted at the edge of the recruit hallway within sight of my door as Second Year Arsenault came around from behind me. "I suppose you think you're allowed to saunter down the halls, laughing out loud and doing whatever you please?" he said, looming over me.

"No, Mr. Arsenault," I said. His nose nearly touched between my eyebrows. I held my ground and did not lean away even when his chest brushed lightly against my breasts.

"Do you think this is a fucking joke!" he barked.

No, but I think you're a fucking asshole.

"No, Mr. Arsenault!" I said.

Behind him, down the hall, Mr. Kendall was smiling as he tiptoed up behind Arsenault.

"This is no place for a woman. Maybe you're not really a woman. A real woman wouldn't want to come here and pretend to be a man. If you had a reason to be laughing to yourself, you don't now. I'm going to make your life hell."

I cracked a half-smile at Mr. Kendall, who stood right behind Arsenault.

"What the fuck?" Arsenault's face turned beet red. "Take five circles, recruit. Report them to Mr. Morgan."

"That won't be necessary, Louis," said Kendall.

Arsenault spun around.

"I witnessed the whole thing," Kendall said. He pulled out his notebook and wrote the circles down. "I'll record Recruit Armstrong's circles, and you'll run along and learn how to play nice instead of lurking around the entrance to my recruit hallway."

"Fine, as long as you know that she was laughing," he complained. He turned on his heel and stomped off.

"If I didn't know better, I'd say he is sweet on you, Recruit Armstrong. What do you think?"

"Please, Mr. Kendall. That is simply too vile to contemplate."

"Of course, it is. You have to watch out for the handsome ones. They can be especially cruel," he said. "Even so, we can't have the rest of the squadron thinking that you're enjoying recruit term. So I'll add another two circles for creating a false impression."

Back in my room, safe at last, I slumped at my desk. I was staying. It was decided, but the moment of exhilaration I'd felt before Arsenault accosted me was gone. I was being punished more than anyone else. There had to be something else to it, something unreachable by me, because I was trying my hardest. I felt pushed to the limit, as if they were waiting to see if I could keep up. I always could. So what was I doing wrong? I was nearly killing myself trying to gain my superiors' approval.

My mother always told me that I asked for trouble. Maybe she was right, but for some reason I was blind to my mistakes. I rested my head on the cool surface of my desk and made myself a promise: *Just keep going through the motions until things calm down.*

10

THE BET

"Are you okay, Kate?" Kurt Samson asked. We were running back from basketball practice alone together for the first time.

"I hardly know. I can barely stay awake in class. I struggle with my homework. I'm running eight circles a night." It seemed like my answers were always the same. I didn't dare criticize my own classmates and their treatment. "And the spiders."

"It gets better. You're almost done the worst part," he said. "Soon you'll be a regular cadet — one weekend parade a month, the occasional room inspection, lots of sports events and parties and balls to enjoy. The main focus becomes academics. Every year gets slacker. Next thing you know, you'll be a fourth year celebrating at your one hundred days to grad party."

"If I complete the obstacle course."

"You're fit. You'll do great," he said. "Say, Kate, do you mind if I ask you some personal stuff?"

"I guess not."

"What are you doing here? You could do anything. Why this place?" he asked.

I stopped dead in my tracks. It took Kurt a stride or two to react. He turned back toward me with a bewildered look.

"No one has ever said anything like that to me before. Is that really what you think?"

"Absolutely."

I looked down at my feet. A scattering of red leaves lay around. I thought about admitting that, given my childhood, I was statistically more likely to be a drug addict or a prostitute than a successful military officer, but I wasn't going to say that to anyone. I soaked up my tears with the sleeve of my sweater. Nobody had ever told me I had *anything* to offer before. I was always too loud and worthless and ungrateful and a little slut. I started to jog again at a lope.

"Kate, for what it's worth, I am glad you're here."

"It's worth everything," I said. I gathered my courage and looked over at him. Our eyes met. I liked how he said my name so often.

"Listen. I … I want to tell you something," he stuttered. "Shit. I know I shouldn't do this. But I want you to know."

"Uh-oh." A tingle ran through me. I wanted to know and didn't want to know in the same breath.

"It's the bet. I want to tell you about the bet," he said, looking around as if there might be spies in the bushes.

"What bet? What do you mean?" I asked, trying not to let my disappointment show.

"The fourth years have a bet to see who can sleep with the most female cadets."

"*What?*"

"Look, I'm not part of it. I didn't know if I should say anything, but I wouldn't forgive myself if anything bad happened to you. I think you're probably at high risk."

"What do you mean? From who?"

"I don't know. Let's face it, you're pretty and you have a great personality. You act tough, but you seem kind of ... innocent to me."

I felt my hair prickle along my scalp. "I am not sleeping with anyone," I said from between clenched teeth.

"Just be careful. I'm not telling you what to do. But I wanted you to know. Plus, there's something else. The Frigate has a new nickname."

"The Love Boat," I said. Kurt blinked. Now I had surprised him.

"Pretty much everyone is saying the Frigate has the best-looking women," he said. "Just keep your chin up and your wits about you."

I broke into a disdainful rendition of the chorus of the college song: "Life's but a march, and it's easy if your spirit's willing."

He laughed and we ran in silence down the stairs passing under the overhead walkway connecting the buildings of the Sawyer complex. The parade square came into view. Without a word, we increased the distance between us and become more formal with each other. Playing on the same team was okay, but people might be watching for fraternization.

"See ya at dinner," he said. We parted at the statue of Brucie.

I approached the white line at the edge of the parade square, halted at attention, and did the pre-run check. I raised my forearms to ninety degrees and stared straight ahead for a moment as Kurt ran away. I felt pissed off, as if I'd been cheated somehow. The recruiters had sold me on an image of this place being filled with the leadership elite of Canada, but I was having another experience.

Right then, a voice bellowed from a third-floor window in Wing Headquarters. "Recruit Armstrong! HALT!"

I dropped my arms to my side and stared straight ahead. *I'm such an idiot. Why didn't I just run away instead of watching Kurt?*

In a few moments, Mr. Helstone, the cadet wing training officer, flew out the front doors of Fort LaSalle Dormitory and marched toward me with an air of supreme self-importance, his blakeys — the metal plates affixed to the bottom of his boots — clicking with each step. The CWTO was the cruellest guy of them all, and I was alone. I braced myself for the worst.

"Good evening, Recruit Armstrong," he said. He was grinning like a maniac.

"Good evening, Mr. Helstone," I said, staring straight through him, avoiding eye contact while trying to keep myself from shaking with fear.

"Do you know why I've stopped you?"

"No, Mr. Helstone."

"Try harder, Recruit Armstrong. At least take a guess."

"For talking outside, Mr. Helstone?"

"No. I missed that part. Thanks for telling me. Take three circles for talking outside, Recruit Armstrong."

"Aye aye, Mr. Helstone."

"*Aye aye.* A simple 'Yes, Mr. Helstone' or 'No, Mr. Helstone' will suffice. You Frigateers and your eccentric little ways. Do you feel special, Recruit Armstrong?"

"Yes, Mr. Helstone. No, Mr. Helstone."

"Now I'm confused."

"Yes, Mr. Helstone, to answering you directly without an *aye aye.* No, Mr. Helstone, I don't feel special."

"Would you like another guess as to why you're standing here, Recruit Armstrong?"

"No, Mr. Helstone."

"Right. That could be dangerous. You can't be too sure what I've seen and what I haven't seen. Well, I see or know pretty much everything going on around this college. That's my job, Recruit Armstrong, to uphold college rules."

How about stopping your own classmates and their stupid bet?

He surprised me by holding up his hand and looking at

his fingernails. He spread his fingers wide, cocked his head, and admired the back of his right hand.

He's killing time. Dragging it out. A cat with a mouse.

"Are you homesick, Miss Armstrong?"

No. In this moment, RMC feels too much *like home.* "No, Mr. Helstone."

After a moment, he spoke again. "You were standing outside in your PT gear staring at a fourth-year cadet."

My face flushed crimson; I *had* been watching Kurt as he ran away.

"You understand that we don't *punish* your behaviour here, Recruit Armstrong. Circles are corrective in nature. Take five circles to correct your behaviour of ogling a fourth-year cadet. No, wait. I suppose that is a matter of opinion. Take the circles for standing around outside in PT gear. We'll keep the ogling as our little secret. Would that please you, Recruit Armstrong?"

He leaned in toward me as if he were trying to smell me.

"Yes, Mr. Helstone."

"Report to Mr. Morgan and let him know about your circles. Three for talking outside and five for standing around in PT gear, and we'll let bygones be bygones. Carry on, Recruit Armstrong."

Several cadets from my squadron were on the parade square heading for dinner. I felt the burn of their stares as I sprinted back to the Frigate.

News of the bet spread like wildfire amongst the women. Besides the obvious vileness of the wager, having sex with female subordinates couldn't possibly be acceptable in the college code of conduct and leadership ethics. But whom could we tell and how could we prove it?

11

SKYLARKS

The bet stripped away a layer of my trust in the fourth-year class. Up until then I had believed they had our highest good in mind despite their horrific treatment of us, that we were just being indoctrinated like every class before us. I was willing to take my knocks alongside the guys. But now life took on a new edge and increased my sense of separation from the male cadets. I felt like an object of prey, and the daily barrage of licentious glances and lewd comments took on new gravity. It became more difficult to keep quiet, play along, and pretend it didn't matter, and more important than ever not to let them know it was getting to me.

Not everything was negative. Recruit term had brought the members of A Flight together in a way nothing else could, and we closed ranks against whatever the fourth years threw at us. We celebrated our wins. Sometimes we fought amongst ourselves, but the bitterness evaporated with a handshake after the explosion of energy was released. A recruit folklore was developing around the funny stories. We teased each other relentlessly for mishaps or lapses in thinking, retelling the tales with the fervour of drunks keeping the laughter going at the bar. We shared stories about waking in a sweat from nightmares about lost pieces of kit when it was time to fall in, nearly shitting ourselves on parade when there was no possible way to get to the toilet, and cracks in the fourth years' armour that accidentally let signs of their humanity slip out. We praised each other for small victories.

As our confidence grew, recruit term became a testament to human adaptability, and our collective attitude took a turn toward the lighter side of the situation. Suddenly, we were on the offensive and looking for entertainment at the expense of the fourth years.

The noon meal was mandatory, the one time of day when the entire cadet wing was in the same place at the same time, seated by squadron, to hear announcements. A simple happy birthday wish to a fourth-year cadet set off crazed chanting within the dining hall: "LAKE! LAKE! LAKE!" An eruption of scrambling recruits would chase down the birthday boy — who was usually making a mad dash for the doors — and then drag his thrashing body down to the Kingston Harbour and literally toss him into the lake.

One day at lunch, I chose fish sticks. I made a fork sandwich with a chunk of fish bookended by two carrots. The combo was an inch from my mouth.

"Do you think you're Georgia Fucking O'Keeffe, Recruit Armstrong?" Mr. Jansen asked, mad-dogging me from the other end of the table. I took the bite, put down my cutlery, and chewed sitting neatly at attention with my hands in my lap. My eyes bugged out with the effort to chew quickly.

The whole time I was chewing, Maxwell and Fitzroy, straight across the table from me, sat with their faces bent toward their plates, gut laughing without making a sound. When Fitzroy looked up, he had tears on his cheeks. *Bring it.*

I choked down the mouthful. "No, Mr. Jansen," I replied.

"Fine. Take three circles. Carry on, and quit making art with your lunch." Jansen had lost interest in me. Fitzroy was more interesting. "Kill that yuk, Fitzroy."

Grant leapt to his feet, his chair crashing loudly on the floor behind him. Recruits at other tables looked our way.

To kill that yuk, he had to wipe the smile off his face and crush it underfoot like a cigarette butt. Grant executed the move with natural precision. His hand flew up to his forehead and slid down his face, shutting down all expression as it passed. Then he trounced on the yuk and left it for dead. He snapped back to attention wearing a calm, cold expression.

"The yuk is dead, Mr. Jansen," Fitzroy reported.

No one moved.

After a few seconds, Mr. Theroux counted aloud from his end of the table. "Five, four, t'ree …"

Fitzroy bared his teeth like a donkey and snorted.

"I fucking knew it!" Mr. Theroux yelled. "'Dat yuk is not really dead, is it, Fitzroy? Take five circle." Fitzroy repeated the drill and stood like a stone. "Carry on, Fitzroy."

Mr. Theroux picked up his knife and fork to resume eating. He stabbed a small piece of chicken and loaded it with mashed potatoes. As soon as he had safely placed the food in his mouth, Becker piped up. We had a strategy to kill time at meals to prevent the fourth years from eating too quickly so that the rest of us could stuff our faces with square meals.

"Excuse me, Mr. Theroux, 14454, Recruit Becker, T., One Squadron, A Flight, Three Section reporting." He sat at attention to address a fourth year.

Mr. Theroux's eyes narrowed. He placed his utensils properly on his plate and glared at Becker while he chewed, his lips jutting out with the motion. Becker sat quietly waiting with a shit-eating grin on his face.

"Yes, Mr. Becker. Dis better be good," Theroux said. He shoved his hand through his thick, wavy bangs.

"I was wondering, Mr. Theroux. Have you ever killed anyone?"

"No. Eat your lunch, Becker. Take two circle for asking a stupid question."

Mr. Theroux looked around the table. He reached for his flatware and took another bite.

I sat to attention. "Excuse me, Mr. Theroux, 14390, Recruit Armstrong, K.A., One Squadron, A Flight, Three Section reporting."

He chewed and swallowed. I sat at attention and stared straight ahead waiting. "Yes, Miss Armstrong?"

"I was wondering, Mr. Theroux, when is your birthday?"

"Like I would tell you. Take five circle."

The next morning during room inspection, my spider-basher stick whooshed past my head and bounced in the hall. I had fashioned it from a broken bit of broom handle by attaching a yellow Kiwi shoe-polishing cloth to one end with an elastic band. The cloth was stained with squished spider juice, and one or two stray legs stuck in the fabric like thorns. I didn't dare look over at Meg. She was going to kill me. I had forgotten it behind the door.

Mr. Kendall was out in the hall in a flash, waving the retrieved stick in my face. "What's the explanation of this?"

"I'm afraid of spiders, Mr. Kendall."

Now Mr. Morgan was beside him. "You're killing our squadron mascots?"

"Yes, Mr. Morgan," I said, "but only if they come into our room."

He grabbed the spider basher from Mr. Kendall, opened the door to the women's washroom, and tossed it in there. "Make this disappear. Take five circles. Just you. Not Miss Carter."

The skylark rule was that absolutely anything was fair game, so long as the trick, joke, or horseplay could be reversed and everything restored to normal by noon the next day and no one got hurt and nothing got permanently damaged.

At midnight, we snuck quietly down the fire escape stairs and met in the shadow of the boathouse. "Where the hell are Colbert and Duval?" Richie asked. He checked his watch and stared at the fire escape.

"They're not coming," said Plourde.

"Why not? We need everyone," exclaimed Richie.

"They said to tell you it's bullshit and they're sleeping tonight. They're not into skylarks," replied Plourde with a shrug.

"Fuckers. Okay, let's go," said Richie.

Even in the dark, it was easy to make out the large gaggle of people gathering near the edge of the road about a block away from the commandant's residence as we crested the slope.

Holbrook, Becker, and Bristow made their way over to the paint cans that had been pre-arranged by some of the guys in Six Squadron, who were stashing cans of white paint against a bush nearby and piling leaves over them in preparation for restoration painting tomorrow. In no time at all, the brushes and paint cans were divided up. According to the recruit handbook, the commandant's fence had 1,876 pickets, corresponding to the year the college was established. It worked out to ten or fifteen slats per recruit. We split up and took up our posts as the organizers counted out the sections and signalled the groupings using our silent field signals from basic training.

The painting was fast and easy. One coat of colour per picket, on the outside only, so that it could quickly be returned to white after the joke was over. I imagined General Horton looking out his window in the morning, seeing his white picket fence the same as always from the inside, only to be surprised as he closed the gate behind him on his walk over to the office. Within a matter of minutes, the small tins, paint pails, and brushes were stashed next to the white paint cache. We headed back to the Frigate and were back in bed within an hour.

"Let's move it, A Flight! Wear your sweaters today. It's fucking cold out dere," yelled Mr. Theroux. As we cleared the edge of the Sawyer Building, we peeked left to see if our handiwork from last night could be seen in dawn's light.

"What da —" Mr. Theroux exclaimed. "A Flight, halt! Left turn."

We were in the middle of the road looking up the hill. The multicoloured pickets spanned the commandant's yard like a playground fence.

"What da hell is dis, A Flight!" Mr. Theroux motioned toward the fence. "Was dis you?"

No one said anything.

"Speak up!" he hollered.

"Aye aye, Mr. Theroux," Richie shouted.

"AR, AR, AR," roared Mr. Theroux. "Fuck da run dis morning. Dat's a beautiful ting. Let's go 'ome."

We looked around at each other, stunned. *Was he for real?*

"Left turn! Double time!" he ordered. "Dis is what I h'am talking about. All da time we wait for you to show some spirit, take some h'initiative around 'ere. I reward you for dat. One more hour sleep, to make up for your late night last night, 'ell yeah."

I felt like pointing out that Colbert and Duval should still go for their run, but didn't. Meg and I crawled on top of our made beds. I threw my housecoat over me and slept at attention until the call came from the hall to wake up again.

At breakfast, the dining hall was buzzing with the skylark story. While we were eating, the microphone speakers crackled to life.

"Wing," Cadet Wing Commander Dansen's voice rang through the loudspeakers. Everyone stopped eating and sat at attention. "Sit easy. During the night, the fence to General Horton's residence was renovated. Although he admits that the new colour scheme has a certain allure to it, he thanks you very much for the effort and says to please feel free to restore his fence to its original state by noon today. Effective immediately, the requirement for recruits to eat square meals has been lifted."

"Three cheers for the class of eighty-four!" someone yelled from one of the nonrecruit tables. As the entire wing chanted, we sat smiling and looking very smug. The end of square meals was the best thing to happen in my life, maybe ever. At that moment, I was proud to be there.

"Give me a beer!" roared someone else.

"BEER ESSES EMMA. TDV! WHO CAN STOP OLD RMC? SCHRAPNEL. CORDITE. NCT! RMC!"

I was hungry and gobbled down my pancakes. No cunt tonight. I tried not to hear those words, only the letters. I was safe; it was going to work out. This place was all right. Maybe there was no bet. Maybe it was just a joke and Kurt had taken it wrong. This place, I realized, wasn't anything like home. Here, the demeaning, the name-calling, and the yelling had a higher purpose, a purpose aimed to help me see myself, my real self, not to hurt me.

12

DOGGIE NIGHT

Suddenly it was the end of recruit term, and the culmination of all our training was a series of competitions. Each recruit was awarded individual points that counted toward an overall team score. The winning squadron held *right of the line* on parade, which meant marching in the place of honour during Ex-Cadet Weekend. In the frenzy, I forgot about everything — the bet; the constant stream of punishment that had me running circles every night; the creepiness of Helstone's obsession with me, although he never let up for a moment and continued to dog my every step; and the continuing onslaught of cheap shots about being a female cadet — everything except the looming obstacle course.

As we competed in each event, the madness of recruit term took on a new perspective. Recruit harriers was an individual running competition that followed the exact route of our morning run. The recruit inspection by the cadet wing commander followed the exact layout of every critical morning inspection we had endured. The recruit drill competition, the recruit college history exams, and *Cadet Wing Instructions* exams covered our learning from the limitless drill practices, pop quizzes, and questions of the day that had been cemented in our heads.

Our worst showing was in the passing off the square competition, which combined drill and etiquette questions, judged by CWC Dansen and CWTO Helstone. Each recruit had to be cleared for the privilege to sign out and leave college grounds after recruit term, the idea being that we needed to be deemed fit to represent the college in public. Still, after all the competitions, Hudson Squadron was in first place. *Now* came the obstacle course, which scared the shit out of me, out of all of us.

The recruit obstacle course would be run the next afternoon to kick off Ex-Cadet Weekend. A loss by us and a concurrent win by Eight Squadron could bump the Frigate out of right of the line into the oblivion of mediocrity.

The most infamous death on the obstacle course was a cadet who had been trampled underwater at the bottom of an A-frame in Navy Bay and not found until after the race was run. Since then, each recruit had been assigned a kind of chaperone, who followed, from the sidelines, the progress of that recruit through the course. This person was called a *mother*.

"Fall in for mothers!" called out Mr. Morgan. "Let's go, people." We scrambled into the recruit hallway and wound our way down the circular staircase to the gunroom.

Our names were unceremoniously read off a list followed by the name of a fourth-year cadet. A small, delicate-looking man approached me. I shook his hand; his skin was softer than mine. *This guy is supposed to save my life?* I stood a head taller than him.

"Luka Chownyk," he said and beamed. "I was hoping I'd be assigned as your mother!" He dragged two chairs into a corner and made room for us to sit.

"You were?" I croaked incredulously.

"Kevin Blackwood is my best friend. He talks about you from basketball."

"Um," I stuttered. "He's not that nice to me."

"That's just Woodsie. He's a great guy underneath. He's just a bit shy, is all," he said. Chownyk squeezed my knee in friendly encouragement.

Mr. Morgan shot me a glare. I sat up a bit straighter and pulled my knees together.

"So, I'm your spotter for the obstacle course," he said, as if this was reassuring news.

"Thank you, Mr. Chownyk." My voice was tight.

"Oh! Don't worry," he smiled. "Nothing bad is going to happen to you. Call me Luka."

"Yes, Mr. Chownyk," I said. He was nuts if he thought I was going to openly address a fourth year by his first name.

Mr. Morgan shouted that our time was up.

"You'll do great. Don't lose any sleep over it," Chownyk said.

The expression made me smile. Two more sleeps and the longest six weeks of my life would be behind me. Outwardly, I imagined I looked relaxed and confident, but inwardly I knew my thoughts were fogged with fear of the one thing that shadowed every waking moment — surviving the obstacle course.

Today was Hell Day, our last full day as recruits, which culminated in Doggie Night, the recruit-term open-season night for the fourth-year cadets to take a final run at us.

The dark, chill October air was the perfect backdrop for our final morning run. The obstacle course handiwork of the LCWB loomed along the route like beasts, shrouded from prying eyes by tarps weighted down with small boulders.

We'd been forewarned to expect a white-glove inspection and had been up most of the night making silent preparations. Meg and I had scrubbed, dusted, shone, touched up, ironed, folded, and polished every possible surface of our space, our uniforms, and ourselves.

Our room was first today. Morgan and Kendall breezed past us without checking our uniforms. My eyeballs involuntarily shot over toward Meg, but I didn't move another muscle as I tracked them with a practised ear. I heard a drawer open and some whispering. Mr. Morgan stood directly before us holding a pair of white gloves in each hand.

"Top marks, recruits," he said. "Your white gloves have passed inspection." The fourth years doubled over together, laughing and slapping each other's backs.

After classes, the recruit flight staff greeted us in the hallway. Morgan was wearing standard-issue green long johns, a jock-strap on the outside, a navy-blue squadron SFMA jersey with the spider emblem, and the college toque. "You're late! Get out of your work dress and into your PT gear NOW, A Flight." We tossed our books into their spots in our bookshelves, changed, and jumped into the hall at attention.

"Welcome to Doggie Night! We promise that no one will be permanently disfigured, but we won't be held responsible for lasting psychological damage," said Mr. Morgan. "First order of business, Mr. Jamieson offered to take you out for a warm-up run and get you limber!"

The light was bad and the weather had turned, the sky leaden, threatening. As we set out it started to mist, and by the time we hit Fort Henry Hill rain was coming down in sheets and the sky was black. The rain had softened the earth, muffling the sounds of our movement. On the way back, Mr. Jamieson ran us straight into an ankle-deep mud puddle on the sports field and halted us there. "Down and give me twenty, recruits!" We dropped into the water; the fug of body odour and wet wool hung above us. Twenty face-soaking push-ups later, we were moving again.

Back in recruit hallway, our blotched faces were smeared with mud and sweat. By now, the fourth years had all changed into costumes, dressed up in various military outfits, a mishmash of field combat gear and PT gear with personal items added as flourish.

I took a deep breath and surrendered to whatever came this night. Recruit term had taught me that I was a risk taker. I was always testing boundaries: talking at unauthorized times, laughing too loudly, cracking inappropriate jokes to let the fourth years know they didn't have total control over me. I wanted to stop. But I couldn't. My mind flashed vivid images of the absurd beyond the obvious of a situation and I regularly blurted out what I was thinking. I vowed to be quieter from now on if I made it through the obstacle course tomorrow.

"A Flight, stand on your heads," commanded Morgan.

Without missing a beat, we turned to face the wall and kicked up into a headstand.

"Stand up," he said. "Close your eyes. Spin five times around to the right." My head swirled with my body. I bumped into walls and bodies. "Open your eyes." I was several feet down and across the hall, inches away from Holbrook; we grinned at each other. "Close your eyes. Spin five times the other direction!

"Stop. Get back to your room, get out of that wet gear, and put on every single piece of recruit uniform. Go!"

We staggered back to our rooms as though on a ship in a storm. My legs dropped out beneath me as if the floor was falling away. Meg and I crashed drunkenly around our room, stripping down and jamming every conceivable piece of kit onto our clammy bodies. We turned out in the hall wearing double socks in our boots; pants, skirts over pants, layered shirts; CF tunics, raincoats, winter coats, tripling up; on our heads, toque, beret, and CF hat. Socks covered our gloved hands stuffed into shoes. Our brand-new RMC cadet uniforms remained untouched in the game, fitted and tailored weeks previously in anticipation of our becoming first-year cadets tomorrow afternoon.

Now I was hot. For the next fifteen minutes, Mr. Morgan stood in a door frame at the end of the hall and yelled out drill commands as we marched around in one big circle, forwards and backwards drill, and then he ordered us to come back out dressed in a clean set of PT gear.

McDonald's takeout bags sat on a display table when we got back into the hall. Mr. Morgan ordered us to form one long line down the hall. I was head of the line with Meg on my immediate left. He held open a bag full of Quarter Pounders for me; I took one. "Take a bite, Recruit Armstrong, and pass it along," he said.

My jaw cracked as I took the biggest bite possible, hoping to catch some extra pickles. I breathed through my nose, turned to Meg, and offered her the hamburger.

"Not the burger, recruit. Pass the bite."

"Huh?" I gurgled through my mouthful of food.

"PASS THE BITE, Recruit Armstrong!"

I turned toward Meg — her eyes were huge — and the sting of tears tickled the back of my nose. I closed my eyes, opened my mouth, and leaned in.

"Wait!" Morgan cried out. I froze. "Christ, how evil do you think I am?" The fourth years cackled amongst themselves. He held the bag out for Meg to take her own burger. "If you can't take a joke, you shouldn't have joined, people!"

We ate at breakneck speed and then spent the next five hours as pawns for fourth-year amusement. We camouflaged each other; did pit drill in our beds, trashing our sheets with the freshly applied camo; and competed in sit-ups, wall sits, chin-ups, hall sprints, and burpee, dive-bomber, and handclap push-ups. They forced us through a series of contact games in which our mattresses were their favourite prop; the most dangerous involved sliding under the mattress cover and lifting the mattress off the floor, then charging blindly, running full tilt toward another recruit coming from the opposite end of the hall until we collided. After we'd all had a turn, it was time to stand in a row holding up our mattresses and be repeatedly shoved over like dominoes up and down the hall. Finally, we piled the mattresses at one end of the hall, on the floor and against the walls, and made mad sprints, flinging ourselves into the mattress pit, following the aircraft carrier landing signals being made by Mr. Theroux with a set of Ping-Pong paddles.

At lights out, Morgan ordered us to clean up. The hallway was littered with sheets, mattresses, and random pieces of kit from our rooms. It stank like hockey gear, a pungent odour of sweat, smelly feet, and jockstraps.

"This night marks the end of an era for each of you. Recruit term comes only once in a lifetime," he said.

"Thank God!" yelled Becker. Everyone laughed.

Morgan continued: "Not everyone makes it through recruit term. I am proud that this year we started with twenty people and we've ended with twenty people. You've done something above and beyond what most people will ever attempt, much less accomplish, in their entire lifetimes. Seven minutes for showers and lights out. Fall out!"

The good-night song played over the stereo for the final time. Every inch of my body hurt. I lay in bed and cried.

13

OBSTACLE COURSE

Speakers crackled. Vivaldi blasted for the last wake-up call of recruit term. I smiled. *Fuck you, Vivaldi.*

Blooming in fresh bruises after Doggie Night, I sat with my fellow recruits on a stone wall alongside the Frigate to pose for the "before" photo. We looked like a greaser gang from the fifties, hair slicked back, Converse high-top runners, and pant legs wrapped and taped closed into stovetops around our ankles. Earlier in the week, somehow, I had taken the time to paint one white letter, using the gooey white belt paste, on each of my fellow recruits' navy-blue jerseys, except on Plourde's shirt, which had the word *of.* Now we organized ourselves in the photo to spell our identity: Stone Frigate Class of '84.

Luka Chownyk lingered nearby in the group of cheering Frigateer spectators, ready to spot me through the course. A mix of other onlookers crowded around, as well — a few parents of recruits and ex-cadet Frigate alumni.

Mr. Morgan said his final words to us as recruits. "As it was in the beginning, so it is in the end. This is no time for superstars. Hudson

Squadron is not done until everyone is done. Work as a team. Do not leave anyone behind at the mercy of another squadron. Be strategic. Make us proud. Whatever you do, don't stop thinking!"

The race started in front of the Frigate. As we crested the rise to the start line on the parade square, a sea of recruit flights ran toward us in solid blocks of colour, trailing matching sprays of squadron spectators along behind them. The storm had passed. The sun was out. It was a gorgeous fall day and spirits were high. My fear shifted to determination. I was either ready or not. Recruit flights formed up along the front of the Frigate, the different squadron colours mashed together like a painter's palette. The parade square was crowded with a thousand people dressed in civilian clothes, the ex-cadet blue blazer and grey flannel pants, and military uniforms. Even reporters from the local press were on scene.

We were the show.

CWC Dansen said a few formal words of greeting, welcoming guests and visitors and wishing us well. Then, our very own Second Year Arsenault took over as the master of ceremonies. A rush of adrenaline pulsed through me as I bounced on the spot and shook out my arms like a boxer priming for the prize fight.

Several second-year cadets came into view from the side of the square, dragging a charged firehose. "Proceed with the dousing!" commanded Arsenault. The front man opened the spout, and the force of the water wrestled them like a writhing powerful snake as a wide, white arc of spray tore at our skin and clothes. When the torrent pointed at me, the water shocked me with a punch in the gut. We crouched into huddles with our backs as a shield until it was over and the second-year cadets were panting over the dripping hose.

General Horton stepped front and centre, dressed in his alumni blazer. He raised a starter's pistol over his head and paused for effect. *Nobody dies.*

BANG!

Every recruit flight ran off in a different direction, like a riot gone wrong. We pushed through the crowd and emerged in front of the senior staff mess. I kept to the centre of the group as it spread out. My heart was beating in dark terror as I wondered what I was about to face and if I could conquer it.

Our first obstacle was a ten-foot wall at the edge of Fort Frederick, covered in plastic and some kind of oily tar. Bristow leaned against the greased plywood frame and planted his feet and made a step with cupped hands. Holbrook scrambled up Bristow's body with a boost and straddled the frame at the top. Tate joined him. One by one, we climbed up Bristow and were tossed over by Holbrook and Tate onto thin gymnastic mats. Finally, Bristow jumped up to Holbrook's and Tate's waiting arms and the three of them scrambled over together.

Once a recruit had passed over an obstacle, it was against the rules to go back and help. The last person had to make it on their own or depend upon the generosity of the other squadrons coming up behind to lend a hand.

The marshal compelled us forward toward the steep walls of Fort Frederick where two thirty-foot ropes, with knots tied at five-foot intervals, hung down from the top of the hill onto the slope of the field below. The ropes rested on sheets of industrial grade plastic covered in the same tarry substance as the wall.

I rushed up the rope and slipped in the tar, and my chin hit the hill with a neck-snapping thud. I skidded back down the terrain to the foot of the hill. Holbrook took charge and started barking out orders. We made a human chain up, securing ourselves on the line and standing on one another's shoulders. Six of us formed a body bridge for the others to climb up. I was third up the line, holding on for dear life. I held my ground while others climbed up and over.

Fitzroy kicked me in the face when his foot slipped, and I tasted the metal trickle of blood in my mouth. Time seemed to slow down.

The human rope scrambled up from the bottom. Becker was holding anchor at the top of the hill while powerful arms yanked the rest of us up and over, and in the process my cotton knit squadron jersey was ripped off my back.

Luka burst through the crowd and threw an indestructible navy-blue nylon shirt in my face. I peeled off my torn one and threw it back as I stumbled, half running and half staggering, along the path on the embankment toward the next obstacle.

Two obstacles and I've already lost my shirt. We faced six more kilometres of torn-up terrain.

We crouched down and scuttled through a tunnel, climbed up tires tied to the stairs for the Martello Tower, down into the moat, back up the stairs, over to the hill, back down the hill, back up the hill, and finally scaled the fort wall on a knot rope and leapt onto puffy gymnastic mats on the other side. Exhaustion dragged at my limbs, but every time I faced a new challenge adrenaline came to the rescue.

We emerged from the fort, followed the water's edge along Kingston Harbour, scooted under bleachers, negotiated unstable no-touch single-rope bridges that required a redo if a foot touched the ground, leopard-crawled under brush, swung between tires on the sports field goalposts at a height of five feet, and clambered up a ceaseless series of rope nets. In between obstacles, we sprinted across the gaps.

Eventually, the muddy sports field behind the Sawyer Building came into view. We slogged through the mud. But where was the obstacle? As we got close, a frothy mouthed second-year marshal yelled in our faces.

"Get in the hole, you fuckers!" He pointed down at the wet, dark, muddy entrance to a cave under a network of camouflage tarps spread across the ground, weighted on the outside edges with sandbags and covered in dirt. I slithered in behind Nigel Maxwell and stayed right on his heels in the pitch black, crawling on my hands and knees through dank mud, my back chafing against the weighted tarp above us.

"It stinks like piss in here," he moaned.

I didn't care. *Move it move it move it.* Light returned as we neared the end. Maxwell popped out of the hole and I oozed out after him.

After the next sprint, we hit the storm culvert ditch under the road leading up to Fort Henry Hill, filled three feet deep with water. I splashed down into it and started running, my legs burning with effort. The water pushed back and it was like being sucked into quicksand. I made swimming strokes on the surface with my hands to pull myself along.

Finally, up and out of the ditch, we raced back onto the muddy field alongside Navy Bay. My pants were heavy, my pockets draining. *I could just stop. And then what? Give up on the last day after working so hard? And go where? Home?*

Luka was right there cheering from the sidelines. "You're doing great. You're gonna make it. All the hard ones are done now. Take a break whenever you get the chance. Recharge."

I was caked in mud and tar and panting so hard that I could barely hear him. My spirit rallied. I was doing this. I didn't give a shit what anyone thought of me. *Fuck everyone.*

Next was a maze of coarse rope pegged tight to the ground and secured with huge rocks. Holbrook squeezed under the lip of the net into the muddy slop beneath it. I threw my head back, hands on my hips, and greedily sucked in air.

"Get down, sweat," the second-year marshal growled at me.

I dove under and leopard-crawled forward. The rough netting pulled through my greased hair and forced my face into the mud. I roared my frustration.

Luka stopped cheering and I became the ninja woman on the bathroom door, a mind floating above my body as my legs kept pumping, my lungs heaving.

The Frigate loomed ahead and the marshal sent us down into the moat to navigate obstacles around the base of the building. Surfacing around the back of the Frigate, I trailed after Fitzroy up the slope and toward the red bleachers edging the far side of the parade square. A crowd of spectators had gathered in the area, near the finish line.

Luka was beside me yelling again. "GO! GO! GO! This is it! Last one! Finish hard. Finish hard!"

I hit the bleachers at full speed and followed Fitzroy's route up the ten rows of awkwardly spaced, slimy bench seats streaked with footprints. From the top, I hurled myself down ten feet onto a thin pile of gym mats and broke into a run. Mentally I was urging my body to speed up, but physically I was already moving at full tilt.

I pushed through the last hundred metres and crossed the finish line, collapsing onto my hands and knees, my forehead on the ground as I sobbed. It was done. I had passed the test. I could stay and become a first-year cadet.

Holbrook grabbed my arm and literally lifted me to my feet. His piercing blue eyes were framed with mud and tar. "Come on! We gotta go back and cheer on the others!"

A second wind hit as Holbrook and I ran side by side upstream through the throng, encouraging our teammates as they passed in the other direction. We were looking for the last person wearing a blue jersey on the course: Nancy Sloane.

Her exhaustion was evident in her rolling eyes and spastic leg movements as she bounced up from the mats at the bottom of the bleachers, and pushed on, her short legs flailing through the hundred metres to the finish, a crowd of Frigateers running alongside, cheering as she staggered across the line and the official timer hit the button on his stopwatch. We had all finished. It was over.

Luka hugged an arm around my waist and braced me to him. Rumours flashed through the crowd that one recruit had broken his leg and another had stalled out, unable to go on. Both were men.

When every squadron had finished, it didn't take long to sort out the winners. "Wing!" CWC Dansen yelled into the megaphone. The silence was immediate. Luka held fast in his support of me, but I edged out of his embrace to stand alone.

"Congratulations to all recruits of the Class of 1984. It is my great honour to officially welcome you as *first-year cadets* of the Royal Military College of Canada."

A roar broke out amongst all years. "Gimme a beer!" The college cheer rang out.

"Today is a day you'll never forget. Each of you has faced the most challenging physical test you are likely to ever encounter in your lifetime. The winners are:

"Third place, BRANT SQUADRON!

"Second place, WOLFE SQUADRON!"

I held my breath.

"First place, HUDSON SQUADRON!"

YEA STONE!

Holbrook and I ran at each other and leapt into the air with a chest-crashing hug. "That was freaking brilliant! We did it. We won," Holbrook sang out. I howled in joy.

Luka slapped my shoulder and I pulled him toward me for a filthy, tarry, stinking hug. "You were a great mother!"

"Mothers are for life!" he said, laughing and wiping my muck off his chest.

"I'll hold you to that!" I said. He put his arm around my waist and supported me in a slow stagger back to the Frigate.

Three hours after the first photo, we reformed to pose for the "after" shot, a cluster of smiling, triumphant, bleary faces with bodies covered in filthy, torn, and bedraggled clothes. It seemed, at this moment, that I had found my only possible life and these people were my only possible friends.

14

SWEATS

I waited until last for showers after the obstacle course. Then I sequestered myself in the washroom alone and ran a bath. While the tub filled, I showered to remove the main grime and took a look at myself in the full-length mirror. I had bags under my eyes and was covered in bruises and scratches. I skimmed my gaze over my entire body and admired my long legs, graceful-fingered hands, grapefruit-like breasts with quarter-sized nipples, newly defined stomach, Irish-green eyes, and auburn hair. My focus shifted easily to parts that I hated: the shortness of my neck, my left shoulder sitting higher than my right, the extra flap of skin on my left ear helix identical to my great-grandmother's in her wedding photo, and my hammertoes.

I slid into the hot water with a groan, assuring myself that I would hold on to some of my femininity and feistiness through the next four years, against any pressure to be otherwise. I closed my eyes, sank my head below the surface, and felt my freshly washed hair float gently in the water. I was happy, mostly, with how I looked, maybe for the first time ever, and at the same time I felt uncomfortable. This was no place to be a girl. No one here welcomed the feminine side of anything, and wanting to look good felt dangerous, like I would be asking for trouble by being attractive.

I didn't know what mattered to me anymore. I didn't know what my politics were. I didn't really know what to think of myself or who I was trying to become. I felt afraid. This place wasn't normal. I knew that much. So that meant I couldn't be normal to be here. I had done everything they had thrown at me so far, but did I really want it? Just because I could, did that mean I should?

When I got back to the room, Meg was in bed. The wind had picked up, bringing a fresh storm off the lake, and rain blew hard against our window. The sky darkened to pitch black and great blinding flashes of lightning broke against the night. Growing up in British Columbia, I had never seen the likes of the thunderstorms that come off Lake Ontario. I remained captivated. In a spur-of-the-moment decision, I listened to the teenage girl in me. I whipped off my housecoat, dressed in my PT gear, rushed out onto the parade square barefoot, threw my arms wide, hung my head back to feel the rain on my face, and danced in a circle to the booming of the thunder. Suddenly, Meg was beside me. We whirled in laughter for several minutes until we crashed against each other in a hug and held on tight.

The remainder of Ex-Cadet Weekend went off without a glitch. After the countless practice sessions of the past six weeks, the members of A Flight were finally integrated as full-fledged cadets of Hudson Squadron in an elaborate parade procession on Saturday morning. The wind from the storm had blown itself out and a soaked Hudson Squadron burgee hung limp from the college yardarm declaring to the world that we were right of the line coming out of recruit term. I felt surges of pride. My skin tingled as I joined the precise movements of those around me. All the squadrons were dressed in perfect rows, perfect squares, perfectly organized. Eight hundred cadets making clicks, slaps, stomps, and stamps in unison created a sense of power as one unit. After being dismissed as newly badged first-year cadets, we were met by an impromptu receiving line formed on both sides of the double doors to the Frigate. The senior-year cadets of the squadron, most of whom we had never met, welcomed us with handshakes and backslaps.

We reached the A Flight hallway and found Mr. Morgan waiting. He held his notebook and was reading aloud the official tally of our final circles count as each person passed him.

"Two hundred and eighty-two circles to run off, First Year Armstrong."

"Aye aye, Mr. Morgan."

I already knew that. I smiled. My sleepwalking days were over.

On Saturday afternoon, we went up to the attic to retrieve our personal belongings. At lights out, I placed the headphones of my precious Walkman over my ears, plugged in my Simon and Garfunkel cassette, and created my own bedtime-song ritual. Tears streamed down my face as I replayed and mouthed the words to "The Boxer" over and over.

Later in the week, a special meeting was arranged for all the female cadets to have a private discussion with Captain Bernice Palomer, Eight Squadron Commander, in her squadron's lounge. In her military career, she was a food services officer and, of course, had never attended RMC. Although I had never spoken with her, in my mind she was our de facto protector. It was our first gathering alone with all thirty-two of the female cadets and the only female squadron commander.

"There is no sex allowed on college grounds. You may date within one year of your year. That means this year, you may date a first year or a second year. Marriage is forbidden without the written approval of the commandant. Any infraction of the dating rules may lead to expulsion." Captain Palomer read from a piece of paper without looking at us, her face tight, voice restricted. She had a shock of grey hair, skunk-like, pulled back left of centre to her tidy black bun.

"If you're approached by the press, direct them to your squadron commander. He will take appropriate action to channel the request. Under no circumstances shall you speak to the press without permission or make disparaging remarks about the college in public."

She stopped reading. "Let me say another word about the press. One of the main complaints made by the male classmates about the first women at West Point, in the Class of 1980, was related to the attention the women were getting in the press. I suggest you downplay any references to considering yourself special and keep the focus on being in this together with your male classmates if you want to avoid the same conflict."

After reading through a long list of rules, she concluded with a crisp "Any questions?" We all looked around to see if anyone was going to speak up. No one said a word.

My lips parted and I took a breath, summoning the courage to say something about the bet.

Before I could speak, she rushed on. "I have an open-door policy," she said. "If you have any concerns related to being a female cadet, please bring them to my attention. If it is something that needs my follow-up, I will take it on. Otherwise, any questions or concerns are more properly funnelled through your own chain of command." She was making eye contact now; I sighed and looked down as her gaze swept over me.

She dismissed us. Not one of us had spoken up, nor had she asked us any direct personal questions. The meeting had lasted all of ten minutes.

Meg and I halted simultaneously at the edge of the parade square, completed a perfunctory area check, and broke into a run. Recruit term was over but first years ran the square all year.

"We can get permission to be engaged but we're not allowed to kiss," I said, keeping my voice low.

Meg laughed.

"How has it been so far, ladies?" I asked in a singsong voice. "Oh wonderful, ma'am. Thank you for asking."

"Do you think she knows about the bet?" Meg asked.

"Doubtful," I said. "And she doesn't want to know, either."

We ran the rest of the way in silence. I thought about my helplessness as a little girl and not knowing how to take care of myself. I did now. Nothing like that would ever happen to me again. I would fucking kill anyone who tried.

The following week, Meg closed our door during study hours and pulled her chair beside me. "Do you know why they call us 'sweats'?" she asked.

I shook my head.

"Two jerks at dinner were talking about how sweats were ruining the college. One guy was saying that at first he'd thought it was a good idea to let sweats in, but only the 'Love Boat' had women good looking enough to consider *banging*, like I wasn't sitting right there."

"Well, you are pretty cute," I said.

"Be serious."

"Okay. So who were they?"

"I'm guessing hockey guys. Fencing and hockey are usually the last ones at dinner. I just got up and left."

"I'm gonna ask Luka," I said.

Still dressed in my PT gear after circle parade, I stood outside Luka's door, knuckles poised. I hesitated. I could hear voices as I rapped on the door.

"Come in?" His invitation was hesitant.

I opened the door slowly and stood still without entering the room. Kevin Blackwood, from basketball, was folded up on cushions in the bay window, back against one wall and feet high against the opposing wall. He had started out in the Class of 1981 with Luka but was repeating third year. If you failed a single course, you had one chance to write a supplemental exam, and if you failed that, you had to repeat the entire academic year.

"I am sorry to bother you, Mr. Chownyk," I said. "Is this a good time to speak with you alone?"

"Sure," he said. "Hey, Woodsie, come back later, okay?"

Blackwood grunted his disapproval, uncoiled himself, and left without saying a word. I looked down as he left the room.

"Have a seat," Luka said, not getting up from his lounge chair. He gestured toward the bay window.

I sat on the still-warm cushions and rearranged myself so I didn't touch them. I cut to the chase. "Have you ever heard the expression 'sweats'?"

He dropped his chin to his chest and sighed. "Yes."

"Why are they calling us sweats? I don't get it."

"In the Old English lexicon, 'old sweat' referred to a soldier who had a lot of experience in a certain area."

"How does that apply to female cadets?"

"It's about sex."

"Huh?"

Luka picked at the arm of his chair. "Basically, it's a way of calling the lady cadets whores. The running joke is that you came here for sex and break out in a sweat whenever you think about it because you're all so ugly and want sex with the male cadets so badly. That you're old sweats in the sack," he explained in a rush.

"Are you kidding me?"

Luka laughed nervously.

"Do you think it's funny?" I said.

"What! Me? No," he said, horrified.

"Do you think I'm ugly?"

"No, Kate. You're not."

"Does everyone call us sweats?" I asked.

"I don't think so."

"Is anyone stopping it?"

"I don't think so," he said and dropped his head again.

"What disgusting pigs. This place is like *Lord of the Flies*."

"It's sad, I agree."

"Why don't you do something?"

"I don't know what to do."

"Tell someone. You know about the bet, right?"

He nodded.

"Tell the squad comm — tell Norwalk." Lieutenant (Naval), or Lt(N), Norwalk was our squadron commander, a regular-force officer responsible for the oversight and functioning of cadet life within the squadron.

"Kate, he doesn't want to hear anything except that the integration of women is going smoothly."

I looked out his window at the night view of Navy Bay. Fort Henry was lit up. I could hear the lazy clank of sailboat rigging from the pier. The sound comforted me. I stared out for a few moments and we didn't speak. *I had no idea it would be like this.*

"You'd better get going back to your room; it's nearly eleven. I don't want any trouble about us being alone together," said Luka, breaking the silence.

With a quick head snap, I glared in his direction. "You're my *mother.* That was the whole purpose, wasn't it? You're a mentor to me, right?"

"Yes. Except some people like to make trouble."

I stomped back to my room. I quickly showered, cleaned my teeth, and crawled into bed.

"So?" Meg whispered when the lights went out.

"It's worse than you can even imagine."

15

REGULAR LIFE

The first Friday night after recruit term, we were allowed to go to town. Signing out gave me a rare break from circle parade. Holbrook, Fitzroy, and I met in the squadron orderly room at 6:00 p.m. wearing our first-year walking-out dress, or No. 4 uniform of a bellhop-looking navy-blue tunic and our gold-trimmed pillbox hat. *Monkey grinders.*

Late fall, and the colour was gone. I was shocked at the number of bare trees in contrast to the evergreen forests at home. We walked over the LaSalle Causeway straight into town. A car passed us midspan on the bridge. I stopped and grabbed Richie's arm.

"One to beam up!" I exclaimed. A short portion of the drawbridge was made of metal grating with gaps large enough to look down into the water below. When cars passed over that section, their tires hummed briefly with the *Star Trek* transporter sound. "That noise has been coming from this grating on the bridge!"

When we reached the shops along Ontario Street, my uniformed reflection in store windows surprised me. I looked serious, devoid of personality. Richie pulled back the heavy wooden door to Muldoon's Irish Pub and music, cigarette smoke, and the smell of stale beer wafted out. *This is perfect.*

We pulled off our pillboxes. Richie elbowed me and made a head gesture toward the bar, where the bartender was pulling pints into frosted glasses from a series of taps.

"Oh my god, it's a GIRL!" a voice roared over the noise of the crowd. Nearly every table was full.

I turned and saw a young man standing in a gold-coloured Queen's jacket stained with purple dye, holding a beer in one hand and pointing an accusing finger with the other.

Our eyes met. The pub went quiet. Chairs scrapped the floor as various RMC cadets and Queen's students around the room stood up, ready for whatever happened next.

"Please, buddy, I just want to have a beer. You have no idea what I've been through," I said as calmly as I could. Besides, I was only eighteen and didn't want to get asked for ID.

Nobody moved.

"Welcome!" he roared and held up his glass in salute. Laughter broke out as he sat down.

Fitzroy and Holbrook fell in alongside me as we bellied up to the bar. The bartender pushed a pint of dark beer with a thick head of foam toward me, my first Guinness.

"On the house," he said.

We found three seats together at a small table by a wall and settled in. We grinned at each other like idiots and pretended to be normal university students for a few hours. Then we caught a cab back to the college in time to sign in before our 23:00 hours curfew. The driver dropped us off at the gatehouse. It was a second-year privilege to be dropped off at the Frigate; it was deking to avoid running the square. We halted at the edge of the square, did the check, and started to run across. It was late and dark and I was tipsy.

"Last one is a rotten egg," whispered Fitzroy.

"Cadet Armstrong! HALT!" Mr. Helstone's voice rang out from somewhere above and behind us.

I screeched to a halt while Richie and Grant kept running. "See ya!" they called.

My friends were used to leaving me alone with Helstone. *Why does he hate me?* At least he couldn't give me circles anymore, which was a good thing since I still had about 240 circles left to run off and wouldn't finish until November as it was.

"Good evening, First Year Armstrong," he said as he stepped in front of me. He was dressed in a plaid shirt, buttoned up to his throat, a few chest hairs curling over the collar button. I suppressed a shudder and averted my eyes.

"Good evening, Mr. Helstone."

"Do you have any idea why I've stopped you, Miss Armstrong?" he asked. Not giving me time to answer, he went on, "I'm concerned about you, Miss Armstrong. Do you believe me?"

I don't believe you, and quit saying my name every fucking sentence. "Yes, Mr. Helstone."

"Good. We're building trust. I like that. Tell me this. Do you think drinking is an impediment or a danger to your ability to successfully navigate the parade square?"

"No, Mr. Helstone."

"Okay. Just checking. Dismissed, Miss Armstrong. I don't want you to be late signing in." He nodded and walked away.

I did the prescribed checks and bolted toward the blue doors of the Frigate. The guys were waiting in the hall foyer. "Two minutes!" they exclaimed simultaneously.

I signed in at 22:58 hours. We high-fived and headed upstairs.

"What's with that guy?" asked Richie.

"He hates me?"

"Bad luck," said Grant. "What did you do to him?"

"Nothing. I've never even talked to him. He wanted to know if I thought it was safe to drink and run the square."

"Yeah, right," Richie said. "How did he know we went to town for drinks?"

"Creepy. Maybe he spies on you," Grant said.

The next day, right after breakfast, Meg and I had run just ten steps onto the square after leaving the Yeo Hall dining room when Helstone bawled at me from right behind us. Meg kept going, as usual.

"Miss Armstrong, do you know why I have stopped you today?" he asked.

"Please don't make me late for class, Mr. Helstone."

"Oh, all right, since you said please. I'm in a good mood today. Dismissed."

In the Sawyer Building hallway, Meg was walking ahead of me, passing a group of fourth years loitering outside their classroom. A hail of catcalls and whistles broke out. Meg's shoulders tensed and she kept walking without turning her head. One of the fourth years drawled, "I'd like to break a sweat with her!"

Meg stopped in her tracks, turned, and said, "Why don't you go fuck yourselves?" Then she continued walking.

They yelled at her: "Halt!" "Come back!" "Get back here!"

She ignored them. I'd never seen her disobey a command before.

I still had to clear them. My stomach was riding tight against my spine. I kept my eyes front and clung to the far wall as I marched past. An argument had broken out and they were focused on each other.

"That was not appropriate behaviour toward her superiors."

"She failed to show proper respect to a more senior cadet."

"It looked like proper respect to me, you jerks," our cadet squadron training officer, Mr. Jamieson, said. "You were offside."

I sat down next to Meg in class. "Are you okay?" I asked. She looked pale and shaken and didn't answer. "Why don't you tell on them?"

"Are you nuts?" she asked angrily. "Who is going to stand up for me? They're all buddies. I'll be lucky if I don't get charged."

She wasn't charged and never reported it. And of course no one apologized to her.

Early November, I formed up for circle parade amongst a handful of classmates left from other squadrons. As we rounded the homestretch turn, the second-year duty cadet was standing alone in the dark. "All those with two circles, fall out," he said.

I fell out. Tears welled up in my eyes.

Recruit term finally ended for me in that moment. I had run over five hundred circles in total, more than 125 kilometres. Meg had run less than 150 circles. In Eight Squadron, Penny Miller hadn't even come close to a hundred.

I ran home across the square as it started to snow. Simple star-shaped snowflakes streaked through the spotlights beaming up from the moat. Winter was coming. This snow planned to stick around. *Just like me.*

As my head hit the pillow that night, I felt relief that my recruit-term atonements were over and that life would be more manageable from now on. I could join my peers on the hamster wheel, trying to get good grades, to become bilingual, to earn crossed clubs for fitness — if I could ever do more than two chin-ups. This was the most hopeful I'd felt since I got here, when I had been so happy to escape my mother.

I was still happy about that. Even getting circles, brutal as they were, had been more or less predictable; my mother's temper was wild and mercurial, and her punishments often painful and humiliating. I hid my bruises and pretended to the rest of the family and to my friends that nothing was wrong. My mother was a beautiful woman and my friends admired her. I liked it that way. I never dreamt of telling anyone the truth.

One night, I went into the kitchen while my mother was alone making dinner and forced myself to tell her what my brother Robert had been doing to me. I was only nine years old, but I knew well enough that the help I needed could come only from her.

I didn't know how to tell her, so I just blurted it out. "Robert puts his thing in me," I said.

"What thing?" she said.

"His thing." I pointed to my crotch.

Her face darkened. "You're not making any sense."

"It's true. I swear." I knew she understood.

She rushed toward me and gripped a fingertip full of soft skin under my arm through my shirt. The pain shot like electricity up into the back of my eye. "Your brother would never do something like that," she said giving my flesh a twist.

"He does." I pulled my arm away.

She grabbed my bicep in her fist and snapped me closer, her face contorted with contempt. "Have you told anyone else?"

"No."

"Don't tell that story again. Go to your room and don't come out until you're ready to behave." She released me, and I stumbled away.

I ran to my room and threw myself onto my bed. I crawled to the far corner against the wall and huddled into a ball. I rocked to calm myself and watched the tears soak into my pant legs. "I'll be good. I'll be good," I whispered over and over. I never told another person and my mother did nothing to help me. I was on my own.

Now I had gotten away from her for good.

First thing the next morning, I jumped up and peeked out the Frigate window. Large stellar flakes were still floating down, hazing the view across the square. Several inches had accumulated overnight, forming a thick covering of blinding white. This meant tonight would be the wing snowball fight, all seven squadrons across the square against the Frigate. They would attack us and try to breach our walls and steal our kye.

They would fail. We would be prepared.

16

GREET THE MEAT

"**A**re you going to greet the meat?" Richie asked me over lunch.

The RMC–Queen's meet-and-greet was an annual date drive advertised in all the women's university dorms as a free party and drinks night hosted by RMC. It was mandatory for every cadet to bring a date to the RMC Christmas ball, held every year on the last Saturday of November before exam routine. The ball was a Kingston social calendar event. The meet-and-greet, or "greet the meat," as the cadets called it, was timed as a serving platter for cadets without a date to find one.

"I don't see the point," I replied. "Do you?"

"You need a date."

"Yeah. So, how does greet the meat help me with that? Queen's guys are forbidden to attend," I said.

"Come on. You don't really expect us to host a party with free drinks and food so that Queen's guys can hook up with Queen's girls?"

"But how the hell am *I* supposed to get a date?"

"Go with a cadet," he said, shrugging his shoulders.

"Who? Like you?"

"Ha!"

"I wonder if Queen's girls know that you call them meat?" I said angrily.

Colbert was sitting on the other side of Holbrook. He leaned forward. "I wonder if you know that guys who date female cadets are too lazy to masturbate?"

I'd heard this "joke" before but couldn't believe he had just said it to my face. I leaned back and looked at the other guys at the table. Everyone was abruptly engrossed in eating, except Colbert, who was staring me down, a smug expression on his face. I grabbed my plate and left the table.

I snuck up to Luka's room that night during study hours and threw myself onto his bed. "This place is fucked up," I ranted. "I'm expected to get a date for the Christmas ball, and the guys talk like I'm a pariah. And I am probably going to fail out of engineering when it has nothing to do with my future life!"

"Whoa. One thing at a time," Luka said. He got up from his desk and stood over me.

"I haven't done anything. I've been trying hard."

"You're a girl. That's crime enough for some of these guys."

"What's it to them? If I can make it, why shouldn't I have the same chances in life?"

"You're cheeky? You don't adore them? They love you? You won't date them? How do I know? I don't have the answers. Just watch out. I'll do what I can to help you. First, you need a date for the ball?"

"Yes."

"How about the president of the McMaster student union?"

"Be serious."

"He's my best friend from high school. We're in Ukrainian Scouts together. I can ask him. I'll call him tonight. My date's coming from Stoney Creek and they could drive up together," he said.

"You're a Ukrainian Scout?"

"Yes."

"Now? You're still a scout?"

He nodded. I started laughing.

"Take it easy there!" he said.

"Sorry. It's funny. So, I may have a date for the ball," I said, letting out a big breath.

"Okay. Second," Luka said, "I'll lend you my first-year engineering notes if you promise to return them at the end of the year."

"You have them here?"

"I picked them up for you last weekend when I went home." He pulled a three-inch black binder from under his desk and handed it to me.

I jumped up, kissed his cheek, and hugged the binder to my chest. It was my most optimistic academic moment since I had arrived at RMC. Brad Boulter was still helping me with calculus and I was passing. With Luka's notes, I felt like I had a real chance to make it all the way through the year.

Remembrance Day. We marched out to the Memorial Arch for the 11:00 a.m. service to honour fallen cadets. It was freezing cold and a light snow dusted us. We had a class-free day after the service, and I was looking forward to a nap and doing homework. Downstairs in Yeo Hall, next to the Hudson Squadron hat shelves, Fourth Year Jankovic made fun of my snow cover.

"You were shaking like a leaf out there," he said. "I'm surprised you have any snow left on you."

I laughed, leaned on the shelf to support myself, and shook the tiny snowdrifts off me. Then we walked into the dining room together.

After lunch, Mr. Kendall came to our room holding a piece of paper, looking grim. He asked Meg to give us privacy and she slipped out.

"Read this," he said. It was a typewritten form, filled in with three different styles of handwriting.

> *Significant Performance Observation*
> *11 Nov 80*
> *Officer Cadet Armstrong KA*
> *One Squadron*
>
> *Where did it happen and what were the circumstances?*
> *I Armstrong was seen in an overly casual conversation with IV Jankovic at 12:13hrs in the lower stairwell in Yeo Hall (where 1 Sqn usually put their caps). She was leaning, with elbow resting on the shelves, and both were laughing.*
>
> *Why was Officer Cadet particularly* ~~effective~~/*non-effective?*
> *I-IV overfamiliarity*
>
> *Recognition given/Coaching action taken on the spot?*
> *No action taken on the spot. This SPO is for your info and action.*
>
> *Name of Observer: G. Helstone CWTO*
>
> *2. CFL 'A': Pass it on, then Duncan will keep it in his file in case of similar incidents. C. Favreau CSL*
> *1 Sqn*

3. *CSC #3: Miss Armstrong must be a little more careful about this sort of thing. D. Morgan CFL 'A'*

I looked up at Mr. Kendall, who stood there smiling tensely.

"Is this for real?" I asked. "It hasn't even been two hours since lunch."

"I'm afraid so," said Mr. Kendall.

"Has anyone noticed that Mr. Helstone is terrorizing me?"

"I'm afraid so."

"Isn't anyone going to help me?"

"I'm afraid not."

"Not even you?" I asked. "You're my section commander. You're the one to help me."

"Let me tell you a story," he said. He gestured for me to sit down on the bed and took a seat at my desk. He told me that when he was a recruit, he got circles from his recruit flight section commander for being ugly. He had tried to redress the circles to his cadet flight leader, who concurred that he was ugly and would not retract them. He pushed the redress all the way to the cadet squadron leader. In the end, he ran three circles for being ugly.

"So, sometimes we have to choose. You can try to fight the system, but you won't win," he said. "You're going to have to serve a correctional squadron runner duty."

"Aye aye, Mr. Kendall. Permission to speak freely?" I asked. He nodded.

"Are you a fan of Che Guevara? I looked him up in the library. He's a Marxist revolutionary, a communist."

"That's right."

"But don't we hate communists?"

"How so?"

"Well," I said, "for example, we use them as the enemy

soldier targets on the firing range, complete with fur hats and a communist-star cap badge. Sorta like, um, Che Guevara?"

He slapped his knees and stood up. "You're smart, Kate. You'll need to find your own way to survive this place."

An announcement was made about the weekend winter survival course in January. It would be a four-day cross-country ski expedition; we'd carry equipment packs and our own food and sleep in snow caves built as nightly shelter. I signed up.

"Are you nuts?" Meg asked.

"Mr. Kendall told me to find a way to survive in this place."

"Don't be so literal. He didn't mean going on winter survival training. You couldn't pay me to sleep in an igloo and chase after a bunch of mountaineering guys on cross-country skis through the Algonquin Park outback."

"I like that kind of stuff. I'm not a very good cross-country skier, but I want to learn."

"Jeez, Kate. That would be the last place I'd choose to go learn. It sounds horrible."

A few days later, a sealed note arrived for me in the wing mail. Red block letters were written across the front of it: RETURN TO SENDER — IMPROPER ADDRESS!! My name, also in red pen, was underlined.

The typewritten note began "Dear John" and was addressed to the winter survival organizer and supposedly signed by me. The note was one long paragraph detailing reasons why I had doubts about attending the winter survival course, giving reasons like "Girls don't have the intelligence to climb rocks" and "I don't have the right clothes or makeup, and what if my nails got chipped?" It ended with "We girls just don't have what it takes to hack the tough life.... I guess it's right that we just stay at home and have kids while you men run the world properly. I'm sure you can find any spaz who would more easily fill my high heels! Thanks for giving girls a chance!"

I showed the note to Meg. "You see now that it's imperative for me to go on the winter survival training course."

"That's one perspective," she said. "Who do you think wrote it?"

"No idea. I'm going on that winter survival course, even if it kills me."

"It just might."

For the Christmas ball, I wore my scarlet tunic over the long blue skirt with red piping. It was my first formal ball, but I felt a lot more like the prince than Cinderella. I dreaded mixing in with civilian girls in long, flowing gowns. Female cadets could wear makeup, but only if it was impossible to notice that we were wearing makeup.

The New Gym was unrecognizable, strung with red and green streamers and bunches of white balloons, with chiffon gauze wrapped around the balcony railings and support poles. A sea of scarlet intermingled with dresses of every possible shade, from lavender to peach to gold metal. Young women were flirting with cadets in every corner of the room.

Luka had secured a table along one wall and waved me over. "Kate, I'd like to introduce you to Olek Zelenko," he said, "and my date, the beautiful Miss Diane." They both smiled warmly at me.

Olek was tall, ruggedly handsome in his tuxedo, and, as I soon found out, charming. I had a real date. I wanted Colbert to see me with him, to show him that I had landed a respectable date, after his disgusting comment about masturbating cadets.

While we danced our first waltz together, I asked Olek about McMaster, and he told me about the student union's pro-choice fight. When he asked about life at RMC, I told him that college policy said pregnancy was grounds for expulsion from cadet life until "the matter resolved itself."

The discussion triggered an evening-long comparison of McMaster's forward-thinking political activism with RMC policies. Olek was shocked to learn that being gay or using drugs was grounds for being kicked out of the military altogether. And politically, that communists and Greenpeace activists were considered nearly the lowest forms of life, second only to feminists. Eventually, back at the table, Olek asked, "Why do you stay?"

"I can't give up on my dream of becoming a search-and-rescue helicopter pilot."

He tilted his head and raised his eyebrows. "Why do you really stay?"

"I can't seem to quit. It's worse than I imagined, and yet somehow I don't want to let them drive me out. If I quit, it will be when I'm winning, not when they're winning."

He smiled at me. "I've been telling Luka for years that this place is crazy and he needs to come to McMaster," he said, slapping Luka's back tenderly, "but he won't quit either."

Although I would rather have worn a dress, I was proud of my uniform, despite it being thick, hot, and unflattering — it made me recognizable as a cadet. Luka's date, Diane, was gorgeous in her perfect makeup and teal satin ball gown. I saw the eyes of my fellow cadets follow many beautiful, well-coiffed women onto the dance floor — those same eyes that followed me around the college grounds — and I felt happy to have them on someone else for an evening.

December came fast. The cold made the landscape look fine and sharp. The first Sunday of exam routine fell on December 7, the anniversary of the Japanese attack on Pearl Harbor. At noon, the handful of Asian and Asian-looking cadets in the cadet wing walked into the dining hall together wearing kamikaze headbands and were promptly "laked" in the last explosion of noise before the silence of exam routine shrouded the grounds.

The New Gym had been transformed again, this time with row upon row of desks placed as far apart as possible to prevent cheating, but close together enough to fit over 230 desks in one room. In high school, my marks had always been high enough that I'd had exemptions from exams, so just the sight of all those desks was daunting. The two weeks of exam routine flew past in a whirlwind of meals and studying interspersed with the actual exams and the sense of helpless finality.

17

HOME AGAIN, HOME AGAIN

I stared out the aircraft window at the frozen expanse of Canada, looking down on the innumerable kilometres of the snow-covered grid, a patchwork quilt of farms and roads. We were chasing the setting sun. I felt a sense of dread, though I wasn't sure why. I'd been looking forward to these two weeks of escape for months.

Mom and Dad were waiting at the baggage carousel of the Vancouver airport. When our eyes met, I spread my arms and pirouetted in my navy-blue No. 4 uniform and gold-trimmed pillbox. They smiled and we hugged in greeting.

My mother's first words to me were "Are you eating enough?" I ignored the dig and gave her a warm smile.

The temperature was hovering around freezing, but it was mild and there was no sign of snow — typical West Coast winter weather. Our black Pomeranian, Trixie, excitedly greeted me in the car and settled in my lap for the drive home. We set out on the highway toward Abbotsford.

Mom turned around to me in the back seat. "Now that you're home, do you really want to go back to camp?"

"Mom! I'm attending the Royal Military College of Canada. It is not cadet camp. You should be proud of me," I said. She turned around to face straight ahead and I stared at her never-changing brown hair: dyed, cut, and curled in the same style as Queen Elizabeth's. "I am not going to quit. The only way I will leave RMC is if I fail out trying."

"You've moved across the country alone to go through who knows what sort of crazy stuff. You said you wanted to quit," she persisted.

"I thought I did, for a while. I still do, lots of days. Most days. But I'm not quitting," I said fiercely. Her criticism made me suddenly fond of RMC. "There's a cadet expression that says RMC is a good place to be *from.*"

"You're not making sense," she snipped. We drove in silence for a bit; the warmth I had felt for her at the airport was already dissolving.

"Any news on pilot opening up to women?" Dad asked.

"Not yet. It could take years. I might graduate and get my commission before it happens. Maybe our success at RMC will help open the doors of other career opportunities for women."

Mother blew an audibly dismissive blast of air from her nose. I turned my attention to petting my dog.

I came into the dark house with a sense of trepidation — it was after seven at night — and caught the scent of Dad's pipe tobacco. I didn't even have to look. In my mind's eye I could see his chair and the end table with the tobacco pouch resting next to the black glass ashtray holding his upside-down pipe. Nothing had changed on the surface, but inside everything had changed. My dread evaporated. I felt lucky. I'd survived and made it out unscathed. I had escaped; I never had to live here again. I could continue into my adult life as a normal person, leave the past here. From now on, I was a guest in my old life. Only two other people knew the truth, my mother and my brother, and they weren't talking. Childhood stories could be anecdotal, even in my own mind, and focus on the good stuff. I knew how to play along in this house.

Suddenly, I was exhausted. A surge of disorientation passed through me. In truth, I didn't know how to be home anymore. I wondered if I ever had.

I took my time changing into my jeans and a sweater and hanging my uniform in the closet of my old room. I thumbed through my clothes that had been sitting undisturbed for months and lay back on my queen-sized bed, arms flung wide in the peach and lime-green cloud of comfortable duvet bedding.

"Come on down, and I'll beat you at cribbage," Dad's warm voice called up to me. When I walked into the dining room, he was at the table with the board set up. "You're looking fit."

"Are you eating enough?" Mom called out from the kitchen. I rolled my eyes, smiled, and shook my head at my dad.

We played a few rounds of cribbage. My earlier sense of exhaustion became acute, and I used the three-hour time change as an excuse to go to bed early. On my way up the stairs, I imagined the sound of Gary's car driving past the house. I hurtled into my bedroom, desperate for a glimpse of him. In the dark room, I peeked from behind my bedroom curtain, face pressed against the glass, hoping to catch him driving past, looking up at my room. The street was quiet, empty of traffic. *He's not coming.*

Trixie came in and curled up on my bed. I closed my door and pulled the drapes. Then I crawled under my duvet, cuddled my feather pillows, and sprawled out in the luxury of a queen-sized bed. I slept for ten hours.

I awoke to the smell of coffee brewing and bacon cooking, stretched, threw back the duvet, and padded downstairs barefoot in my pyjamas. Mom rounded the corner coming out of the kitchen.

"I was just coming to get you. I'm making scrambled eggs. Can you do the toast?"

"Sure. Hey, Mom, all that stuff in my closet is exactly where I left it. It's as though I still live here. Do you want me to clear it out?"

"There's no rush."

"I'm not coming home," I said, pushing down the first two pieces of bread and staring down at the glow of the filaments inside the toaster. The simple act of making my own toast pleased me.

"We'll see," she muttered. "Can you call your brother?"

"Craig! Breakfast," I hollered up the stairs. My brother Craig was three years older than me and still lived at home, despite being fully recovered from his childhood head injury and capable of making his own way in the world. He had worked at the local Keg Steakhouse since high school and was a manager there now.

By the time he got to the table, we were already eating, but Mom got up to make his breakfast.

"Hey," he said. "Welcome home."

"Hey." I stood for a perfunctory hug. "How've you been?"

"Good," he said. He sat at the table waiting for Mom to serve him. "Nothing new." She came in with a plate of hot sliced toast covered in peanut butter and jam.

"Mom, can't he make his own toast?"

"I'm right here. You can ask me directly," Craig said.

"Can't you make your own toast?"

"Mom does it better than me."

"Don't get started, you two," Dad said, snapping his newspaper in front of him.

On Christmas Eve, Mother always served a traditional holiday meal — roast turkey, dressing, gravy, yams, mashed potatoes, corn, green Jell-O salad, cranberries, pickles, and all the fixings.

My sister and brother-in-law, Ellen and Doug, arrived with their ten-year-old daughter and seven-year-old son. Appetizers were served and Dad and I shared our annual plate full of toothpick-skewered smoked oysters.

"I miss your hair," Doug said, tousling my pixie cut. He grabbed my arm and squeezed my bicep. "Impressive."

"You have no idea," I said. "I bet I could take you in an arm wrestle now."

"That will require quite a few more drinks before you'll convince me."

Ellen joined in. "It's so surreal. I can't believe you actually went to military college."

"It was your idea," I said.

"What? How do you figure?"

"Remember when I was in grade nine, you showed me that magazine article about the first women at West Point and said that I should do something like that? Somehow I've gone and done it."

"Well, don't blame me!" she said.

"I don't. I've done it to myself. But still. Tell the truth. Do I seem different to you?"

"I don't think so." She stepped back and looked me up and down. "Maybe you look even more fit?"

"I feel tense. Intense. Like I'm not funny anymore."

"You're funny looking," Craig cracked from the couch.

We sat down to eat. I filled my plate to overflowing and ate with gusto. When I was nearly done eating, I glanced around the table. Most plates were still full, and some were seemingly untouched. Everyone's mouths hung open and they were all staring at me. My niece and nephew giggled.

"What?" I asked defensively.

"I *had* heard that you learned extreme table manners at RMC," said Ellen.

The whole family burst out laughing, and then, while they ate, I told my stories about recruit term, demonstrating square meals, describing circle parade and the quirky facts we had to memorize and sleepwalking each night to do my ironing.

For a split second, I felt the thrill of success. I finally felt seen by my family for my real self: a strong, capable woman.

I leaned back in my chair and took it all in. Mother appeared in the kitchen doorway, holding hot bread pudding and hard sauce. She looked right through me and said, "Too bad Kate isn't here. She always loved this pudding."

The words punched me in the gut. "Knock it off," I said. "I hate that game. I never found it funny."

Right on cue, the laughter turned on me. The others around the table ignored me and joined in the teasing, pretending they were saying nice things about me in my absence. Instantly, I was ten years old again and collapsed into a sulking posture.

"Would anyone like Kate's share of Auntie Alma's bread pudding and sauce? It was always her favourite," said Mother, persisting.

Doug spoke up, "I would!"

I stood up from my slouch, pushed in my chair RMC style, and said, "Why don't you go fuck yourselves?" They were still laughing as I closed my bedroom door.

The holiday weeks sped past. I was rested again and eager to get back to RMC. I had seen my friends who were still living in Abbotsford and had spent time with Gary. He had mentioned getting back together but it didn't go anywhere. It was hard to believe that four unremarkable months had passed in their lives, months that felt like an eternity in mine. When my friends reacted with shock and amazement at what I had endured, I felt proud but couldn't really answer their questions about how I'd done it. I remembered having the feeling at RMC that I was missing out on something really good going on at home, that life was continuing on here without me. Well, now I knew that I wasn't a part of this world anymore. A future sprawled out before me, one in which I would continue on the path I had chosen, away from Abbotsford.

The day before heading back to RMC, I went downstairs to do my laundry. Even though my older brothers had left home years ago, Dad always built every house with a large basement bedroom furnished with their matching pine twin beds and orange bedspreads. I couldn't stop myself from peeking in. Almost like a test. That's when I saw the blue-covered book *Be Here Now* by Ram Dass sitting on the bedside table. My brother Robert had brought it home from his second year at UBC that last Christmas, right after I had told Mother about him. I remembered the weird lettering and drawings, like the sketch of two penises on one page framing the words for the path to enlightenment.

I walked into the room, sat on the bed, and picked up the book, remembering the scene with Robert that Christmas in 1971. He'd given me the promise of being special to buy my silence, to guard his secret. When I got older, I struggled with feelings of being dirty and frightened. I was afraid to stop him and be alone. His long absences at university had been plagued with shame and promises to myself that I would make him stop. In the summer after his first year of university, he had been especially attentive toward me and I didn't want to give that up.

I don't know what I had expected to happen when I finally said no that Christmas, but it had been so anticlimactic. "I don't want to do it anymore. It makes me feel bad," I had said when he told me to go to his room.

He looked shocked, but all he said was "Okay," and he never pressed the issue.

"I still love you." I hugged his side, hoping he would say he loved me, too. He silently patted my back the way Dad did when he hugged us.

In the new year, Robert went back to UBC, immediately dropped out of his second-year studies, packed his bags, and emigrated to Australia. He was twenty years old. I was nine.

When I was eleven years old, I would learn about having my period and how babies were conceived. Then I started to understand what he had been doing to me. Still, I felt like a bad person, like it was my fault. What I said had made him go away. I had still wanted him to be my brother; I just wanted him to stop. From the time he fled the country, it would be twenty-eight years, in 1999, before I would see Robert again.

18

THE BOSS

I shuffled my suitcase into the main foyer of the Frigate, dropped it at my feet, put my hands on my hips, and beamed a big smile. I had been nervous to go home to Abbotsford for fear of being overcome with a desire to stay, but I knew that the Frigate was home now.

In the orderly room, I glanced at the fourth-year bar slate for winter term: Mr. Jansen was cadet squadron leader, the top cadet in the Frigate. Mr. Morgan was moving into Wing HQ as the new cadet wing training officer to replace Helstone. No more Helstone! And effective immediately, first years were granted the privilege of no longer being required to make the side-to-side checks at the edge of the square. We could simply run across. Things were looking up.

Room reassignment moves were underway and the hallways were full of cadets traipsing armloads of bedding, unpacked belongings, boxes, and luggage to their new rooms. With only four women, there were limited roommate possibilities for second term. Meg and Nanette would be together on the second floor in a room overlooking the water. Nancy and I were in the largest room on the third floor overlooking the square. I was as tall and willowy as she was petite and curvy, which landed me in the top bunk that term. We would be the only women in C Flight. In second term, all the flights were a mix of first-, second-, and third-year students. Only first years shared rooms.

After class on the first day, we went directly to a large bulletin board in Mackenzie Building to check for exam results. My main concern had been chemistry, but I had passed. Barely. I had passed all my courses. Barely. How had life seemed so easy in high school? I was going to have to work harder this term.

I couldn't believe the day would ever come, but basketball was on the chopping block. There was no point pretending or being sentimental. Besides, ever since Kurt had sprained his ankle and had to sit out for the season, my enjoyment of practice had lost its edge. My chronic exhaustion had spawned an unnatural obsession with sleep. I would count every moment of sleep per day and rush to my room during any block of spare time longer than forty-five minutes and power nap while laying at attention on my bed, fully dressed in my uniform without taking off my boots. I also developed an aversion to unnecessary exercise — I simply didn't have the time or energy to keep practising in the hopes of fourteen other women basketball players coming to RMC in the future. Especially if I failed out and wasn't even here to play anyhow. But I did feel sentimental. Ever since I had sprouted in grade five, being a basketball player had been part of my identity. On this team, I wasn't even allowed to play in the real games. But who was I without basketball? *Time to find out.* I ran the parade square back to the Frigate, went straight into the orderly room, and signed up for intramural floor hockey.

Contrary to my resolve to conserve energy, here I was going alone, as the only woman, on winter survival training with ten men to Algonquin Park, where the snow was four feet deep and I was easily the most inexperienced cross-country skier of the group. Luckily, Jerry Stawski and his best friend, Bill, from Eight Squadron, had taken me under their wing and agreed to watch out for me. I carpooled with them and one other guy. I kept wondering who had written that stupid note about why I didn't want to come on this trip. Whoever it was didn't mention the only real reason — I should be back at the college doing homework instead of chasing after a bunch of guys through the wilderness to prove something.

At each rest break, I would glide toward them, soaked with sweat through my layers, and they would start skiing ahead again. They took turns blazing trail while I slogged away at the back for the entire four days. I started counting my strides. *Just get through the next fifty.*

At one point, I lost sight of the group and despaired that I might collapse and die of hypothermia, when the tracks broke out of the trees onto a frozen lake covered in several feet of pristine powder. There wasn't another mark in the snow within eyeshot, just a rolling plain of perfection cut by our trail. The guys stood still in the middle of the lake as I panted up to them. No one spoke. Jerry turned and held his fingers to his lips. I held my breath and then I heard it. The silence was so heavy it had gravity. A tear of awe leaked from the corner of one eye, crystallizing in my lower lash. For a split second, I remembered that the real world still existed outside of RMC and would always continue to exist.

On the way home, I resolved to never sign up as a member of the mountaineering club. I was glad I'd done this trip, but once was enough. It was time to quit trying to prove that I belonged. I dozed in a semi-lucid state as Jerry and Bill sang along at the top of their lungs to the Doors cassette blasting over the stereo. In concert with the lyrics, Bill made a comical display of keeping his eyes on the road and his hands upon the wheel.

I fell asleep with a smile on my windburned face, grateful to be in a car full of laughter and heading home.

Bruce Springsteen was on tour for his new album, *The River*, and had a concert booked in Ottawa in January. I had signed up to go. On the bus, an unfamiliar voice said, "Mind if I sit here?" I looked up to see a tall man with fine features gesturing toward the empty aisle seat next to me. Dangerously handsome.

"Sure," I said. He introduced himself as Fourth Year Eddie Byrne of Six Squadron.

"So, how shall we begin?" he asked in a light teasing voice as the bus began to roll. "How about we start with whatever made you decide to join the military and come to this godforsaken place?" He beamed at me and I felt lit up. I instantly trusted him.

For the entire two-hour bus ride, we shared our stories. Hometowns. Growing-up experiences. Family structures. Hopes. Dreams. When the bus stopped at the stadium, I was smitten.

"See you on the ride home?" he asked.

"Um. Sure." As we shuffled down the aisle, I stood as close as possible and breathed in the citrus smell of him.

I spent nearly the entire concert on my feet, screaming and singing along — especially loudly to the title song, and my favourite on the new album, "The River." The Boss came right down into the crowd, working the fans on the floor into a frothing frenzy. From our seats, we overlooked a sea of swaying arms. I wondered where Eddie was sitting and scanned the audience for a glimpse of him.

In the crush of leaving the stadium, I caught sight of Eddie walking with another guy. Eddie looked back and I waved, but he didn't acknowledge me. I felt a pinch under my arm and wheeled around angrily, ready to punch whoever it was.

Heidi Gottlieb from Seven Squadron grinned at me.

"Don't pinch me," I said. "I hate it."

"Whoa, okay." She pulled back from me. Her expression made me feel ashamed of my reaction.

"Sorry, I have an emotional allergy to being pinched, especially under my arm."

She pointed ahead to Eddie and his friend. "Hey, do you know who that guy is?" she asked. "The short, stocky guy," she added, pointing to the grinning cadet at Eddie's elbow. "Mike Spears. He's a fucking pig."

"How so?"

"He's the guy who started the bet," she said.

Back on the bus in the dark, Eddie reached down and touched my hand, but I pulled away. "That was weird," I whispered, staring straight ahead. "I know you saw me."

"Yeah, sorry. Spears is a prick and I have to be careful," he said, keeping his voice low.

"So, he *is* a friend of yours?"

"He's a real jerk about having women at the college. Let me just leave it at that."

Eddie placed his hand on my thigh and squeezed gently. I felt myself softening. *Who cares? If this is about the bet, I'll be the one who decides if and when.*

The next day, a manila envelope arrived for me in the wing mail. My hands trembled as I opened it. He had gorgeous cursive handwriting.

> K.
> *I can't stop thinking of you.*
> E.

I had never cared much about wing mail. Outside of my performing the first-year squadron runner duty, the mail hadn't really factored into my day-to-day life. That all changed with my simple reply.

> E.
> *Me too.*
> K.

This was the beginning of our correspondence. I became mail obsessed. Our notes contained questions for one another, snippets of poetry, quotes, cards, cartoons cut from the local paper, and details like what time we were going to be at the dining hall at the next meal. We carefully cloaked any open declarations of affection and rarely saw one another in person, though I was constantly on the watch to catch glimpses of him. Now I went to school as if seeing Eddie, even from afar, was the only real reason to go. Every day I hoped to arrive at dinner at the same time and to eat at the same table — that was the extent of our physical contact. When I had the rare chance to sit beside him, the space between us felt charged with the mingling of our vibrations. I would soak in his presence and later replay our interactions over and over in my mind. For over a month, we had nearly daily contact by mail but rarely ever saw each other in person or spoke to each other. But that didn't stop me from thinking about him constantly.

One evening during study hours, in early March, Fitzroy knocked on my door. "Armstrong! Phone!"

"Who is it?" I asked, stupidly, of his retreating back.

"How the hell should I know?" he said. I ran past him on the stairs.

"Stone Frigate. First Year Armstrong speaking."

"Can you talk?" Eddie asked.

"Hey, Dad!" I exclaimed. "Is everything okay?"

"Never better. I'm crazy about you." He gave me a phone number to call.

"I'll call you back," I said. I ran downstairs to the phones in the gunroom.

"Sorry to drag you away from your books," he said, "but I had to tell you I love you."

"I love you, too." My heart pounded against my ribs. It seemed crazy to say it after so little time together, but I meant it with my whole being. We talked on the phone for nearly an hour. After that first call, we arranged call times through the wing mail and sent fewer risky notes.

One day, Luka left a message on my desk asking me to come to his room. He was more solemn than usual. I sat down on his bed.

"Is there anything you want to tell me?" he asked.

I shrugged, shook my head in bewilderment, and didn't say anything.

"Eddie Byrne?" he added eventually.

"What about him?" I asked warily.

"Are you dating him?" he asked. *He knows.* They were classmates in mechanical engineering.

"No," I replied. Technically, this was true. We had an *intention* to date. "Why do you ask?"

"He will land you in the worst kind of trouble. I asked because two pieces of information came to me today and I connected the dots. At lunch, Woodsie told me that he noticed you're getting a lot of wing mail these days —"

"What? Is he watching me?" I said. "That's creepy."

"Hold on. Let me finish," he said. "Then after lunch, I was walking through Sawyer Building behind Eddie Byrne and Mike Spears. Mike asked Eddie, 'How is your little Love Boat project going?' And Eddie just laughed. Then, I knew. It's you, isn't it?"

I stared at him.

"So, are you?" he asked again.

I flushed. "What do you want me to say?"

"I know you're aware of the bet."

"We're not dating. We plan to date after he graduates. Right now, I would call our relationship … covert flirting."

"Just be careful."

"Nothing has happened. Nothing will happen until after grad."

"Is he the reason you don't come here anymore?"

"I really need to go. Blackwood probably has his nose buried under your door, eavesdropping," I said. "Please, don't tell anyone."

"I won't," he promised.

One Saturday evening in the middle of March, Eddie and I happened to end up at the same dinner table. After everyone else had finished eating and left, we lingered.

"Can you come to my room?" Eddie asked in a low voice.

"Are you nuts?"

"I don't mean now. I have something for you. Can you come, say a week from tomorrow?" he grinned at me.

"That's my birthday," I said, trying not to grin back.

"Well, that's a crazy coincidence," he said. "Let's say you come at two thirty for half an hour and I'll wish you a proper happy birthday."

We had never been alone. "If you promise not to try anything."

He leaned toward me and smiled while under the table he pushed hard against my leg. "Promise. Now, I'm going to get up and walk away all casual-like, as though I couldn't care less about you," he said. His chair shuddered loudly across the floor.

The weather on my birthday was bright and calm as I ran across the square. By now, the days were getting longer, the light felt warmer, less strident than in February, and the snow already seemed to be gone for good. There had been a weekend winter parade this morning and the guys from Three Squadron had pulled a skylark; they staged a faux coup to depose the commandant and install a Central American dictator to run the college. It had been well executed and exciting to watch, but I had panicked about the impact it might have on my plans to meet up with Eddie.

I disappeared into Yeo Hall and took a winding route through the maze of dorm hallways en route to Fort Champlain Dormitory rather than risk walking in the front door to his squadron. As I approached Eddie's door, I checked up and down the corridors to be sure no one was watching. I tapped lightly twice and barged straight in.

Eddie rose up from his desk. I closed the door behind me and plastered myself back against it.

"Bold," he said.

"I don't think anyone saw me," I whispered.

"No need to whisper, but it's a good idea to keep our voices low," he said. He pressed his full body onto mine and clasped fingers with me, pinning me against the door. I was breathless.

On first contact, his lips were soft; I closed my eyes and breathed in his clean smell. He cradled my face and he kissed me again. My breasts tingled at the pressure of his chest brushing against mine.

"Happy birthday," he said hoarsely. "I've been thinking about that kiss for a long time."

"Me too," I said. Voices in the hall jarred me and I ducked under his arm and threw myself across the room, as far as I could get from him.

"Whoa. Skittish filly."

"Sorry."

"I have two presents for you today. One you can open and take home, and the other is good news. Which do you want first?" He stepped toward me.

"Good news first," I answered as I moved away from him and sat on the bed.

He flipped his desk chair around, placed it in front of me, and straddled it. "My F-18 training starts in September, which means I'll spend the summer in some lame time-killer job. You're going to summer French immersion at CMR in Saint-Jean. So my news is … I intend to fail my final French qualifying exam, so that I'll be at language training in Saint-Jean, too." Eddie was effectively bilingual. He had spent the first three years of military college at the Collège militaire royal. "We can spend the summer together."

"Oh my god, really?" I exclaimed, then added cautiously, "But what if you get caught?"

"Failing my French exam won't raise huge flags. I'm border-line to obtain level five, which is required for exemption," he said. "Besides, how else can we really get to know each other?"

I covered my face and fought tears.

"What's wrong? Don't you want me there?"

I took a deep breath and looked up. Eddie was looking a little pale. "I've been terrified that your attention was all about the bet. Even today, I didn't want to consider that you might have invited me here to try to have sex with me."

Eddie hung his head and rested his forehead on the chair back. When he finally looked up, a red ridge marked his brow.

"Kate, when this whole thing started on the bus, I was being an ass. Showing off to Spears, pretending that I was part of the bet."

"Have you slept with anyone else?" I asked.

"What? No. Trust me — I am really lame at getting girls to sleep with me. The truth is I *want* to spend the summer with you. I have years of pilot training ahead and you have years left here. We can spend the summer and see how we get along, away from this place." He moved the chair aside, took my hands, and raised me to my feet, hugging me close. "I want to be your guy. I know I can be a jerk and am going to have to earn it. Will you let me?"

"Yes," I said, half crying and half laughing. I ignored the slight tremor of foreboding in my belly.

"Good. Ready for the gift you can take home? Keep your eyes closed and open your arms wide."

A soft furry body pressed against me, and when I opened my eyes I was hugging a four-foot-tall dark-brown bear with a head the size of a throw pillow.

"A little someone for your empty bed," he said.

One month until final exams; review time had started. I didn't see Eddie and I stayed clear of Luka. I spent more and more time with my books, panicking about my mediocre results. Nancy spent all her time, except for the nights, studying with her second-year boyfriend, fellow Frigateer Will Cross, in his room. I had our room pretty much to myself.

Midterms had come and gone. Somehow, I had managed a passing grade in everything, but chemistry was scaring me. I didn't really understand the lab work. My real problem wasn't the material; it was my inability to think clearly. I had trouble concentrating for more than a few moments at a time and would sometimes just sit and daydream about Eddie.

19

FATHER-SON TIME

The snowdrifts on the edge of the parade square were melting, sending streams of dirty water down the drains. Loud cracking sounds came from the bay as ice floes broke apart and heaved up onto the shores of the St. Lawrence River in chaotic piles. The days seemed to be growing exponentially longer; the trees sprouted green buds.

In early April, the traditional father-son mess dinner was held, even though some of us were not sons. My dad flew out from the West Coast for the weekend. The mess dinner was held in the senior staff mess. We were a regal-looking crowd, cadets in scarlet dress and all the fathers in their finest. I had never seen my dad in a tuxedo. It was fun to play grown-up and host him at such an elite affair.

When people asked me about my dad, I always said, "I love my dad. He's the best." In saying this, I didn't feel like a liar. He was great in so many ways: a warm, funny, handsome, socially comfortable person. He was a kind man, prone to seeing the best in everyone. I had followed his lead in being gregarious and people-pleasing by nature. When I was a kid and Dad was home, an unconscious ceasefire with Mom permeated the house. But I could sense a weakness in him that frightened me, because I saw in myself the same tendencies that had cowed him. He failed to stand up for himself, or us. My mother saw to that.

I wanted to be closer to him and make him proud of me, but in fact, I had no idea what he expected or what I should expect from him. We spent the whole day together, the only one in my entire life, touring the historic sites of Kingston and then having lunch at Chez Piggy, my treat. I played at being lighthearted with him, but it felt like a show.

That evening, at the start of the mess dinner, a piper wailed out a short rift on his bagpipes to signal the five-minute warning to prepare for entering the dining room. Dad led me in on his arm. We were seated at the middle of three long, white-linen-covered tables butted up along the span of a head table. The seven-course meal, served on fine china set between cascading rows of silverware, included a fleet of wines and finished with the passing of the port.

Three hours later, after all the speeches were done and the regimental marches had been played, the crowd spilled into the lounge area of the senior staff mess. It was tradition for the first years to remain behind and finish off the port. When I staggered out of the dining room, I found my dad chatting with Luka and I felt a surge of pride. He was behaving with grace and a relaxed courtesy that I never really saw at home, his head bent, politely listening as Luka talked animatedly to him.

I dragged him to the billiards room where a game of crud was underway. Crud was a rowdy, physical game, involving teams and two billiard balls, in which each player had three lives. Dad played one round and bowed out after losing his lives; I kept going. All the players were getting drunker and louder as we played well into the night. At one point, I glanced over at my dad and his mood had shifted — he seemed sad. I had been a swearing, yelling, pushing, competitive hooligan playing toe to toe with the men. Shame triggered the suspicion that, even though I had been a tomboy as a young girl, my dad didn't recognize me now, like there was no part of him in me.

The next morning, we went for a farewell breakfast at Morrison's Restaurant. He was quiet. I burned with the shame of a hangover, not because of anything I'd done exactly, but because of who I was.

"Did you have a good time this weekend?" I asked.

"It was really interesting," he said neutrally, "but I'm ready to go home today."

I tried not to sound hurt. "Aren't you glad you came?"

"Oh, for sure. It's just that I miss your mother. I'm not used to being away from her. I woke up in the night and my shoulders were cold, and I realized that she's the one who keeps the blankets over me," he said. "She's a good woman, the best there is."

I don't know what possessed me, but I said, "You know she used to hit and pinch me, right?"

His gaze hardened. "It's always been the same with you and your sister. I don't know why you girls have to constantly upset your mother. Why can't you just behave?"

"She's horrible when you aren't around, you know."

"If she is, I'm sure you've done something to upset her," he said. He shifted away from me in his chair and pursed his lips. They stayed that way until the moment he drove off.

After lights out that night, I thought about what someone had once told me, that we only have four choices in life: to be like our mother, to be like our father, to be not like our mother, or to be not like our father. And we instinctively knew our choice when asked the question of who we want to be.

My answer had been instant: not like my mother. I was constantly told that I looked exactly like her. But I didn't have to behave like her. I would never be like her.

I imagined Dad back home, getting into bed, lying helpless beside my mother, his shoulders cold, waiting for her to pull the blankets up and cover them. That was my father: the man who had been so focused on my mother that he didn't seem to really notice me. I always blamed my mother for standing between us. I thought that if he only knew the truth, things would be different. I thought back to the time a few weeks after my brother had left for Australia, when my mother turned on me. She never said it, but I think she knew that it was my fault he'd run away — and he was her favourite. Her physical attacks were sudden and inexplicable, except for one constant: they happened only when my father wasn't home. She hit me with innocuous items: acrylic hairbrushes over my head, croquet mallets on my legs, wooden spoons everywhere. But her favourite assault was up close and personal. She loved to pinch half-moon-shaped bruises into the soft skin under my arms, her face twisted with my flesh. It was understood that these secret marks must be kept hidden from my father.

At twelve, I was a head taller than her and finally raised my fist in defence. "Do that again and I'll fucking kill you," I said. Her expression told me that she was just as shocked as me. From that moment, the physical attacks stopped and her verbal tirades ramped up.

"You don't have any friends," she would say. Her features contorted with spite. "Anyone spending time with you is just using you. You're nothing but a little slut. A plain whore. A selfish bitch." She treated me like I was impossible to endure, which I easily accepted. I felt horrible that Robert had run away.

I wanted to prove her wrong about me. I started doing things that would force her to see that she loved me after all, just for being me, hoping that she would be proud of me. I did well in school, excelled in air cadets, and earned my glider pilot licence at sixteen. I was a high-school basketball all-star and MVP, worked part-time at McDonald's, and had a cadre of friends through the house on a weekly basis. Above all else, I refused to have sex with my high-school boyfriend, terrified that he would know I was not a virgin and tell everyone. He dumped me for it. She never had a word of praise for me, no matter how well I did.

20

MY CHANCE

One day in late April, my flight leader handed me a slip of paper during breakfast and waited while I read the note from Major Hardie, Staff Officer Careers. I was summoned to his office at 12:45 hours that day.

"Do you know why?" I asked.

"I was going to ask you. Come see me after class and let me know," he said with a sympathetic smile.

Major Hardie was seated at his desk, leaning back casually in his chair smoking a cigarette. He waved me to take a seat. I sat stiffly, hands on my knees. My eyes followed his hand to an open file folder.

"This message just arrived from NDHQ," he said, referring to National Defence Headquarters. "The Canadian Armed Forces are ready to open up the pilot classification to women." He slid the message across the desk.

I jumped out of my seat, grabbed the message, and screeched, "Really?"

"Holy shit." He reeled back and smiled. "You scared me. You can keep that copy. It says the plan is to start training twenty-five women pilots this summer in a four-year trial. Candidates will complete two years of continuous pilot training followed immediately by two years of observation flying in a squadron."

"How will this work for me?" I asked.

"That's the catch. You'll have to choose. Finish RMC or apply to enter the pilot trial as a female candidate starting this summer."

My whole purpose for joining the military, for agreeing to come to RMC in the first place, was to fulfill my dream of becoming a pilot. Now the choice felt complicated.

"Sir, I came here to be a pilot. To help my chances of reclassifying when this day came. Now I find myself afraid to quit RMC."

"Understood, Miss Armstrong. Why don't you sleep on it?" he said.

I joined the stream of cadets heading for the Sawyer Building classrooms after lunch. A few senior cadets looked sideways at me and scowled. I stared back intently so they would feel my gaze and be shocked. *Fuck you. I am outta here. I'm gonna be a pilot.* I smiled at them in a mocking way and another thought hit me. *I would be quitting and that's all that matters to them.* However valid the actual reasons, the final score would be a simple tally of women graduates and quitters. Every woman who left could be used as evidence that women couldn't complete the curriculum.

Not my problem.

What if I left here and then failed the pilot training trial? *Oh shit. I'll be in another trial with the first group of women.* What if I said no to pilot and then failed out of RMC? What if the trial failed? Would I regret leaving RMC for the rest of my life?

By the time I sat down in class, I had surprised myself. *I can always reclassify to pilot after I graduate and the trial is complete.* If pilot training wouldn't make me quit, nothing would. I sat up a bit taller, determined to pay closer attention in class that afternoon. *I'd better pass my exams and get the hell out of engineering.*

Meg slid into her desk beside me. "So?" she asked as class was just about to start.

I told her what had happened. She grabbed my arm. "Are you going?"

"No, damn it. I can't seem to convince myself to quit," I said.

"Thank God," she said and loosened her grip on me. "Please don't leave me here alone."

Next day after class, I gave Major Hardie my decision.

The atmosphere at lunch was electric. The fourth-year cadets were finishing their last day of undergraduate classes. I felt a twinge of emptiness — I wasn't living my dream of pilot anymore. *This place better be worth it.*

After class, the Frigate hallways resembled a madhouse more than a dormitory at military college. Wherever I looked, cadets were running up and down, cheering, roughhousing, and wrestling. A morning announcement in Hudson Squadron had ordered us to gather on the pier behind the Frigate immediately after class. First-year dress was squadron jersey, work dress pants, and running shoes.

The ice had barely melted off the bay. The air was still crisp with winter's chill, and a brisk, metallic breeze stirred at the water's edge.

Lt(N) Norwalk stood on the pier with shoulders raised to fend off the wind at his back. He wore a delighted grin. "Congratulations, Hudson Squadron. You're officially finished classes for the year and that can only mean one thing: it's time for first years to jump in the lake!"

A thunderous cheer rang out. We first years looked at each other in horror. The second years handed us overstuffed green life jackets that looked like relics from the Second World War and smelled like wet dog.

"First years!" Mr. Jansen yelled. "You will run off the edge in pairs. Hold hands if you're scared." The senior cadets laughed. It was recruit term all over again. I paired off with Fitzroy. "LAUNCH!"

Maxwell and Holbrook ran to the edge and hurled themselves into the six-foot drop. Fitzroy and I launched in fourth place. It was over so quickly that the biting cold didn't register until I was standing back on the dock. Nancy and Nanette jumped last, and when they were safely up the ladder, the entire squadron yelled out our cheer: "Yea stone! Yea boat! Yea, yea, stone boat!"

Ghostly echoes of "Stone boats don't float" drifted over us from across the square. I ran straight up to Norwalk, hugged him, and squeezed a puddle from my life jacket into his sweater. Jansen smiled from the edge and jumped into the water, followed quickly by all of our recruit flight staff. No pairs, no life jackets, no boot removal.

Exam routine officially started that night after dinner.

21

BLINDSIDED

"**M**arks are posted!" someone was running up and down the halls yelling. By the time I made it to the notice board in Mackenzie Building, a crowd was swarming the list. I looked over Penny Miller's shoulder for my name.

Chemistry: Supplemental exam. *I failed.* I passed everything else, but failed chemistry. If I failed my sup exam, it meant repeating the entire first-year process, including recruit term. *There's no fucking way.*

I ran straight home to my mother. I flew into Luka's room, barely pausing for an invitation to enter. He was sitting on his bed, red-eyed.

"What happened?" I asked.

"I have three sups. After all this, I might not graduate." He sobbed, took a deep breath, and made an obvious effort to pull himself together. "I'm sorry," he said. "Sorry. I don't mean to put this on you." I tried to interrupt, but he raised his hand to stop me. "How did you do?"

"I supped chem," I said, raising my palms toward the sky and shrugging my shoulders.

Our eyes met. Unexpectedly, I laughed at the absurdity of our situation. Luka joined in briefly.

His face collapsed into sadness again. "I'm going to miss my own convocation and grad parade," he said. Sups were written the week after graduation.

"Oh shit."

"Make sure you go see your chemistry prof and ask for help. Let him know you care."

"I will. I promise." I got up to leave, embarrassed that I had barged in with my drama when he was facing a worse situation. "Is it bad that I'm glad we're in this together?"

The door flew open and Blackwood came in. He moved to block my exit. I sidestepped him. He blocked me again. "Why do you leave as soon as I show up?" he asked.

"I was leaving. It's nothing personal," I said. He blocked me again. I stood still, staring straight ahead.

Luka put his hand on Blackwood's arm. "Come on, Woodsie."

I beamed a plastic smile and ducked around him. "See you." I slammed the door behind me.

A few days later, I stood at attention in front of Lt(N) Norwalk's desk to receive my year-end performance review. For some reason, Jansen stood behind him off to the side. Norwalk cleared his throat, leaned back, placed his elbows on the arms of his chair, and tented his fingers. The lazy rattling sounds of sailboat rigging floated on a light breeze. His office seemed small and dank in the evening light.

"Well, Miss Armstrong. I'm impressed with your progress. Your standing has bumped to the high side of the middle third," he said. I smiled.

"Thank you, sir," I replied.

He reviewed the performance categories and my strengths and weaknesses. "Keep putting in the effort. You're gaining ground. Maybe train over the summer to get that third chin-up. Pass your chemistry sup and come back to a fresh start next year in commerce."

"Yes, sir." I didn't see the point of telling him that I had been training all year and could still rarely do two chin-ups. It would just make me look even worse.

"The formal assessment is complete. But before you leave, there's one more serious topic to discuss." He frowned and nodded to Jansen, who moved from his place behind the chair and stood alongside Norwalk. I felt uneasy.

"Do you have anything you would like to share with us?" Norwalk asked.

"I'm sorry, sir?"

"Miss Armstrong," said Norwalk, "let me be blunt. Do you intend to date Fourth Year Eddie Byrne?"

I gasped. "No, sir. I have no intention of dating Fourth Year Byrne. He will be Second Lieutenant Byrne and cleared of RMC before anything happens between us."

"Don't get smart with me! Let me be direct. You're forbidden to date him. I don't care if he's a graduate or not."

"Sir, I don't understand. It's not against college rules for me to date a junior officer."

"If I catch wind that you date him this summer and return next fall having disobeyed me, I will personally see you kicked out of RMC. Do you understand?" Norwalk slammed both hands down on his desk and rose out of his seat. "You've heard my decision."

I tried a softer approach. "Sir, please. Why does it matter to you?"

"He's not suitable. End of story," he replied.

Not suitable? My own dad doesn't even tell me who to date.

"Permission to speak freely, sir?"

"Go."

"Sir, with all due respect, I'm nineteen. I'm old enough to make my own choice. How can you stop me from dating him?"

He glanced at Jansen and back at me. His face was strangely devoid of expression.

"Don't fucking try me, Miss Armstrong. I mean it," he said. He snapped my personnel file shut. I looked toward Jansen, but he wouldn't meet my eyes. "You're forbidden to date Eddie Byrne. That's final."

I crashed through the blue double doors of the Frigate and ran directly to the cadet safe haven of Fort Frederick — a hats-off area designated as a refuge in which college rules were purportedly suspended, a concept which had never been tested by me. Once inside the gates, I bolted up to the Armstrong Gun, a cannon mounted during the War of 1812 to guard the mouth of the St. Lawrence River, and screamed out across the water. "FUUUCK YOOOUUU!" I beat my hands on the grass mound along the edge of the limestone encasement wall. "Fuck! Fuck! Fuck!"

I drew in a deep breath of resolve. I would date Eddie Byrne. No one was going to stop me. We would decide if we were suitable for each other, no one else. Norwalk was resolved? I was resolved. I had followed their stupid rules. I knew for a fact that some of my female classmates were secretly dating cadets in third and fourth year; they didn't wait. They were even having sex in their rooms.

In a split second, I made a decision to ignore Norwalk's order. *I'm not even going to tell Eddie.*

After the three-hour graduation parade, we marched off the square, taking the route behind Fort LaSalle cadet dorms. Our passage was lined with recent graduates holding their swords aloft, forming a seemingly endless arch for us to march under as a farewell salute to honour us. We were dismissed, out of sight from the crowds; cheers erupted and parade guests flowed in around us. Children ran here and there, chattering and squealing.

Eddie found me. He picked me up off my feet and swung me around.

"One more night," he said, "and we can openly date. I wish you could come to the grad ball. I hope you know that."

"I believe you. I wish I could meet your family," I said, hoping to be swept off with him right then to search them out.

"You'll meet them during the summer. We'll go stay at the cottage," he said. "Good luck on your sup, and see you in Saint-Jean." Eddie was heading home to Ottawa the next day with his parents.

I watched him walk away. He turned and waved. I lifted my arm to wave back and a hand grabbed my shoulder. My face fell when I looked into the eyes of Graham Helstone.

"Kate," he said. "I'm glad I caught you."

"Caught me what?" I said, bracing myself.

He laughed. "No, I mean before you left. I ... I wanted to say sorry ... for being extra hard on you this year."

"Pardon?"

"I'm saying that I feel bad for how I treated you."

He had graduated; I didn't have to be the dutiful cadet anymore. "You feel bad? You made life hell for me."

He flushed red. "It was the only way I could talk to you."

"What?"

"I really like you…. You're my favourite cadet."

"You have a funny way of showing it."

"I know," he said. "I'm sorry. I didn't know what else to do."
I shook my head, dumbfounded.

"Now that it's over, I wanted you to know. I thought maybe
if you knew …" He paused and looked down at his feet and
then back up at me. "Say, I was wondering if you're interested
in rowing?"

"Rowing?" I asked, half laughing.

"You have a perfect build for rowing. If you want to try out
for the Queen's rowing team, my younger brother is on the team.
They allow cadets to row with Queen's. I could ask him to help
you out," he said, a hopeful look on his face.

I stepped back. "That's okay. I really need to get going. I want
to say goodbye to some of the guys from my squadron."

His smile collapsed. "Oh, of course. Well, take care."

"You too," I said. "Congratulations."

"Thanks, Kate," he said.

Richie and Meg were hanging out in a loose circle with
Jamieson and Morgan. As I approached, they made space for me
to join them.

"What was that all about? He wanted one last kick at the
can?" Jamieson asked.

"That was just Mr. Helstone saying sorry for treating me so
badly this year. Apparently, he had a crush on me and it was the
only way he could talk to me," I said with a casual shrug.

Meg's jaw dropped, and Mr. Jamieson croaked, "Are you
fucking kidding me! He did not just say that to you."

"I swear on my mother's grave."

22

ALREADY DONE

On Wednesday morning, I wrote my chemistry exam. After lunch, I went out to Fort Freddie and sat at the Armstrong Gun. The wind whipped off the water and tousled my hair — I had started letting it grow out. A ridge of dark clouds advanced along the lake toward the college. My skin got damp in the oppressive humidity.

At two o'clock, I walked back to the Mackenzie Building to get my mark. I scored 71 percent. The sup mark was not factored into my overall final mark, so my transcript mark would always read 51 percent. I didn't care. I had passed!

A warm rain hit the college amidst loud claps of thunder. The storm passed, the rain broke the back of the humidity, and the college was washed clean.

I slept for two days, read in Fort Freddie on a blanket, and waited for Luka. He was driving me to Saint-Jean when he was done.

——————

On Friday afternoon, as soon as Luka had seen his final mark and knew that he had graduated, we left RMC. We drove down the highway in his white 1968 MGB with the top down and the sun beaming on us as we sang along to a mixed tape he had made for me. We wore Vuarnet sunglasses and had our collars up on our Lacoste shirts, mine pink and his white. The wind whipped our hair in every direction. I leaned my head back and soaked it all in.

Three hours later, we arrived at the CMR dorms outside of Montreal. Luka pulled up in front of the three-storey red brick building, grabbed my bags out of the trunk, and set them on the sidewalk.

"See you soon," I said, telling myself that this was true. "I never would have made it without all your support. You're the best mother ever."

"Now you're my little chickadee and I'm shoving you from the nest," he said. "Remember to write to me."

We hugged goodbye, holding on a little too long. I loved him like a brother.

I spent the afternoon settling into my room at CMR. Eddie picked me up at five to go for dinner in Montreal. That evening, after our first real date together, Eddie stopped the car in the parking lot of his building on CFB Saint-Jean, part of a complex called The Mega due to its gigantic footprint, where the commissioned officers were staying. He cleared his throat. "Wanna come up to my room?"

"Now?" I asked.

"I have my own room, and we've been on a four-month journey getting to know each other," he said gently. "We've had a nice dinner in Montreal and a romantic drive. So, to me, it seems like now is a good moment."

I started to cry.

He sat up in shock. "Are you okay? What's wrong?" He took my hand and raised it to his lips.

"I can't do this," I said.

"Are you a virgin?" he asked.

I couldn't help but laugh ruefully at his assumption even though I had spent my youth avoiding sex and aspiring to be mistaken for one.

"I won't hurt you. I want to make you feel amazing," he said.

"It's Norwalk," I cried. "During my year-end performance review, he ordered me not to date you. He threatened to kick me out of the college if I did."

"I've graduated. We waited. How can he kick you out? We can be together if *we* choose. It's not his decision!"

"That is exactly what I said. He said, 'Don't fucking try me.' Just like that. I'm scared. I haven't told anyone."

"When were you planning to tell *me*?"

"I don't know," I said. "Never. Later. I wanted to disobey him."

"So why are you crying?"

"If they kick me out, I lose everything"

Eddie exploded. "Fuck! Norwalk can't tell you who to love outside of the college."

"I gave up my chance at pilot to stay. If we date, he'll find a way to kick me out."

"I failed my French test to be here this summer." Eddie took a deep breath and spoke more calmly. "Kate, I love you. I want to be with you."

"How could this ever work? What if I get kicked out? What then?" I wailed.

"You *know* how I feel about you, Kate. Trust that."

"I can't," I said.

"Please don't do this." He leaned over and nuzzled my neck. My body was on fire to be with him. I pulled back. He slid his fingers through my hair along the base of my skull and gently took a handful. He pulled me to him and kissed me hard and let me go. "Okay. I guess we'd better get you home."

As he drove, I tried to hold back the panic. I placed my hand high on his inner thigh and he intertwined his fingers with mine and said nothing.

At my dorm, he got out and opened my car door for me. I slid out, leaned against his car, and held on. He took my face in his hands and kissed me so tenderly that I felt faint.

"Well. See you around, Kate Armstrong," he said, smiling half-heartedly. "I'm going to miss you."

"I can't do this," I said. My legs wobbled under me.

"It's already done."

He took my elbow and led me to the doors of the dorm. I forced myself to walk down the hall without looking back, but when I heard his car start, I bolted into my room, pressed my face against the window, and peered out, hoping to catch a glimpse of him driving away.

He was already gone.

23

DISHONOURABLE INTENTIONS

Second year. After a listless summer of French immersion and a few weeks at home doing nothing much, I was back at the college. I was startled awake at 05:30 hours. "Another One Bites the Dust" by Queen. Three minutes and thirty-one seconds of annoying pounding followed by blissful silence as the new recruits headed out for their morning run. I rolled over.

I had a first-floor corner room all to myself, next to the fire escape door and as far away as possible from the recruit hallway. My room had two bay windows. One looked out over the parade square; the other looked over the fire escape stairs at the red brick wall of the Old Gym across the alley. Second-year privileges allowed me to use the fire escape, which meant I could avoid the foyer next to the orderly room almost entirely. I was allowed my own bedding, so I had shipped my goose feather duvet set — a pastel green and pink flower print cover with matching pillowcases — and two feather pillows from home. My military uniforms and gear needed to be regulation for inspections: properly measured, organized, and sorted in my closet and drawers and on my shelves. But with no roommate, the extra space could be filled with my personal clothing and effects. Second-year walking-out dress for trips to town was the No. 6 uniform, a navy-blue college-crested blazer and grey flannels.

We'd lost four of our original twenty recruits in A Flight at the end of last year. Two guys had failed and two others had quit. Of the thirty-two first women who had started last fall, we'd lost eight: one for medical reasons and one for voluntary release; Mary Tyler had failed for fitness reasons, and five more had failed academically. All four women of the Frigate were back.

In my clearing-in package was the 1981 yearbook. I held off unpacking my things and excitedly flipped the book open to look at Eddie's photo. I'd seen him only twice from a distance all summer and had heard he was windsurfing a lot. I touched his photo and felt a familiar twinge of sadness. I read his graduation write-up.

One line stopped my heart cold: "He's going to catch up with Spears even if it means a quick visit to Crazy Linda's place." Crazy Linda was a woman from town rumoured to be available for sex with cadets. I had never paid much attention to the story. I flipped over to Mike Spears' write-up and read, "Spears let the 'Big Guy' take over, and he began to rack up the numbers, much to Byrne's dismay."

Eddie had said back in March that he wasn't really part of the bet. The yearbook was assembled in May, before he knew we weren't going to date. *Maybe Norwalk did me a favour after all?* I slammed the book shut. A wave of relief washed through me — I could admit it now. I loved the idea of him but had never really believed that we could make it work. *He's a fighter pilot and I'm a cadet for the next three years.* Fighter pilots had a bad reputation as cheaters. "Now I don't have to find out the hard way," I said aloud.

I was in the midst of setting up my new tuner and cassette player, with stand-alone speakers, when there was a knock on my door. I hollered, "Come in!"

The new cadet squadron training officer, Kevin Blackwood, stood at my bedroom door dressed in full No. 4 uniform of blues, pillbox, red sash, and gaiters.

"Yes?" I said coolly.

He beamed. "Hello, Kate," he said with a bow, taking off his pillbox and sweeping it nearly to the ground. "Welcome back, my lady."

"Please don't call me that."

He made another less formal bow. "As you wish."

I was flummoxed. He brushed a lock of hair off his brow and grinned smugly, his hat pressed to his chest.

"How may I help you, Mr. Blackwood?" I asked. He closed the door and stepped forward. I backed away until my legs brushed against the bed frame.

He moved forward again. I leaned away. "No need to be so formal. Call me Woodsie. I've come directly from my afternoon duties with the recruits of A Flight to attend to another matter of utmost import," he said. "I've given our situation a considerable amount of thought over the summer. I have a proposal to make."

"I'm sorry? What situation?"

"Kate, I am attracted to you. No need to play coy." He reached his right hand toward me with his fingers spread, as if trying to catch a butterfly, and squeezed my shoulder. I scurried out from under his touch and slammed back against my closet door. "I want you to be my girlfriend. I want us to be a couple this year."

"What? No, thank you."

"Why? Don't you want to think about it?"

"You're two years senior to me and the CSTO. You know we're not allowed to date. Right?"

"We-eeell, yes," he said, "but you were willing to work it out for Eddie Byrne."

"What? I *liked* Eddie and I was ordered *not* to date him. So I didn't exactly work it out, did I?"

"Okay, well that's good. I was checking," he said.

"What are you talking about? Is this a game?" I asked.

"No, I'm not trying to trick you. I want to date you," he whined. "I've thought about it all summer."

"I didn't come to RMC to be *your* girlfriend." I took a deep breath. "I'm not attracted to you. Please leave my room."

His face darkened. I was prepared to scream at the top of my lungs if he touched me again. "I'm warning you," he growled, "if you don't date me, I'll make you very unhappy this year."

"Can you hear yourself?" I asked, emboldened by his threat. "I would never date you, even if I could." I walked over, pulled open my door, and with a flourish invited him out onto the green carpet of the hallway.

Richie and Meg came by my room on the way to dinner. We clanged down the metal fire escape stairs and walked casually across the square. I told them what had happened with Blackwood.

"Are you fucking kidding?" Richie asked. "That guy is a nut job."

"He kinda scared me," I said.

Richie grabbed Meg's arm protectively. "Seriously, if that guy even looks at you sideways, I want to know. I'm keeping my eye on Blackballs."

"Our knight," Meg said.

24

DON'T GET CAUGHT

The dining hall echoed with yelling directed at the new recruits, the Class of 1985. The newest crop of cadets seemed frantic in their urgency to prove themselves; they hurried, scampered, and shouted on command with enthusiasm, seemingly eager to earn favour. It was strange to see what had been our third years running the racket on the new candidates. A Flight marched past us looking scared and confused.

"Did we look that frightened?" I asked.

"Maybe. But you didn't look that hot," said Bristow, elbowing Fitzroy to look up. "I'll take the blond one."

"I prefer the tiny one with dark hair. She's sassy," said Fitzroy. I followed their gaze. There were only three women in the group.

"Holy shit, you guys. They're not commodities," I said.

"Don't worry, Kate. You're still cute," said Richie.

"That's not what I am talking about."

"We're guys. Guys look at girls," said Fitzroy dismissively.

"Fine," I said, looking at them now myself. I was surprised to feel a pang of jealousy and self-doubt about my attractiveness compared to the new women, an ugly feeling. I promised myself I'd offer the new women the friendship and support of senior cadets that was not available to us last year.

A letter arrived in wing mail from a classmate in Five Squadron. He wrote an eloquent condolence advising me that an old boyfriend of mine, Shawn, had been killed in an accident on the West Coast and had repeatedly called my name from his hospital bed in the intensive care unit before dying. Shawn and I had worked together as staff at the Air Cadet Gliding Program in 1979, the year after I earned my glider pilot licence. He'd been a crush during the summer after grade eleven, when Gary had dumped me for refusing to have sex. I was gutted by the news. I rushed downstairs and called his mom.

"Mrs. Baker, I hope you won't consider me insensitive for calling so long after Shawn's accident. I've only just received the news and want to offer my condolences. I'm devastated that he's gone," I said, holding back from sobbing.

"Kate, what are you talking about, dear? What accident?"

I was confused. How could she not know? "His hang-gliding accident three weeks ago?"

She was quiet for a moment. "I think someone has played a very mean trick on you. Shawn's right here. Would you like to speak to him?"

Shawn came on the line. "Kate, what's going on?"

"Oh, thank God," I exclaimed and told him about the letter.

"That bastard. He told me he'd get even!"

"What could make anyone be so cruel?"

Shawn told me that they'd been training on the same base over the summer. He had asked the cadet about me. The cadet replied with a description of various ways he would like to fuck me.

"So I beat the shit out of him," Shawn said. "It was worth the ten days of extra duty officer."

The next morning, I cornered my letter-writing classmate at breakfast. I got right up in his face.

"How could you do that?" I asked. "That was evil."

"He deserved it. I have no use for him."

"Why bring me into it? I haven't done anything to you."

"Will you fuck me?"

"What? No!"

"Then I have no use for you either," he said and walked away. That was the end of it.

I spun around in disgust and crashed right into Blackwood. He smirked at me, stepped aside, and bowed low as I passed.

As second years, we worked every spare moment on building the recruit obstacle course. As the end of recruit term drew near, we fudged study hours to make more time. One night I got back to my room just before lights out. I closed my door and drapes and stripped off my filthy clothes. That's when I spotted a note on the floor that had been slid under my door. Jeff Dillon, my section commander, wanted to see me immediately upon my return. I threw on my housecoat and went next door to his room.

Jeff stood in front of his sink; he wore a housecoat, too. The intimacy embarrassed me. "Close the door. It seems you're facing a breach parade," he said bluntly.

Breach parade meant being charged for a misdemeanour. There was a code of conduct in the *Cadet Wing Instructions* and a whole chapter assigned to breaches of conduct. If found guilty — of whatever I was being accused of doing — I'd be confined to quarters and stripped of all privileges, pretty much like being grounded or under house arrest, for however many days on charge.

"What did I do?" I was baffled.

"You're being charged with an insecure bayonet. Mr. Blackwood found the key to your gash drawer, opened it, and found your bayonet. In his world, this means someone could break into your room and steal your weapon."

"He was searching through my personal stuff while I was out of my room?" I felt a wave of disgust.

Jeff gave me a blank look and doubled over in laughter. "You should see your face right now."

"You're kidding, right? This is a joke?" I laughed nervously.

"Sorry. I shouldn't laugh. I'm just shocked at the lengths some people will go to make other people miserable. Blackwood definitely seemed pleased with himself when he came by earlier to tell me."

"But I hid my key," I said. *Do I tell him about Blackwood's threat to me?*

"Not well enough. The breach parade is on Sunday afternoon. You'll need a peer to act as an escort for you. Blackwood will present his case against you to CSL Toller and you'll have the chance to give your side of the story. I'll be there, as your CSC and support at — let's call it what it is — kangaroo court."

"Have you ever been charged?"

"Nope. And I can tell you Blackwood is purposely making trouble," he said. "I bet I can find every gash drawer key in our section within minutes — if anyone bothered to hide them at all."

After a silence, I said, "Blackwood told me on my first day back that he wants to date me. When I refused, he said he would punish me."

Jeff grimaced. "He's the type to play dirty. I wouldn't say anything if I was you. He could make you look crazy. Do you want me to step in?"

"No, I can handle it," I answered resignedly.

"Okay. Well, for now, keep this between us."

"At least now you know. I promised myself not to screw up this year," I said. "I plan to stick to it."

The college motto drilled values into us: Truth, duty, valour. The fourth was tacit, but everyone knew it: *Don't get caught.*

I went directly back to my room and tossed all my underwear into my laundry bag.

The next morning on the way to class, I told Holbrook what had happened. "So, will you do it?"

"Is it like being your best man?"

"Something like that," I said.

He agreed enthusiastically.

"You don't have to look so fucking delighted."

"Look, the easiest way to keep my eye on Blackballs is to be in the room when he's pulling his shit," Richie said. "Besides, I think it will be fun to see a breach parade."

I elbowed him in the ribs.

Sunday afternoon, Richie and I stood before Cadet Squadron Leader Toller, who was seated at a desk in the gunroom, flanked by CSC Dillon and CSTO Blackwood.

"Miss Armstrong, you are called before me today to answer to the charge of having an insecure weapon. This process is internal to the college. Any findings here will remain on your file for the duration of your time at RMC and be expunged upon graduation. Do you understand?" he asked smoothly.

"Yes, Mr. Toller."

"Further, upon hearing both sides of the situation, it is at my discretion to make a determination of the appropriate correction under the circumstances. I will ask Mr. Blackwood to give his account. You may speak when invited to share any mitigating circumstances. Do you understand?"

"Yes, Mr. Toller."

Toller read aloud the several columns on the page in front of him, making a show of consulting the conduct sheet: "An Act to the Prejudice of Good Order and Discipline in that Second Year Armstrong, on 24 September 1981, at approximately 08:50 hours, left the key to her security drawer, which contains her bayonet, insecure.

"These charges are being brought against you by Mr. Blackwood," Toller concluded. There was a pause. I tried to breathe deeply and evenly. Richie stood beside me like a stone statue.

"Mr. Blackwood, proceed with your findings."

Blackwood nodded and snapped to attention. "Certainly, Mr. Toller. I was conducting a routine squadron walk-through of rooms when I discovered the key to Second Year Armstrong's lock-up drawer, where I found her FN breechblock, unloaded magazines, and a bayonet secured inside. The key to her rifle was not found. In my view, the disposition of her room, being adjacent to the first-floor fire escape stairs, greatly increases the risk of the bayonet being stolen. I step back in deference to your decision on appropriate action."

He is such a fucking sycophant.

"Thank you, Mr. Blackwood." Mr. Toller's eyes narrowed almost imperceptibly as he cast a sideways glance at Blackwood. "Where did you find the key?"

"In a drawer containing articles of clothing, Mr. Toller," he said.

Mr. Toller made a few notes. "Miss Armstrong, you've heard the formal charge brought against you. I understand that you were not in your room at the time, is that correct?"

"Yes, that is correct, Mr. Toller."

"You had no knowledge of Mr. Blackwood's intention to conduct a thorough inspection of your room in your absence?" he asked.

"No, Mr. Toller."

"Where exactly was the key to your lock-up drawer hidden, Miss Armstrong?"

"Amongst my personal underwear, Mr. Toller."

Toller frowned. "I beg your pardon?" he asked.

"With my panties, Mr. Toller."

He leaned back, grasped the wooden arms of his chair, and stared hard at Blackwood.

"Permission to speak freely, Mr. Toller?" I asked.

"Go."

"One pair is missing," I said.

Mr. Toller's face flushed. "I am *not* pleased with what is being disclosed," he said in an icy tone.

I waited. Holbrook stood so still, I had almost forgotten he was there.

"Miss Armstrong," Mr. Toller continued, "regardless of the tactics used, which I find suspect, nothing has been revealed to refute the facts. You left your lock-up key hidden but unprotected in your room, resulting in a serious breach of conduct, an insecure bayonet. Taking into consideration the circumstances disclosed and that this is your first breach of conduct, I am awarding three days on charge to be served on October second, third, and fourth. Do you have any questions?"

Ex-Cadet Weekend. I would be on charge for all of Ex-Cadet Weekend.

"No, Mr. Toller," I replied.

Three days in jail.

Blackwood smirked.

"Mr. Dillon, please remove the accused and debrief her on the process to be followed during those three days. Mr. Blackwood, please remain for a word," Mr. Toller ordered. "Breach parade dismissed!"

I caught a glimpse of Toller addressing Blackwood intently as the door closed on them. Dillon turned to me. "What the fuck? Are you for real? Your key was hidden in your gonch?"

"Yes!" I hissed.

"Why didn't you tell me?"

"I didn't think it would matter," I said. I didn't admit that I had wanted some advantage, and the element of surprise seemed to have worked in my favour.

"So creepy," Richie said.

"I have a feeling that whether or not it matters is being determined right now, behind that door," Jeff whispered.

"I still got three days."

Richie accompanied me back to my room, where I threw myself on my bed and stared at the pipes on the ceiling. "I have to do all the shit preparing for Ex-Cadet Weekend and now I'll miss all the parties and have to run around in my white belt and gaiters like an idiot in front of all the ex-cadets."

"Based on what just happened in the basement, you have bigger things to worry about. I'd be scared of him if I was you," Richie said.

"I am," I said. I looked Richie in the eye. "But no one can know that I'm afraid."

25

ON CHARGE

The word *panties* floated in my wake wherever I went over the next few days. I had hoped for sympathy for the violation of my personal privacy, but none came. I was the joke.

Blackwood became a shadow over my already minuscule sense of privacy. Whenever I came back to my room I checked to see if anyone had been there. I looked under my bed, in the closet, and behind my door. I left traps: a pen placed just so on a book, a hair on the edge of my drawer, one thing offset from another. I thought about locking up my panties in my gash drawer, but I didn't. *I need to pretend he's not getting to me.*

Friday morning, 05:30 hours. "Another One Bites the Dust" shook the Frigate for the last time. This time, I got up with the recruits. I was on charge. It was pitch dark. I dressed in the winter version of No. 5s — battle blouse jacket, blue pants with red piping, and a light-green shirt — adorned with the formal white belt, parade boots, and gaiters normally worn only on dress uniforms, but in this case the hallmark of a cadet on charge.

There was an art to putting on gaiters, the polished, hard, black leather puttees strapped over the lower pant leg. First, I put on pants and boots. Then I lined up the pant seams, secured the gaiter around my leg, and did up the buckles. Next, I pulled my pants down, tied my pants to the gaiter tops with crudely fashioned bootlaces stuffed with fishing weights that we had made during recruit term, pulled my pants up, and bloused them with perfectly aligned seams front and back. All the while being careful not to make any creases.

On charge, I had to run everywhere when I was outside. My second-year privileges were suspended: no use of common rooms or fire escapes; no phone calls, mail, or social interaction; four inspections a day; and remedial duties at the discretion of the duty cadet. My first inspection was at 06:20 hours, followed by corrective drill.

Drill lasted an entire half hour. The duty cadet belted out a new command every third pace: right turn, left turn, halt, quick march, about turn, halt, stand at ease, attention, quick march, slow march, quick march. By the time he dismissed me for breakfast at 07:00 hours, I was sweating.

I ran back to the Frigate and locked up my rifle. Now I kept my gash drawer key with my rifle key on my dog tags, which I wore around my neck at all times.

I ran to Yeo Hall for breakfast.

I ran to Massey Library for class.

At noon, I ran back to the Frigate to re-iron my uniform and unlock my weapon for midday inspection. And so the day went, running every time I set foot outside and doing what felt like an eternal round of inspections and menial tasks. That afternoon, I was granted special permission to fulfill my second-year duties on the obstacle course and dress in work dress.

———

At 23:00 hours on Saturday night, I ran back to the Frigate after a defaulter parade spent scrubbing the commandant's private toilet with a toothbrush. The badging parade for the recruits was over and everyone was partying with the new first years. Music and laughter wafted up the stairs from the gunroom. I skulked to my room and threw myself on the bed in the dark and watched lights track across the ceiling from cars leaving the ex-cadet party at the senior staff mess. My door cracked opened. A bare-hand puppet poked in with thumb and fingers pressed straight out together in the form of a beak and scanned the room.

Richie and Meg stumbled in a moment later, drunk and giggling, and flicked on the light. It was just past midnight. "We came to let you know the party sucked because you weren't there. It was no fun at all," Meg said.

"Thanks, you guys. I'm feeling pretty sorry for myself," I said.

"We brought you kye," Richie said, grinning and holding out a tinfoil packet of lukewarm soggy toast slathered in peanut butter and jam. I gobbled it down.

The following week, the new director of cadets, or DCdts, Colonel George Gilmore, called a meeting for the first- and second-year female cadets. I walked up the stairs to the Currie Hall theatre alongside the other second-year Frigate women, Meg, Nancy, and Nanette. At the top of the stairs, I stopped in my tracks in front of a pale marble statue of a goddess guarding the entrance to the theatre.

"Why have I never noticed this statue?" I asked. The rest of them shrugged and kept walking. I stared at her for a moment. The word *PAX* was engraved on the marble base under her sandalled feet. She was seated, draped in a robe, and wearing a dove-adorned helmet and an elaborate metal breastplate. Across her knees, she gingerly held a sword that was partially wrapped in olive branches. A tarnished silver plaque said the statue was a gift from the French government in 1923 in gratitude for RMC graduates and their contributions in the First World War.

The expanse of Currie Hall, able to accommodate the entire cadet wing, accentuated how few seats in the college were actually taken up by female cadets. We barely filled the first two rows.

Colonel Gilmore was gruff. He stood with his hands on his hips, and he reminded me of Elmer Fudd with his balding head, glossy skin, and fat body, which stretched the seams of his uniform.

"Ladies," he said, "I've called you here today for a blunt discussion about sexual attraction and sexual conduct in the cadet wing. I want to be clear that the responsibility rests squarely on your shoulders. Each one of you must take this responsibility seriously. Sexual intimacy is forbidden on the college grounds. The onus is on you to maintain strict vigilance about your conduct and appearance, to ensure that your integration into the cadet wing is as seamless as possible. It is your job to prevent trouble and to not invite unwanted sexual attention."

What the fuck? Who is this guy? Does he know about the bet from last year? I looked around at the faces of my peers and saw that other women seemed pissed off, too.

"Am I clear?" he asked.

"Yes, sir," we answered lamely. I was keeping my mouth shut after my recent trouble with Blackwood.

"Good. If there are no questions, you're dismissed."

"Excuse me, sir?" Janice Bellamy put up her hand. "Second Year Janice Bellamy, Two Squadron." *Go, Janice!* Janice was the only second-year female cadet remaining in Two Squadron. Last year, Bellamy's recruit-term roommate had been infamous for having sex with senior cadets. We all paid the price for it. Much to the terror and horror of Bellamy, her roommate had been publicly presented with a dildo at a squadron party and their squadron commander had simply laughed along with the male cadets. The roommate didn't last the year.

"Yes, Miss Bellamy."

"Sir, to be honest, I'm not sure that I am clear."

"What part confuses you?"

"Permission to speak freely, sir?" she asked.

"Go."

"Sir, aren't the male cadets responsible for their own thoughts and behaviours?"

"Of course, Miss Bellamy. The trouble is, women are the more mature sex in these matters. We can't count on the guys to keep a grip on themselves, especially at this age. It's just the way they're wired."

"*Sir*," Janice said, "how is it even possible for the female cadets to take responsibility for male cadets' thoughts and behaviours?"

"You need to keep your hormones in check. You're the gate-keepers, as it were," he said with a tight little smile.

Janice sat down. It was a pointless argument. He hadn't called us here to ask us; he'd called us here to tell us. Red blotches mottled her neck.

"If there are no further questions, you may carry on, ladies."

As we trudged down the stairs past Pax, I gave the marble goddess a sideways glance. The Frigate first-year women ran across the square, leaving the four of us second-year women alone, marching side by side. Once we were definitely out of earshot of anyone, I spoke up. "Next thing you know, they'll have us wearing black tablecloths over our heads and face scarves to protect the guys from their thoughts," I said. I was thinking of the images I'd seen on the news of women in Iran.

Between Colonel Gilmore's speech and Blackwood's unwanted attention, I wasn't very keen these days on taking part in extracurricular events. My tolerance for blatant sexist remarks and stupid jokes was depleted. Last year, I had enjoyed the rough-and-tumble activities with a first year's sense of wonder and amusement: the Navy Bay regatta, the annual cadet wing snowball fight against the Frigate on the night of the first big snowstorm, the winter carnival, cheering at varsity sporting events, and all the seasonal parties and formal balls. Now I had lost interest in participating, but I wanted to keep up the appearance of having a good attitude, so I forced myself to go through the motions and lumped it all into one general category: mandatory fun.

November blew in the first winter storms. It was cold and snowing hard. I'd just had a nice meal out with Kurt Samson, my favourite fourth year from the basketball team last year, who had been on his way through town and invited me out for dinner. We'd had a friendly, meandering chat at a local upscale restaurant on the edge of town and had lost track of time. When the waiter delivered the cheque, it was starting to feel late.

"My treat," Kurt said and grabbed the bill. "I'm a rich second lieutenant now." I opened my mouth to argue, but he held the bill out of reach and looked at his watch. "Whoa, it's eleven forty. I'm pushing your curfew to the limit."

"It's only a ten-minute drive. We should be fine," I said, but I was immediately nervous. I had been living by the book, making every effort not to break any rules.

On the drive back, we rounded the curve along the limestone walls of Fort Frontenac and saw the LaSalle Causeway lift bridge was up and still rising as a tugboat waited for clear passage from the Rideau Canal side.

"In all my years, I've never been caught by the bridge," Kurt said, "and now, of all times."

I looked at my watch. "It's okay. I still have twelve minutes."

For several minutes, we watch the bridge in action. It cantilevered up and then down, and within minutes Kurt zoomed along Precision Drive and around the rear of the Sawyer Building complex, slowing at the Frigate. He squeezed my hand and I leaned over to kiss his cheek.

"I hate rushing away like this. Thank you so much again for a lovely evening," I said. The instant the tires stopped crunching in the snow, I was out of the car.

I charged up the fire escape stairs two at a time and walked quickly down the dark first-floor hallway. It was a nondescript night without any big event happening, so there was no reason to be concerned about the duty office being manned past 22:30 hours. In second year, we signed in and out on the honour system.

The orderly room lights were out, the door was half closed, and I sighed in relief. I flicked on the lights and yelped: Blackwood was sitting there on the desk. He was wearing a Scrooge-style striped nightshirt, and a pair of shower sandals hung from his bare feet.

"Good evening, Miss Armstrong," he said. "What time do you have?"

I took a deep breath, and looked up at the standard-issue white-faced orderly room clock. "Twelve-oh-two," I said. I wrote it down as I signed in.

"You're late," Blackwood said cheerfully. "It looks like you're AWOL. Being AWOL is a serious offence."

"Yes, Mr. Blackwood," I said, completely deadpan. "Permission to carry on?"

"Carry on, Miss Armstrong."

I walked away, resisting my impulse to punch a wall or scream in frustration, anger stiffening my every stride. I placed my hand on the doorknob to my room and looked back down the hall. Blackwood stood in the beam of light from the orderly room with his hands on his hips, watching me. I closed my door behind me and locked it.

I couldn't sleep, so at 01:30 hours I wrote a note to my section commander, Jeff Dillon, about the incident and slid it under his door. The golden rule in the military is if you're in trouble, make sure your superior officer hears the news from you first.

I awoke to a knock on my door at 07:00 hours. I put on my housecoat and opened the door. Dillon came in and sat down in my lounge chair uninvited.

"Got your note. This is worse than I thought," he said. I half-sat on my desk and braced myself. "The key thing was bad enough, but this is ridiculous. Waiting in the orderly room for a second year? He definitely has it in for you."

"You think?"

Jeff asked me for the details. We went over the whole story. I had no real defence. I was late. Bad luck. Bad planning. End of story.

"Yes, best to take your lumps and move on," he said. "The good news is, only six more weeks of Blackwood as CSTO until the new bar slate for second term."

We left it at that.

Next stop, Richie's room. He was totally hungover and still in bed. His blue eyes were bloodshot. I told him I had some bad news.

"Let me guess, Blackballs?" he said.

Richie listened to my story while he lay back in bed, head in his hands, staring at the ceiling. When I was done, he propped up on one elbow. "Okay, do you want the bad news or the worse news first?"

"Bad news."

"Bristow and I went out last night. We didn't sign out. We got home at three a.m. That is the true definition of AWOL."

"Fuckers!" I said it with a laugh but felt the sting of unfairness. "Crap. So, what's the worse news?"

"This is going to make you really angry, so brace yourself," Richie said. "Last night, Blackballs was on the rampage in town looking for you. We saw him a couple times and he kept grilling us, wanting us to say where you were. His eyes were all crazy. Have you ever noticed that he walks kinda sideways like a rabid dog?"

I stared at Richie. "Oh my god. He must have seen that I signed out for dinner with Kurt. *Shit.* Wait. He saw you and didn't even notice that you weren't signed out?"

"I didn't even think about that. We were already feeling no pain by the first time he showed up. I wonder if he'll remember?"

"I don't think he cares," I said. "So, can you guess why I'm here?"

"You need a best man?"

"Uh huh."

"Agreed."

"Thank you. You're a true friend and a lucky bastard. Details to follow." I leaned over to hug him but I reeled back to avoid breathing in the booze cloud around him.

Seven days.

That was the price I paid for being two minutes late. Blackwood charged me for being ten minutes late on the official paperwork. I didn't contest the amount of time because it wouldn't have changed anything. Late was late.

The breach parade was a repeat performance, all the same characters playing their roles. The only change was the content. Once again, the details on the surface of the incident supported the punishment. Or rather, the *correction*.

26

SECOND CHANCES

Truth, duty, valour. *Don't get caught.* I avoided the limelight with new fervour. The idea of Blackwood storming around town looking for me had frightened me. I couldn't trust the system and I had been naive to think that rules were applied objectively.

In an effort to stay out of harm's way, I re-created my room as a local tea emporium. One of the first-year guys lent me a teal and yellow windsurfer sail to tie to my ceiling pipes, and I added throw pillows in the bay windows and a few potted ferns. It worked. I had a lot of visitors, mostly the first-year women but also a few men.

Penny Miller, my classmate from Eight Squadron, was my most frequent visitor. Penny was thin and walked with her hips forward like a supermodel, but on her the overall effect was more like an old woman walking into a strong wind. I looked up to her, and more than once someone suggested, "If you could be more ladylike, like Penny, you'd be more attractive and in less trouble all the time." But I couldn't. We were opposite in nearly every way and, outside of RMC, would have been unlikely friends. At first I found it curious that she was willing to come all the way over to the Frigate to study with me, but once she admitted her crush on Nigel Maxwell, it made more sense. When they started to date, I saw less of Penny, and I saw more of Meg again after she broke up with Richie.

Christmas exams came and went and I passed everything, but my academic performance remained unremarkable, even though I was studying commerce this year. I couldn't seem to shake my academic entropy and eagerly left my books lying open unattended whenever someone stopped by to visit. I told myself that I'd do some serious studying later, a time that never came.

In the new year, Blackwood became the cadet wing training officer and moved across the square to live in Wing HQ. He seemed to lose interest, or perhaps opportunity, in making me miserable. I was assigned a new room facing Navy Bay, and college life settled into a near peace.

A message came down from Norwalk that I was scheduled to travel to NDHQ in Ottawa on Saturday, January 23, for a photo shoot. I'd been chosen as the female cadet to model every uniform combination for the RMC clothing stores catalogue.

I felt a flash of pride at being chosen, which was quickly dashed in the next section of the travel order. The male model, and my travel companion, would be Third Year Louis Arsenault. Only Blackwood would have been worse.

We took an early morning staff car to Ottawa, complete with a driver, all our uniforms and accoutrements loading down the trunk. I didn't make any social effort toward Arsenault, which he reciprocated. We spoke barely ten words the whole way.

The seemingly endless combinations of uniform were captured on film by four thirty. I watched Arsenault interact amicably with the photographer and found myself liking him a bit better despite my determination to hate him. A few times, I stopped myself just in time from speaking to him. When we arrived back in Kingston later that evening, there was a new easiness to our mutual silence.

"That wasn't as bad as I thought it would be," he said in parting.

"Same here."

"Well, good night, Kate."

"Night," I said, feeling off-kilter at his display of near friendliness.

On March 2, I sat down for dinner at a table with three guys in third year. They chatted and laughed together congenially.

One of the guys caught my eye, stuck out his hand, and said, "Excuse me. My name's Bud Dalton. Would you mind sharing your opinion with us?"

"Sure. I always seem to have one." I smiled and shook his hand, introducing myself.

"Well, Jake here," Bud said, poking a guy from Seven Squadron, "is turning twenty tomorrow. He won't go out to celebrate because it's a school night. What do you think?"

"Well, I'd say that if I was allowed to go out on a weeknight, I would go. Especially for my birthday," I said. It was a third-year privilege to sign out during the week and miss study hours.

"Yes!" exclaimed Bud.

The good-looking guy, soon to be the birthday boy, rolled his eyes and laughed. I was struck by his huge smile and sexy gap-toothed grin. "I'm Jake Tatham, the stick in the mud. This is Jimmy Tolbert." He thumbed at the other friend. "So? First class of women, eh? How's that been for you?"

"More fun than the brochure said," I deadpanned. They surprised me with their warm laughter. They were new to RMC this year from Royal Roads Military College in Victoria.

"I gotta admit, I like having you girls here," said Jake. "Makes it feel more like regular university."

"That's a bit of a stretch," I teased.

"I'm just glad that I didn't end up in the Frigate." He pointed at my navy-blue second-year shoulder patch.

"To tell the truth, I love living in the Frigate."

They guffawed. "Come on!" Jimmy roared. "You can't be serious?"

"Seriously," I said. "Have you even been there?"

They all shook their head. "Nope," said Jake. "I guess we haven't."

"Come check it out sometime," I said, smiling directly at Jake.

At lunch the next day, I scanned the Seven Squadron tables for Jake and spotted him on the other side of the dining hall. After announcements, I said to Richie, "See you in class." When I reached Jake, he was headed for the exit and I squeezed his elbow.

"Happy birthday," I said. I gave him a big smile when he turned around, and then I reversed my course back across the dining hall to my normal exit.

At lunch about a week later, Richie stared at me. "What the fuck is going on with you?" he demanded.

I tried to look baffled. "What are you talking about, Holbrook?"

He took a big mouthful, looked up, elbow on the table, and shook his fork at me. "Something is up. I'm gonna figure it out," he said through the food in his mouth.

"If only Mr. Theroux could see you now." I smiled and wagged my head.

He shrugged and chewed while he scanned the dining hall. "Who are you looking for?" he asked.

"Eat your chicken," I replied.

A week later, an unfamiliar knock sounded on my door, and I called out casually to come in.

The door opened slowly and Jake stood there. I leapt up, pulled him in, and shut the door behind him. He stood rigidly to one side, frozen in place with a startled look on his face and hands raised in the international sign of surrender.

"Sorry! There's a backstory. I didn't mean to scare you," I said cheerfully. I took a breath and waited to see what he'd say.

"I ... I thought I'd take you up on your invitation to come check out the Frigate. Hope I didn't come at a bad time." I shook my head and his shoulders relaxed. "Is it okay if I stay for tea?" he asked.

"More than okay." My hands trembled as I poured.

Three weeks after I'd fallen in love with Jake, we lay on crisp sheets in a hotel room in Kingston, naked and spooning. He was treating me to an overnight away for my birthday. It was our first time being alone together — and naked.

"What are you thinking about? I can hear your mind racing," Jake whispered as he nuzzled into my neck.

"I finally feel like a grown-up," I said. My mind flashed to one year before, when I was in Eddie Byrne's room celebrating my nineteenth birthday.

"What else are you thinking?" Jake asked.

"Now that we've been together, I'm wondering how we'll last at the college without being allowed to touch. And I'm wondering when I get to be naked with you again." We had already agreed to never have sex on the college grounds; it would be too dangerous.

"You're naked with me now," he said.

"It's just that I can already feel how hard it'll be to leave here."

"Don't worry," he said. "The waiting will make our time together like this all the more delicious. And in the meantime, we can just mingle."

"Mingle?"

"Combine or bring together two things. Mingle. Not technically sex. Mingling. Second-best option. I don't believe there is a rule at the college against mingling."

I rolled over and looked into his eyes. We kissed again.

"Does this fit the definition of mingling?" I asked.

"Not quite."

We made love again.

On April Fool's Day, Jake invited me to join him for Easter with his family in Streetsville. I bounced on the balls of my feet and said, "Yes! Yes! Yes!"

"April Fools," he said. I crash-landed my last jump and my face fell.

"Really?" I said.

"April Fools," he said again, slapping his knee.

"Crap, Jake. Which is it?" I snapped angrily. "Am I invited or not?"

"Whoa. Yes, you're invited. I see you're taking this very seriously." He dwarfed me in a bear hug.

For the first time in two years, I was going *home* to be with a family for a holiday weekend. Once our plans were set, I wondered why nobody commented on the lightness of my step or noticed my good-natured enjoyment of the littlest things in life.

I instantly loved Jake's parents and his three younger brothers. For the weekend, I was set up in a basement room with a cot, right next door to Jake's old room, which he had shared with his next younger brother and was sharing again for the weekend. Jake came to visit me each night and we slept together on the floor, wrapped in a quilt made by his grandmother. He would get up before dawn and go back to his own bed.

By the time we drove back to Kingston on Monday afternoon, I was sure that Jake was my guy. He was so attractive to me, and funny and creative and interesting. The rest of my life had finally begun; I'd found true love at the perfect age and my place in the family of my dreams. I pictured myself as Kate Tatham, having children with Jake, spending summers at the family cottage on the Lake of Bays, and creating a lifetime of rapturous photo albums together.

Just six more years of my military officer career stood between us and wedded bliss. Jake was attending RMC as a Reserve Entry Training Plan cadet. This meant that he had paid his own way to attend the college and had no military commitment after graduation. I wasn't sure yet how that would complicate our future lives.

27

BILL AND ALFIE'S

Late in April, I whirled into a tailspin of panic. I barged into Richie's room after dinner one night and he flew out of his chair, knocking a pile of books to the floor.

"What the fuck?" he protested. "You're lucky I'm not naked."

"Oh my god. You study naked?"

"No, but I could've been." We squared off, hands on our hips, staring at each other. "Besides, who the *fuck* are you? And what do you want?"

"Touché. I haven't been around much but I'm ready to change all that. Have you been to the library to look at old exams yet?" I asked.

"No. We still have two weeks until exams, so calm down," he replied as he squatted to gather up his books.

"Come with me to the library tomorrow after class and make copies of the old exams? We could study together."

"Oh, so now we're buddies again? I haven't seen you outside of class in months and now you need me." He scowled.

"It's true. I haven't been on charge this term." We both laughed.

I flopped onto my knees in front of him, hands clasped together beseechingly. He struggled to keep a stern look on his face.

"Can you forgive me?" I said. "I fell in love. I seem to remember a certain time last year when I lost my two best friends in one fell swoop to the same disease."

"Touché," he said. He extended his hand and pulled us both to our feet. "Why wait until tomorrow? Let's go now."

Soon we were in the library ransacking old exam binders. My briefcase was brimming by the time I lugged it back to the Frigate.

Next evening, Richie threw another old exam onto the growing stack on the floor. "Holy shit. I was hoping to find a bunch of common questions that we could solve and memorize, but there are no common questions. Even worse, I don't know most of these answers. I'm screwed."

"Let's go to the pub," I said.

"Hell, yeah. Drink tonight. Tomorrow we start serious studies." He glanced at his watch. "It's Thursday. If we hurry, we can catch the end of *Hill Street Blues.*"

We ran to Bill and Alfie's, the college hole-in-the-wall pub out back of the New Gym, and caught our breath at the bar. Richie turned to me. "Thirty-five minutes until closing. I say … four beers each?" He waved to catch the attention of the bartender without waiting for my answer.

After closing, we half staggered and half jogged our way home, laughing loudly. Richie stopped dead in his tracks and hollered "Hey!" at the clock tower, and *Hey hey* echoed back at us. We galumphed up the Frigate stairs and into my room. We were still laughing when someone knocked on my door. I opened it with a flourish.

"Hullo!" I said to Mr. Harbottle. He was a serious sort of cadet, with a great deal of confidence in his future success as an officer. For the moment, he was the second-slate cadet squadron training officer of the Frigate. For some reason, Blackwood stood next to him.

"Miss Armstrong," said Mr. Harbottle, "you're being inappropriately loud. It's after lights out. Other people are trying to sleep. You were making too much noise in the hallway and in your room just now. Keep it down."

I looked over my shoulder at Richie. He had made himself at home on my bed, stocky legs straight out in front of him and back against the wall. He had a blank look on his face. I turned back to Mr. Harbottle.

"Oh, fuck off," I said. "You make noise. I've heard you." I slammed the door in the face of the CSTO and burst out laughing. Seeing that Richie was silent and suddenly white, I opened the door again. Harbottle and Blackwood were still standing there.

"Step aside, Miss Armstrong," said Harbottle, and they strode into my room. "I consider your behaviour gross misconduct and unofficer-like. You're drunk, Miss Armstrong, and will face charges. Mr. Blackwood will act as my witness." Blackwood stood his ground, silent and poker-faced. "Your CSC will provide further direction in regard to this matter. Good evening." Then they were gone.

"Out of the frying pan, into the fire," I said and plunked myself down in my chair. Richie had not so much as flinched during the entire interaction. "Hey, how come you're not in trouble?"

He shrugged. "You kinda stole the show."

In the cadet wing commander's suite a few days later, CWC Fleming, my adjudicator this time, asked, "How many beers did you drink?"

"Four, Mr. Fleming."

"In what amount of time?"

"About thirty-five minutes, Mr. Fleming."

He suppressed a smile and wrote some notes. *This will be my last breach parade, ever.*

Mr. Fleming looked up. "Miss Armstrong, I hope you appreciate the severity of your situation. This is no laughing matter," he said firmly but kindly. "You're standing here today to answer charges of lack of proper respect for a senior cadet, unofficer-like conduct, and drunk and disorderly."

Just tell me my sentence and get me out of here.

"I find you guilty of lack of proper respect for a senior cadet and unofficer-like conduct. I find you not guilty of being drunk and disorderly. Understand, Miss Armstrong, that if I had found you guilty of the last charge, you would be sent to a residential alcohol rehabilitation centre treatment program. That is a career incident, which would remain on your service record beyond RMC." He paused again and held my gaze.

I gasped and heard Holbrook suck in his breath as well. *I did not know that.*

"I don't believe that kind of mar on your career is necessary, under the circumstances. Do you agree with that assessment?" he asked.

"Yes, Mr. Fleming," I agreed. "Thank you."

Ten days.

My days on charge were to be served during Drill Fest, the two weeks of college life considered by some to be the best days of the year, immediately following exam routine. Richie and I walked back to the Frigate together.

"Close call," said Richie.

"No kidding. Can you imagine? I don't need treatment." I looked over at Richie. "Do I?"

We both laughed.

"I gotta say," Richie mused, "what impresses me about me is my ability to have all the fun and dodge the bullet every single time. Besides your telling Harbottle to fuck off, I was a worse actor than you that night."

"Do you ever have survivor's remorse?" I asked.

"Not so far," he replied. I punched him on the arm.

The rest of the term passed uneventfully. By some miracle, I was able to avoid any further contact with Blackwood. I wrote and passed all my exams. I served my ten days on charge during Drill Fest, with a few days to spare before the parade to join in some of the fun. Everyone else had been free to spend nights in town, with exams done and no other responsibilities except daily grad parade practice, for the entire two weeks. Soon enough, I was on my way to CFB Borden for my first phase of logistic officer training, happy that Jake was taking his summer phase training in Borden as well. Blackwood had graduated and disappeared without a trace. Never to be seen again. His departure made my anticipation of a summer full of visits to Lake of Bays and my future life at RMC all that much sweeter.

28

BAN THE SWEATS

Third Year. "Running with the Devil" by Van Halen blared through my dreams. I lurched up in bed. It was all starting again.

I'm getting earplugs this year.

Cleared in and with leave pass approved for the Labour Day weekend, I set out with Jake early on Friday afternoon for one last weekend at his family cottage on Lake of Bays north of Toronto. We had spent the summer together at CFB Borden completing logistics officer classification phase training and rushing up to the cottage nearly every weekend. We were more in love than ever.

That weekend was cottage close-up weekend. When the family's yellow station wagon pulled away on Sunday afternoon leaving us alone for the night, we ran down to the water, tore off our clothes, and skinny-dipped off the end of the dock in broad daylight. That night, we cooked steaks on the grill, baked potatoes in foil, boiled corn on the cob, drank lots of beer, and spent an entire night in the same bed.

Third year was off to a good start. Our new classmates from
Royal Roads and CMR actually seemed less hostile to women,
and right away I did well in all my subjects. My room decor was
understated this year; the pink and green flowered duvet cover
remained the same but my tastes had changed. I liked to think of
myself as more mature and sophisticated. To display this new attitude, my room included a framed Sierra Club poster of an Eliot
Porter photograph of trees at the edge of a forest with the cap-
tion "In Wildness Is the Preservation of the World" and, on my
bulletin board, a magazine photo of a young female Soviet Union
soldier guarding a Second World War memorial. I nicknamed her
Nikita and liked to imagine her life and our similarities despite
being on opposite sides of the Cold War. She made me think
back to Mr. Kendall's poster of Che Guevara in recruit term.

One day in late September I was making my way across the
square, heading for breakfast, when I passed a gang of second-year
cadets outside Yeo Hall. I recognized a few of them from the
Frigate and smiled. They looked right through me.

One of the guys muttered, "Sweat."

I whirled back around to face them. "I beg your pardon?"

"I said 'sweat,'" he repeated with a sarcastic wobble of his
head. He was from Six Squadron. "You heard me."

We stared each other down. *Oh my god, you're a dick.*

"Who the hell do you think you are?" I asked, unable to control the tremble in my voice. "I've been here longer than you."

He straightened his posture. "I *think* I'm Derek Snyder, a
third-generation RMC cadet, and I don't care how long you've
lasted. This is no place for a woman. I'm not the only one who
thinks sweats should be banned." He reached into his pocket and

thrust a button in my face. It had a cartoon head of a girly looking pig on it. The pig was wearing a pillbox hat. The edge of
the button was rimmed in red, with one thick red line slashed
through her pig face. "Ban the sweats," he said. "I've had buttons
made up for Ex-Cadet Weekend." As if on cue, the other guys
straight-armed their buttons into my face.

"You guys need to get a fucking hobby." I walked away.

I took a seat next to Meg, picked at my scrambled eggs, and
grumbled to myself. Snyder's gang of second years was entering
the dining hall, laughing and looking smug. I cocked my head
toward them and said to Meg, "Have you seen the latest bullshit?"

"No. What's going on?" she asked.

I told her about my exchange with Snyder and she rolled her
eyes. I swung around when I heard the sound of blakeys clicking on the marble floor in their wake. The cadet wing training
officer for this term, none other than Fourth Year Louis Arsenault
from the Frigate, was gaining ground on Snyder and his posse.
Arsenault's back was straight and there was purpose in his step. I
watched with glee and nudged Meg with my elbow.

"Second years! Halt!" Arsenault roared at them. "Remove
those buttons this instant and report to my room immediately."

The second years looked stricken, all except for Snyder, who
looked pleased with himself. Mr. Arsenault turned on his heel
and clicked out of the dining hall ahead of them.

"Arsenault's stocks just went up," I said, digging into my eggs.

We heard the rumour later that Snyder had made 250 copies of
the buttons and was selling them for two dollars each. Apparently,
after the meeting with CWTO Arsenault, Snyder had had an
afternoon session with the new commandant, General Howell

C. Pratt, whose claim to fame was that he intended to put the *M* back in RMC. After the meeting, Snyder was madly chasing down the buttons he had sold.

It was a luxury to simply be a spectator at the obstacle course this year. I trailed the Frigate recruits and enjoyed being out of the spotlight. Jake was running as spotter for a recruit in his squadron.

29

CAUGHT

On Thanksgiving weekend, my brother Craig was getting married in Burnaby. It was my first and only weekend trip home from RMC. Jake and I caught a direct flight from Ottawa on Friday afternoon. We had been on the plane for about three hours when a visit to the bathroom confirmed that my period had come — it was late by ten days. When I got back to our row, I crawled over Jake into my window seat, leaned in, and whispered, "I got it." Jake grabbed my hand and squeezed it tight. *Thank you, God.* My lungs eased and I could breathe a full breath again. "Even so, don't forget. My mother is difficult. You might not like her."

"I don't need to like her," said Jake. "I need her to like me — and my chances just got better."

We were staying with my sister, Ellen. She'd put us together in their downstairs guest room, which had a king-sized waterbed and a private bathroom.

My mother arrived while Ellen was helping us get settled. She appeared in the bedroom doorway, hands crossed over her chest. "I'm not sure I approve of this arrangement," she said in a clipped tone. Jake leapt forward and introduced himself. I watched her size him up and soften a bit.

Ellen piped up, "Oh, come on, Mom. By Kate's age, we were both married and having babies. Besides, she said they already sleep together."

I bore a hole in the side of my sister's head with my glare. *Shutupshutupshutup.*

"Oh my lord!" Mother cried indignantly, grabbing my upper arm. "What will people say?"

"Whose business is it?" Ellen asked. "It's not a big deal. It's the eighties, Mom. Get with the times."

I pulled my arm from my mother's grasp, suppressing the urge to strike out at her.

She was nailing me with her stare. "I thought you said you weren't going to be like that."

"Like what?" I asked.

"You know what," she said.

"I'm a grown woman in university. I'm free to make my own choices," I said. I wasn't going to back down; I was sharing a bed with Jake this weekend whether she liked it or not.

"You're not a *married* grown woman," she said, and then stormed back upstairs.

"Well, that went well," Ellen said and laughed. She seemed to enjoy upsetting our mother. Jake stood awkwardly to one side, not saying a thing.

"Seriously, do you have to be so blunt?" I asked.

"She's such a hypocrite," Ellen said. "She was already knocked up with me when they got married."

"Well, at least now we don't have to pretend to get along for Jake's sake. Welcome to *my* family, Jake."

Ellen looked at her watch and said, "It's time to get ready for the rehearsal. I'll see you upstairs."

As soon as Ellen had left, Jake turned to me. "Holy shit. Imagine if you were pregnant? Your mother would've had my nuts."

"I am glad you're getting a clear picture of what I've been telling you all this time," I said. "I tried to warn you. That was actually pretty tame."

Jake hugged me. *He doesn't know the half of it.*

One mid-October evening, after watching *Hill Street Blues* at Bill and Alfie's pub, I went back to Jake's room to grab my jacket before heading home to the Frigate. It had been ten days since our trip to Vancouver, and we were both frustrated at our lack of privacy at the college. Repeats of our first night together in a fancy hotel room were not sustainable on a cadet budget, but when desperate to be alone, we had on occasion borrowed a car and taken a room for the night at the Highway Inn, a grimy roadside hotel just off Highway 15 near CFB Kingston. We ignored the wheezing air-conditioner wall unit loudly circulating damp air and the cheap, worn-out sheets, and revelled in one another's bodies, laughing a lot, and gossiping a while after making love. Sometimes we ordered pizza.

We had not been perfect at abstaining on college grounds. Early on, a few occasions of hurried, fumbling sex were each followed with a solemn promise not to let it happen again. We'd kept that promise for eight months now without incident, even though most college couples weren't bothering. Penny Miller was basically living common-law with Nigel Maxwell in the Frigate and went seemingly unnoticed and undisturbed — she openly joked about being an honorary Frigateer.

"Let's mingle," Jake said. He pulled his sweater and T-shirt over his head in one swift motion and stood bare-chested in front of me. I frowned and stepped back.

"Just shirts," he said, reaching for me and unbuttoning my blouse. After the third button, he turned on his desk lamp and flicked off the overhead light.

We didn't speak while we kissed and undressed each other slowly. By the time we were down to our underwear, our twisted clothes were strewn about us on the floor. My bare breasts pushed against his hot skin. I exhaled tiny gasps of pleasure as Jake slid his hands under the waistband of my panties and scooped up my buttocks. A simple movement of his wrists edged the panties down my hips.

"No," I groaned, grabbing his wrists.

Three loud knocks rapped on the door.

"Oh shit!" Jake whispered. I dropped to my knees and frantically untangled my clothes from Jake's.

More loud knocks.

"Hello?" Jake feigned confusion in a calm voice. He scrambled to untwist the legs of his khaki rugby pants. The door handle rattled. I was shaking so violently that I struggled to fasten my bra and get my limbs back into my clothes.

Jake stuck his legs into his pants. "Who is it?"

"It's Brian Floyd. Open up!"

Brian Floyd and Jake had been classmates for two years at Royal Roads and were members of the same squadron. Brian had a reputation as a jerk who pulled really disgusting stunts on peers and juniors, like getting drunk and pissing under the doors of people he disliked. He was a slimy sort of character with bad skin and he gave off the fug of a greasy diner.

"What the hell do *you* want?" Jake asked, flapping his hands for me to hurry up.

"Open the door! I know Third Year Armstrong is with you!"

Jake opened the door a crack and blocked Floyd from entering. I instinctively hid myself inside the closet, pulled the curtain closed in front of me, crouched down, and trembled as I re-buttoned my shirt.

"What business is that of yours?" Jake said, holding him off.

"You're having sex! Let me in or I'm going for Geoff Hampstead."

"What's your fucking problem? You'd better get Geoff. There is no way I'm letting you in here," Jake roared. He pushed Floyd back and locked the door behind him.

Floyd said to someone outside the door, "Stay here. Make sure she doesn't leave." His footfalls clomped down the hall at a run. More doors opened and voices filled the hallway. I came out of the closet, still shaking. We were both properly dressed and stood looking at each other. We were trapped.

Moments later, a lighter rap sounded on the door. "Jake? It's Geoff. Can you please open up?" Cadet Squadron Leader Geoff Hampstead was the top cadet of their squadron. I was seated in the lounge chair by now and trembling uncontrollably from adrenaline.

Jake put his forehead right against the door with his hand on the knob. "I'll let you in, but there is *no way* Floyd is coming in my room."

"Agreed."

Jake opened the door and Geoff stepped into the room wearing a housecoat and slippers. His expression seemed apologetic as Floyd pushed forward, trying to enter, a shock of greasy black bangs hanging over his shiny, pimpled face. Jake blocked him with the door. "Fuck off, Floyd."

"Hi, Kate," Geoff said to me and then he turned to Jake. "What's going on? Brian said that he caught you having sex on the college grounds. He insisted that I come at once."

"I was hoping *you* could tell *me* what's going on. We're not having sex. The guy is a freak," Jake said.

"He said he followed you back from B and A's just after eleven p.m. He watched in the hall for half an hour to make sure no one came out."

"Holy shit. How creepy," Jake said.

"He said he caught you red-handed," Geoff continued.

"He's a liar."

"He says that he listened at the door and it was quiet in here. That's his story."

I sat in the chair shaking. Jake was red faced and indignant. "Geoff, I'm serious. I question *his* behaviour. Does he seem normal to you?"

Geoff closed his eyes, dropped his chin to his chest, and sighed through his nose. He turned to me. "What do you have to say, Kate?" he asked.

I stood up and faced him squarely. "I swear, Geoff. We did not have sex."

He looked at my face and my clothes and scanned the room. "It looks to me like nothing has happened in here. There are no rules against spending time together in each other's rooms," he said. "The trouble is, he wants to press charges. It's your word against his. I have no choice but to proceed if he wants to push it."

"You have a choice. Don't do it," Jake said.

"Sorry, Jake, my hands are tied."

"Jesus." I fell back into the chair in exasperation. This would be my fourth breach parade.

"You'll receive orders tomorrow for next steps," Geoff said. He opened the door and stepped out. Floyd and two others remained in the hall. "Show's over. You can go back to your rooms."

Jake braced against the closed door and stared at me. "Holy crap," he said. "Listen, Kate. No one knows what happened in here besides us. We tell the truth. No sex, which is true. The only thing we need to keep secret is anything about taking off clothes — which technically is not against the rules, but we don't need to go down that path. Agreed?"

"Absolutely," I said. "What a nightmare. Why us? Others are way worse."

"Who the hell knows?"

I hardly slept a wink, tossing and turning, feeling a mixture of desolation and outrage. This story would crash through the cadet wing rumour mill like a tidal wave.

The summons came early. CSC Jerry Stawski, my cadet section commander this term, knocked on my door just after 07:00 hours. Jake and I were scheduled to meet with the director of cadets, Colonel Gilmore, right after class. *Elmer Fudd's going to blame me as the temptress. Jake's never been in trouble.* General Pratt, the new commandant, would be presiding over our breach parade. My past performance could finish me: three previous charges, average marks, no merit badges. On paper, I was average. *Lacklustre, even.* General Pratt's plans to put the *M* back in RMC meant I could expect severe treatment.

My crimes: being a twenty-year-old woman in love and in a relationship. That's not a crime in the real world — it's an ideal. Why did I feel so much shame?

30

CHOPPED LIVER ROW

"Enter, Miss Armstrong," Colonel Gilmore, Director of Cadets, called from his office. I shakily closed the door behind me, marched to his desk, and stood at attention in front of him, a place I never imagined standing in my cadet career. Jake had just been there. Gilmore was making notes and did not look up at me. I stared over his head and focused on the painting of a C-130 Hercules that was perched on the fireplace mantel behind him. He clicked the lid onto his fountain pen and stared at me across his desk as though I were simply one in an infinite series of trivial problems he must set right.

He looked me up and down and declared, "Well, you're definitely not going to end up in the chopped liver row."

"I beg your pardon, sir?"

"That's our nickname for the less attractive girls, the ones who never get requested by the press for interviews. The press just wants the pretty girls," he said.

I fought a grimace. *What the fuck?*

Gilmore registered my response. "It's meant as a compliment. But never mind all that." He turned his attention to the paper on his desk and read out my charge sheet. The charges claimed I had been disrobed and had shared the bed with Jake and had tried to conceal my presence in the room for approximately one hour in the dark. "Give me your version of what happened last night," he said, shifting away from me in his chair, lips tightening. I said my piece and he pressed for more details. "What were you doing during the half hour while Mr. Floyd was guarding the door?"

"Talking, sir."

"Talking?" he asked, and raised his eyebrows.

"Yes, sir." My heart was thundering in my ears. I hoped that my answers matched Jake's.

"About what?"

"Probably nothing much. I can't recall entirely, sir. Maybe the *Hill Street Blues* episode we'd just seen on TV?" I kept it vague in case Jake had been asked the same question.

"So, did you have sex?" he asked.

I blushed. "No, sir."

"You're sure?"

"Yes, sir. Absolutely sure."

"You don't seem sure."

"I'm sure, sir."

He stared at me in silence. This proud man, so used to giving orders, seemed unsatisfied with this response.

They've got nothing. There is nothing more to do. Make him ask the right questions.

"Do you love him?" he asked.

"I beg your pardon, sir?"

"Do you love Fourth Year Tatham?"

"Yes, sir. Very much."

"The sad thing about these cases, Miss Armstrong, is that regardless of the truth, the damage to your reputation is done. Mr. Tatham becomes the stud, and you're the slut."

I tried not to let the shock show on my face. *He just called me a slut.*

"It's unfair, don't you agree?"

"Yes, sir."

"Do you have anything else to say?" he asked.

"No, sir."

"Right, then. Dismissed. Fall in outside General Pratt's office."

I had never known such terror in my life. Making out with Jake may have cost me everything. When Jake came out of the commandant's office, his gold two-bar section commander pins were gone, leaving pinhole marks in his epaulettes "You'll be okay," he whispered as he went past. "I'll be in my room."

Waves of relief flooded over me. It didn't make sense to kick me out if they hadn't expelled Jake, but he'd never been in trouble. My legs felt weak. My armpits were cold with sweat and my hands hung limp. It was still possible that I would enter this office as a third-year cadet and leave as a civilian, one moment to the next.

General Pratt had the corner office in the Mackenzie Building, complete with a sitting area and a fireplace. He sat behind a massive wooden desk, elbows on the arms of a vintage chair, neck jutted forward, and fingertips tented together. His lips were full and his eyes were framed by Coke-bottle lenses. The curve of his belly pressing against his green uniform looked hard. His hands were plump and thick fingered, like paddles. *He looks like a turtle.* I instantly flushed with embarrassment at my insubordinate thought; my future life rested in his hands.

"Stand at ease, Miss Armstrong," he said. "This is your chance to be heard. Please share your version of the events." General Pratt listened attentively, seeming almost sympathetic as I repeated my story.

"In this case, there is a fine line to be walked. It's a tricky business entering the bedrooms of our cadets. The question is, just how far do we go without interfering with your human right to a personal life? Under the circumstances, I'd say quite far," he said. "All the way, if you will excuse the pun," he added with a little smile.

His style of speaking wasn't quite British but had a similar affected quality. "Naturally, I take a very serious view of any breach of college rules. At the same time, I don't want to be perceived as tacitly sanctioning a witch-hunt mentality."

A small tingle of relief tickled the back of my neck.

"I can't ignore the charges, but without proof, I will not take the correction to the full extent possible, which in your case, given the previous three breaches of conduct, may have tipped the scales to expulsion."

I felt the colour drain from my face.

"Yes, Miss Armstrong. Your career is on the line. Your issues seem to stem from a difficulty in conforming to general conduct expectations. Now that I meet you, I don't get an impression of malicious defiance. Perhaps a better characterization would be 'spirited'?"

I couldn't stop myself. I smirked. *I fucking smirked.*

"It seems you need earnest direction to keep you on course. I'm sentencing you to twenty-one days on charge." My face turned to stone. He saw my reaction and held up a sausage of an index finger. "Hold on, don't panic. The twenty-one days of charge will be given under a ninety-day suspended sentence. If you stay out of trouble for the next ninety days, all this will be behind you. However, if you commit a single infraction which results in fresh charges being laid against you, you will automatically serve the twenty-one days on charge without the courtesy of a breach parade and be expelled from the college upon completion of your sentence."

I trained my eyes on the wall behind his head, trying to regain my inner balance.

"You need a dose of concentrated effort in keeping out of trouble — and in learning how to play the game as if your life depended upon it," he said. "Do you understand?"

"Yes, sir."

"Let me drive home the seriousness of what's at stake." He turned in his chair and read aloud every word of his commissioning scroll, issued by the Queen to all commissioned officers in the Canadian Armed Forces. Then he swung back to me. "I hope one day you will get one of these, Miss Armstrong."

"Me too, sir."

"I suggest that you keep this correction close to your chest. The last thing you need to do is invite additional scrutiny."

"Yes, sir. To tell the truth, sir, I'm terrified of *anyone* finding out."

In Jake's room, we talked in low voices, with the door open a crack. I filled him in, and he told me that the general had given him a ninety-day suspended sentence with no charge days to be served in the event he committed an infraction — he'd just be expelled immediately. Pratt had lectured him about how the cadet wing was both "self-protecting" and "self-cleansing."

Jake said, "I've been sitting here thinking about how the cadets run this place. That's what Pratt said. If my classmates want me gone, I'm gone. They have the rest of the year to make it happen, especially in the next ninety days." We sat in silence for a moment. "I want to fucking kill pizza-face Floyd."

"Why not Geoff?"

"It's not Geoff's fault. He had no choice."

"Are you kidding? He could've talked Floyd down, convinced him to drop it. Geoff was the one who pressed the actual charges."

"It's a game, Kate. Geoff is deep in the game. He wants to be CWC. Talking someone out of pressing charges for a serious conduct breach is not a smart career play to become top cadet."

"Exactly. He did it for his own gain. He didn't protect you." I stood up indignantly. "I'm going now. I hate being here with the door open."

Jake stood and we hugged briefly.

31

HERMIT

One day in early November, General Pratt summoned me back to his office immediately after class. This time, when his matronly secretary led me in, I was surprised to discover a full tea service had been laid out on the coffee table. The general sat in a wingback chair next to it with his legs casually crossed. His tea had already been poured. He motioned me to the couch across the table.

"Anything you'd like to report yourself for?" he asked.

"Being a hermit, sir?" I said.

"Well, that won't do. The whole idea of the suspended sentence was to keep you active in your cadet life. Help yourself to tea and a biscuit. I wanted to chat with you about being a lady cadet at RMC. You struck me as a woman who is willing to say what's on her mind, rather than telling me what you think I want to hear. Are you up for a fireside chat about the college life experience of Miss Kate Armstrong?"

"Of course, sir. If you really want to know."

"Do you mind if I smoke?"

"Of course not, sir," I said, astounded at being asked permission to do *anything* by the most decorated and important person I had ever met in my life. "I consider it an honour to be invited to share my experiences with you."

"The price of admission is the willingness to be honest." He tapped a cigarette against an engraved silver case. As he leaned toward the flame of his lighter, his neck stretched; he really did look like a turtle poking its head out of its shell.

For the next half an hour or so, I told the highlights of my story, without embellishing: the daily glares, lewd comments, and horrible jokes; the nickname "sweats"; the Love Boat; the bet; Eddie Byrne; Blackwood; and my second-year charges. He smoked and asked the occasional question. When I used the "Ban the sweats" buttons as an example of toxic behaviours, he interrupted.

"Would you like to hear how that story ended? Are you able to keep this information to yourself?" he asked sternly.

"Of course, sir," I said.

"By midmorning, Mr. Snyder stood before me, much as you did. I told him to hand in every single button to me by end of day Wednesday or he could pack his things and say goodbye to his military college career," he said.

"In no time at all, I received an urgent phone call from Major General Dickie Snyder," he continued. "Dickie ranted that he would have my job if I dared to threaten his son again, and that I had better get a sense of humour about boyish pranks. I replied that was all very well and good, but it wasn't a threat and I didn't consider this form of prank, at the expense of the lady cadets, as acceptable behaviour for a gentleman cadet."

He took a sip of his tea. "Come Wednesday afternoon, Mr. Snyder appeared in my doorway carrying a box of buttons which he painstakingly counted out in front of me. One button was missing but he was adamant that it must have been lost, so I took his word for it. The entire box is lying on the bottom of Navy Bay as we speak, but that's another story. Carry on, Miss Armstrong, with yours."

I wondered if he would share my secret charge parade details with other cadets as part of their "professional development." I resumed my narrative by saying that I didn't have much more to add except that I thought the dating rules were unfair.

"Sir, I understand that the rules are supposed to protect junior cadets from being preyed upon by senior cadets in positions of authority. The trouble is, we're all young and love is uncontrollable."

General Pratt laughed. "This institution is a *military* college. Nothing is uncontrollable."

"Of course, sir, but we're all officer cadets," I said.

"Yes. Understood," he said. "Fair enough. But the framework of the college is meant as a training model to emulate rising through the ranks as a military officer. Dating subordinates is not on."

"Sir, in our combat motivation class, we were taught that it's natural for men to want to protect women and that a mission might be placed at risk for a 'damsel in distress.' But my experience has been the total opposite. I've been treated with more aggression and malice than my male peers. I know the dating rules are supposed to prevent favouritism, but I've stood by watching hockey, rugby, and football team members advance junior teammates in meal lines, get them out of wing duties, and generally treat them as special for years. If anything, I feel at risk of being fragged — being taken out by any means — for being a woman."

General Pratt glanced at his watch. "I'm familiar with the concept of fragging. You've raised some interesting points. I'll give the matter of dating rules serious consideration. Is there anything else?"

"Sir, there is one thing. The first-year lady cadets have been told that it's mandatory for them to carry their military-issue purse when they have their period."

"That's ridiculous," he said.

"I know, sir. It's like wearing a banner."

"Well, you've brought forward one concern that is immediately rectifiable. That's a good start. With that, let's call it a day. It's time for me to go home for dinner with Mrs. Pratt." He stood and brushed loose ash from his tunic. "Thank you for a frank discussion, Miss Armstrong. It's been illuminating."

"Sir, I'm honoured to have been invited."

"Yes, well, it would be a bit awkward to refuse an invitation for tea from the commandant," he said.

"Yes, sir. Especially when I thought you'd called me here to kick me out."

"If anything else needs my attention, please don't hesitate to contact me. I appreciate your candour and courage. Good luck with your suspended sentence. I'm cheering for you," he said as he opened the door for me on my way out.

32

TIME OUT

Jake and I had agreed not to spend time together until things cooled things down a bit, but I missed him horribly. If I wanted to see him, I had to go to him. I finally broke down and went to his room. He had come to the Frigate only once so far this year.

He barely said hello before turning away and sticking his face back into his textbook.

I dropped my books on his bed and sat down. "Have I done something to upset you?"

"Don't worry about it," he said.

"I don't know what I've done — that's what I'm asking," I said, my eyes brimming with tears. "Tell me what's going on."

He blew a long exhale through his nose and came over to sit beside me. "I feel choked at you. I hate being in trouble, even though it was my idea to mingle. I've lied to my parents. I've lost my bars. I'm living under this fucking suspended sentence."

"I hate it, too. I'm terrified every time I leave my room. Now I come here and we fight," I said. The pretense of everything being normal was taking more energy than I had. I caught my breath. "I can't do this anymore."

"What do you mean? Are you breaking up with me?"

"No. But I feel like a loser," I said. "Like I'm a chump chasing someone who doesn't want to be with me."

"I want to be with you. It's complicated."

"I'm going to leave … and let you show me. Come visit me in the Frigate. From now on, I'll only come here if you invite me."

"Kate," he said, "to tell you the truth, I am terrified of going to the Frigate. It's so … public, walking across the square."

I got up and started collecting my books into a pile. Hastily, he asked what I had been hoping to hear. "Can I walk you home?"

I struggled between longing and fury. I wanted him to come with me; I never wanted to see him again. "It's okay. I'm fine."

"Come on. Let me carry your books," he said.

"Sometimes, I really don't get you." I kissed him on the cheek and left.

Jake and I struggled along. He never came to the Frigate. We argued when we saw each other, and I caught myself acting like my mother, making mean comments or giving him the cold shoulder. Finally, after a month of this, I went to his room and we decided to take a break but not break up. I wanted to feel upset, or passionate disappointment, or fear, or something. But all I felt was numb.

My new social life revolved around sticking close to the Frigate and going to class. I spent more time studying than ever, even forming a mini study group with two fellow commerce classmates, Adam Lennox and Steve McIntyre, both Frigateers newly arrived that year from Royal Roads. Still, it didn't take long before the feelings of being on the outside crept back over me. Richie, Adam, Steve, and a bunch of other guys from across the square formed a group of buddies nicknamed the Groovers.

When I'd pass them in the hall, on their way to class or out to town as a gang, they'd grow loud and boisterous, absorbed in each other. I knew they saw me. I would lower my gaze and walk faster, feigning indifference at being excluded. I hated myself for being too loud and too brash, and even more for pretending I didn't care when I cared more than I thought it was safe to let them know. I revived the tea emporium and even made some unexpected new friends from across the square. A few of the guys in my class started dropping by more often and hanging out, and a first year from Four Squadron, Jane Quigley, became a regular visitor for tea.

After the Christmas holidays, I moved to another room, with a huge amount of floor space, facing the parade square. Geoff Hampstead had been appointed the cadet wing commander for second slate. Nineteen more days and my suspended sentence would be complete. Academically, I was tied for first place in commerce with Adam Lennox, my study buddy from Royal Roads. Walking on eggshells and avoiding Jake was obviously good for my academic performance.

One evening a few weeks into the new term, First Year Jane Quigley showed up at my room, anxious to tell me something about her Christmas vacation. "But you have to swear not to tell anyone," she said. "Do you swear?"

"Of course," I said easily. "I promise." Jane got up, peeked out the door, looked up and down the hall, and closed the door carefully.

"What's going on?" I asked her.

"The most amazing thing happened," she said in a half-whisper. "I haven't told anyone." She sat back in the lounge chair. Her skin was pale and flawless, a touch of pink in her cheeks. "I'm in love with the most amazing man."

"That would have been my first guess," I said, laughing and handing her a hot mug of tea.

"Believe it or not, I met him in my hometown," she said.

"So, he's civilian? Nice." I said, smiling.

"No, he's a cadet. We met at the Oakville Christmas party hosted by the ex-cadets alumni. He noticed me and came over to talk to me. I would never have dreamt of speaking to him."

"Of course he noticed you. You look like freaking Wonder Woman. How could he not notice you?" I said. "You're gorgeous."

"I want to tell you the whole story. You'll definitely know him."

"Uh-oh," I said. "Is he out of bounds for you?"

"Yes. But just wait," she said with an excited wave of her hand. "So, he asked me on a date. We went out together in Oakville, and I can hardly believe that *he* likes *me*. Kate, I'm so in love, I can hardly bear it. We agreed to wait until after his grad to be together, but it's so hard."

"So, he's a fourth year?" I said.

"Yes," she said. "You are not going to tell anyone, right? You promised."

"I promise," I said. "You can trust me. I've been in your exact shoes."

"We've been sending notes back and forth in the wing mail. He gave me a bear for my room."

I laughed out loud. And then I felt a twinge of envy remembering my intense feelings during the early days with Eddie Byrne compared with the current strain between Jake and me.

"What's so funny?" She looked a little hurt.

"I'm having flashbacks. Eddie gave me a bear, too, when we were trying not to — well, you know, *trying not to*."

Jane nodded and continued. "One night, he talked to me in the dining hall and told me to meet him at three a.m. in the women's changing rooms for the pool. I dressed in my sweatpants and running shoes to be super quiet. It was scary sneaking down there at night alone. We made out. It's our secret place to meet up now — no one ever comes there."

"Holy crap, Jane. This is serious. You need to be very careful. You're dating a fourth year and you're having sex on the college? You could get kicked out for both."

"I know, but once we crossed the line, it felt impossible to wait until grad to be together again. I've never felt anything like this in my life," she said. "What am I going to do?"

"You know what to do," I said. "You need to be careful, and really, you need to stop."

"I know, and it's so much worse because of who he is. Especially now."

"What do you mean?"

"I need to tell someone," she said, her face pale.

"Don't tell me. It's best if you don't." I wanted to know and I *did not* want to know. She stared at me in silence.

"Geoff Hampstead," she blurted out.

"Pardon?" I couldn't believe my ears.

"The fourth year is Geoff Hampstead."

"The CWC?" I asked.

"I *know!*" she said. "That's what makes it so awful."

"Holy fuck."

"I know. Right?"

I doubled over to catch my breath.

"You're scaring me. What do you think?"

"I think he's a good guy?" I said.

Her shoulders relaxed and a smile spread across her face. "What would you do?"

"I don't know. I really don't know," I said. "We can talk again later. In the meantime, be careful. I mean it. Don't tell anyone else. Please."

I took her teacup and started cleaning up. She left soon afterward, and minutes later I grabbed my jacket and ran across the square.

"What the fuck?" Jake exclaimed. "Are you certain?"

"Yes."

"I mean *certain*. Do you believe her?"

"Of course. I am so fucking angry with Hampstead that I don't know what to do. Motherfucker!" Of all people, it had to be him, the very person who had turned us in to the commandant. Anyone else and I would have left it alone.

Jake slumped down onto his bed in a defeated posture while I paced the room.

"I promised Jane that I wouldn't tell anyone."

"Yeah, but you promised before you knew who it was."

"I know. So stupid. I could puke right now."

"The women's change room at the pool?" He leapt to his feet. "Let's go down there tonight at three a.m. and catch them!"

"No way! We're not Buddy Biffing Floyd."

"Well, what do *you* suggest, then?" he said angrily.

I sat down on the bed, doubled over, and stared at my feet. RMC was something I had to get through. Where was the profit in developing righteousness and convictions that would make it even harder?

Jake sat quietly beside me until I finally spoke again. "I think I might have a way to deal with it and basically keep my promise to Jane — except for having talked it over with you," I said.

I told him my plan. On the way home, after midnight, I stayed as far as possible from the outdoor lights, following the edge of the square, with my scarf pulled up over my face. I crawled into bed and stole six hours of fitful sleep before my alarm rang to get up for class.

———————

The next evening, at exactly 9:45 p.m., I made my way across the square. I climbed the stairs to the third floor of Fort LaSalle Dormitory, rounded the corner to the Wing HQ hallway and paused. *Back at the door of the CWC.* The last time I had stood before this door, I was facing charges for drunk and disorderly and conduct unbecoming an officer. I could turn back. Jake was the only person who knew anything about my plan.

I could tell by the look on Geoff's face when he opened the door that he didn't know that I knew. "Well, hello, Kate," he said with a friendly smile. A wave of shame washed through me.

"May I speak with you in private?" I asked, my voice tight.

Inside, I gave him the letter I'd written and he read it. "Kate, is there nothing I can say to change your mind?" he asked.

"No. I'm sorry. Like it says, I need you to take the letter to General Pratt so that he can read it for himself. And within one week, I want to meet with him in person. If he hasn't called for me by then, I'll take my copy to him directly."

Geoff started pacing. "I told her not to tell anyone. Of all people, she chose *you*," he said.

"I'm sorry. Truly. I didn't want to know about this. It has been extremely upsetting for me. I don't want to break my promise to Jane, but this approach is the best solution I could think of under the circumstances."

"So, now you'll have revenge upon me?" he said, glaring at me.

"I'm living under the persistent risk of being kicked out for less. That's a huge double standard," I said. "I don't care what the commandant does about it, but I think he should know."

"You can leave now. I'll take your letter to General Pratt tomorrow. I expect you will hear from him shortly," he said stiffly, opening his door.

33

SECRETS

The summons to General Pratt's office came a few days later. There was no tea service this time. We sat in the same spots as we had during my last visit.

"What's this all about, Miss Armstrong?" General Pratt asked, tapping a cigarette on the table and lighting it.

"Sir, I needed you to know." My voice was quivering.

"It's a good letter. It seems well considered," he said. "I understand what might lead you to handle it this way. Would you please read the letter aloud to me? I want to hear the story in your own voice."

"Of course, sir." I shakily read the letter, which explained how I came to know about Geoff and Jane and called Geoff's behaviour a breach of trust. My chest was so tight that I felt winded as I forced out the words on the page. By the time I finished, a light film of sweat had cooled my upper lip.

"Is it true?" General Pratt asked.

"To the best of my knowledge, sir."

"I believe you. Geoff came to my office yesterday morning and admitted the whole thing. What I want to know is this: Is it true that you have no attachment to the outcome of this revelation? It's strictly in my hands to deal with the matter?"

"Of course, sir. It's not for me to decide what's appropriate under the circumstances."

"Okay. So I'll do nothing. Pretend it never happened," he said.

My jaw dropped. I was speechless.

"Oh, so you do care."

"Sir, I won't deny that I brought this issue to your attention because of the charges brought against us by Geoff this fall."

"So you want revenge," he said tersely.

"No, sir. I want fairness of treatment. I'm serving out the final days of my suspended sentence for a lesser charge than the CWC who turned me in. And he's having sex on college grounds with a first-year cadet he's not allowed to date under any and all circumstances. It still makes me question his integrity *and* the validity of the dating rules."

"It questions the validity of the CWC appointment. We can start there," he said. "The rule needs addressing, there is no doubt."

"A few of my good friends aspired to be CWC and have been following the rules and doing all the right things. Geoff Hampstead was appointed to the position in preference over them."

"You know that I appointed Mr. Hampstead, right?"

I closed my eyes. *How could I have been so stupid?* I looked back at the general, who wore a knowing smile. "I guess I didn't think it through, sir."

"I appreciate the choices you've made so far in this process and your good sense to allow me the latitude to handle the situation however I feel is best. I believe it was a wise decision to allow Mr. Hampstead the opportunity to disclose his failings to me, and we can't forget that Miss Quigley is a part of this breach, as well."

"Yes, sir. I feel terrible for not keeping her secret. Does she really need to be implicated?"

He chuckled. "That would present a challenge, would it not, to accuse the CWC of a clandestine — to use your word — relationship and not have the partner exposed? Miss Quigley is a very beautiful and fairly intelligent cadet, and she must accept the consequences of her choices. There is no protecting her from them. She ensured that by disclosing the relationship to you."

"Yes, sir," I said, swallowing hard.

"We have a potential scandal in which you're going to suffer alongside Jane and Geoff," he said.

"Yes, sir. I've considered that my life could become a torment when word gets out that I'm associated with this."

"*If* word gets out." He looked me directly in the eye.

"What do you mean, sir?"

"Have you told anyone?"

"Yes, sir. I talked it over with Jake on the night that Jane told me."

"Let's hope he's better at keeping secrets than you," he said dryly. He lit another cigarette and exhaled a plume of smoke. "If you leave it with me, I may be able to handle the whole matter without implicating you. Your part is to never discuss it with anyone. Get Jake's promise of confidence and don't say anything more about it."

"Yes, sir. But won't Jane or Geoff tell people, sir?"

"If my idea plays out as planned, it won't make sense to involve you, but I am getting ahead of myself. At this point, all you have to do is keep quiet. Okay?"

"Yes, sir," I said, hugely relieved. "Truth be told, I wish she'd never told me. I wish I was never any part of it."

"Well, that ship has sailed," he said. "I'm seeking another agreement from you today, as well. Would you be willing to grant me the grace to deal with this matter after West Point Weekend?"

"Sir?" I said. United States Military Academy West Point and RMC had an annual sports exchange weekend dating back to 1923, which had started with a hockey competition and expanded to include many sports. In early February, RMC would be hosted at West Point this year.

"As you know, Geoff Hampstead, besides representing RMC as the cadet wing commander for the weekend at West Point, is the star goalie of our hockey team. We can avert international attention from our scandal by holding off until we get back from New York. I would hate to cast a shadow over the weekend, wouldn't you?"

"Yes, sir. Whatever you think is best."

"How much time do you have left to serve?" he asked.

"About a week, sir."

"I'm sure you'll be fine."

The last week of my suspended sentence passed without incident. Richie and I went out for beers, though he didn't know why I was so very happy until I drunkenly let the details of the suspended sentence slip on the way home.

34

KING EDWARD

College spirits ran high after the game. Goalie Geoff Hampstead had stopped a record fifty shots on net and led RMC to a 3–2 win against West Point. Hampstead was a hero.

A meeting of the cadet wing was called for Monday after class. I nodded to the statue of Pax as I passed her on my way into Currie Hall, which was filled to the rafters. The fourth-year class filled the upper balcony, standing room only, and the remainder of the wing packed into chairs on the main-floor level.

Hundreds of voices buzzed. No one knew what this gathering was about.

"WING!" shouted a voice from the back of the hall. A final wave of shuffling echoed from the ceiling, and then silence fell. General Pratt, Colonel Gilmore, and CWC Geoff Hampstead marched up the aisle dressed in formal uniforms.

Geoff was wearing his dress scarlet uniform, complete with the royal-purple belt adorned with gold-trimmed curtain tassels unique to the cadet wing commander position.

"At ease," Gilmore breathed into the microphone. A wave of clapping started toward the back of the room and picked up momentum. Soon everyone stood cheering for Hampstead.

General Pratt stepped forward and stared out across the sea of cadets. He did not speak for a few moments. The clapping died down and everyone took their seats.

"You're wondering why we're here. Sports are cancelled. Dinner is delayed. Even the walking wounded have been dragged along for the announcement," he said, making fun of a few people at the back in slings or holding crutches. "Such an occasion for gathering is rare in the history of college life. I hope that many years will pass before such a necessity presents itself again, if ever."

He had our full attention now.

"We're into our third year of having lady cadets at the college, and certain challenges face us during their integration that have never been faced within the cadet wing. Male or female, the foundational structure of college life is designed to produce future officers of the Canadian Armed Forces with deeply ingrained values: truth, duty, valour." He paused and glanced meaningfully around the room. "*And don't get caught*," he added. A few brave cadets chuckled at this.

"I'm talking about truth, duty, valour, about doing the right thing when it is the last thing you want to do." He swept his arm toward Hampstead, inviting him to the podium. "Cadet Wing Commander Geoff Hampstead has an announcement to make today. Mark this moment as a touchstone, the very definition of courage." General Pratt stepped aside.

Geoff leaned toward the microphone and spoke calmly. "I stand before you today as the cadet wing commander and as a humble cadet. From my earliest moments as a recruit, I dreamt of becoming CWC, even though I doubted my ability to fulfill the duties of the post." There were a few knowing nods and laughs around the room. He bowed his head for a moment, as if trying to compose himself. "I've reached that crossroads," he said. "I have broken the very rules that I am intended to model as CWC, by falling in love with a first-year lady cadet."

A dull roar rumbled through the hall, and Hampstead raised his voice over the din. "To that end, I am resigning my position as CWC and surrendering my bars forthwith." He stepped back, undid the ornate belt that was the symbol of his power, and placed it in Colonel Gilmore's outstretched hands.

The roar became angry and rattled the windows of the hall. Bile rose in my throat. *Holy shit. He's pulling a King Edward.*

Colonel Gilmore restored order to the hall with a single word. "Room."

Geoff stood with his head held high. Colonel Gilmore spoke into the microphone. "With the resignation of Fourth Year Hampstead, the cadet wing requires a new CWC. It gives me great honour to announce the appointment of Fourth Year James Tolbert, of Seven Squadron, as cadet wing commander."

My heart lifted. *Perhaps it was all worth it after all.* Jimmy rose from his seat in the front row, and General Pratt presented him with the CWC belt. Jimmy put it on and turned nervously to face the cadet wing.

"May I introduce Cadet Wing Commander James Tolbert," Colonel Gilmore said. "You may cheer." But we were already roaring.

On the way out of Currie Hall, Meg spoke to me in a low voice. "I wonder if he was having sex on college grounds?"

A voice interjected from behind us. "To answer your question, there is a lot of fucking going on at the college." I swivelled around abruptly and nearly tripped on the stairs. Brad Boulter joined us and we kept moving.

"How would you know? You've never dated a cadet, have you?" I asked him.

"I'm not talking cadets with cadets. I'm talking civilian girl-friends." He smiled slyly.

"Are you serious? Cadets bring girlfriends to the college for sex?"

We squeezed through the main doors of the Mackenzie Building with the throng of cadets leaving the assembly and stepped out of the flow to continue our conversation on the edge of the parade square.

"Everyone has been so busy watching you girls and trying to catch you doing something, we're basically doing whatever we want. During cadet parties and balls, every male cadet is trying to get his girlfriend back to his room for sex, and lots are succeeding," he said.

"Seriously!" I said. "I had no idea that was going on."

"Yeah, well, I guess being in the Frigate, it would be harder to sneak girls to your room after walking two hundred and twenty yards across the parade square in full view. So maybe it was happening more on our side of the square."

"Holy crap," I said.

"You must have known?"

"All I know is that every time I try to get away with any-thing, I get busted."

"Based on the rumours, you're getting away with lots."

"Now what?" I asked.

Brad flushed and shuffled his feet. "Never mind."

"That can of worms is open. There's no getting away now," Meg said, rapping Brad on his shoulder.

"Fine. There's a rumour that if you want to get lucky, all you have to do is knock on Kate's door at two a.m."

"What the fuck? That's a load of crap!" I said.

"Has anyone ever knocked?" he asked.

"Not one person. Ever … wait. Oh my god. There have been random guys who came to visit me during evening hours and flirted with me. Nothing ever happened. I wonder if that was why?" The familiar heat of anger burned in my belly. "Do you repeat the rumour?"

"To answer that question, I'll say that I didn't start the rumour."

"Did you ever try to stop it?"

Brad blurted out his staccato laugh. "No! Who do you take me for?"

"The real question is, who do you take me for?"

"That's easy. You're the most unmilitary person I know." He beamed at me like he'd just paid me the greatest of compliments.

Back in the Frigate a few hours later, the rumour mill literally came through my door.

"Did you hear? Jane Quigley is Hampstead's girlfriend," Meg said. "She got thirty days on charge. Neither of them got kicked out."

"What? They charged her?"

"Apparently the charge parade took place in General Pratt's office right after the CWC resignation announcement."

"Oh my god. Poor Jane."

"You know her well, don't you?" Meg asked. "I can't believe Geoff would be so stupid. It's only a matter of months until they could have dated after he graduated. They should have waited."

"Ha. Like Eddie and me?"

"I think they got caught. He blatantly broke the rules, went to such an extent to hide it, and then grabbed a conscience? Doesn't that seem weird to you?"

"Beyond weird," I said, nodding sagely.

"And what guy gives up being CWC for a two-month-old relationship? It doesn't add up. There's more to this story. Aren't you choked?"

"Me? Why?"

"Hampstead turned you in, and then he pulled off this stunt."

"I'm just glad he didn't get away with it." *Prick.*

In March, deep snow was piled high all around the campus. During a rare spare in my schedule, I left Massey Library and leaned my body into the biting wind, intent on getting back to the Frigate for a forty-five-minute nap. I wore my greatcoat — a full-length, double-breasted winter coat — over my battle blouse tunic. The flaps on my cadet astrakhan faux-fur hat covered my ears. Navigating the uneven, icy path, I looked up and saw Jane Quigley approaching me, still on charge, running gingerly on the slippery surface.

"Jane!" I called out. She stopped at attention and stared ahead. I rushed over to her, grateful that the wind was coming off the lake into my face, not hers. "I have no right to ask, but could we talk inside for a moment."

"I prefer not," she said, eyes front.

"Please?" I asked. "Just one minute."

Inside the library foyer, we walked silently straight into the women's washroom.

"Jane," I said, her name catching in my throat as she looked me in the eyes. "I've been hoping for a chance to speak alone."

"What do you want to say?"

"I'm sorry."

She laughed derisively. "Are you kidding?"

"No. I'm so sorry. I didn't know what else to do. I couldn't live with myself otherwise. I'm sure you know the whole story by now."

"Yeah, Geoff told me," she said. "So, I gave you revenge?"

"I wanted things to be fair. I never wanted to hurt you. I don't expect you to forgive me. I needed to say it to your face. I'm so sorry."

"So, would you do it again?"

Her question caught me off guard. After a split second, I nodded. "I would. I did it because I couldn't live with the hypocrisy and unfairness. That hasn't changed."

"Sounds like you've got it all worked out for yourself."

"Jane, I can't take it back. You were innocent in it."

"Funny that you say it like that," she said wearily. "Because I'm not innocent, am I? I did it. I knew the rules. We could have waited. I could have kept my secret to myself. You didn't make up the story."

"He shouldn't have started up with you. You were off limits."

"Don't get me wrong," she said. "I wish I never told you. But it could've been worse. We could have been caught. At least this way, he saved face."

"Every single cadet makes choices and does things around here that are against the rules. It's a matter of who gets caught and who gets punished. I've been punished so often that I hate myself for being a part of your being caught and punished." My minute was running out. "How many days do you have left?"

"A few more days. I'll finish out this year and then decide if I'll quit," she said.

"Jane, I wish the best for you. I'm glad I had the chance to say sorry."

"I should get going."

"Me too," I said, standing awkwardly, not knowing how to end it. She pulled off her glove and I shook her cool hand. "Don't laugh, but if there is anything I can ever do to make this up to you, please let me know."

"I doubt it," she said.

That night I had a visit from Penny Miller. She was enraged and wanted to know if I was going to turn her in for sleeping in the Frigate with Nigel. We argued.

"What are you really doing here?" I asked. I stood up and turned to her with my fists clenched at my sides.

"I want you to know that I know. People know you're a hypocrite for turning them in."

"No. Hypocrite's your forte," I said. "You live here common-law and pretend to be following the rules."

"I'm not pretending anything. You're the one who invited a first year here and tricked her into telling her secrets so that you could punish Geoff for what he did to you and Jake!" she said, raising her voice.

"*Oh my god.* How could I trick someone into telling me a secret that I didn't know about?"

"Well, then, what really happened?"

I opened my mouth and clapped it shut. "Just go." I pulled the door open.

"Not before —"

"Out." I pointed out the door. She glared at me and spun on her heel. I closed the door behind her, turned out the lights, and lay down.

Soon another knock sounded on my door. I didn't answer. The door opened a crack and Richie poked his face in, his body backlit by the hall lights.

"I'm here, Holbrook," I said, my voice hoarse. Meg and Richie came in.

"Watch your eyes," said Meg. I squinted as she flicked on the lights.

"You have balls, Armstrong. I'll give you that," Richie said. I stared at him, my stomach in knots. "Shit, girl. No wonder you've been acting so weird."

"Are we still friends?" I fought the tears spilling over my lower lids.

Meg stepped closer. "We've just heard the rumours and came to let you know —"

Richie cut her off. "You're my friend right now, but if you don't start spilling your guts and bring us up to speed with what the hell happened, you're getting your ass kicked."

"I'll make tea," Meg offered.

"Fuck the tea. Start talking, Armstrong," Richie said, throwing himself down on the foot of my bed.

35

POSTER CHILD

A period of unhappiness began. I wasn't seeing Jake at all — we were still taking a break. I felt exposed, not knowing who knew the role I'd played in the Hampstead debacle. I poured my anxious energy into hitting the books. In May, Adam and I stood together in front of the year-end marks posted on the notice board in Mackenzie Building.

"How can we be tied for first place with a seventy percent overall average? This place is nuts," I said.

"Who cares? First is first. My marks won't matter. I'm going to fly helicopters for a living." Adam grinned.

"I should have gone pilot when I had the chance," I said.

Things were going well on the pilot trial for women; sixteen of the first twenty-five women had passed training and were being posted for two-year flying assignments in squadrons to complete the final phase of the assessment.

A few days later, Adam, Richie, and I sauntered back to the same notice boards in Mackenzie Building. Our fourth-year bar slate positions were posted. The fall-term bar slate was the most competitive and representative of each cadet's status and standing within the class. The squadron appointments were self-contained, a competition amongst squadron peers, based on performance reviews and academic, military, and athletic accomplishments. The wing appointments drew from the entire class.

I didn't have high hopes. I'd be lucky to get two bars.

I was shocked to read my name and see a three-bar position listed beside it: aide-de-camp to the commandant. Richie and Adam were already hugging and backslapping beside me. We all had three-bar positions. Meg did, as well. She would be the deputy cadet squadron leader. That was a feather in her cap.

"Holy shit! Can you believe it?" Richie said to Adam. "I'm the fucking recruit flight CFL and you're going to be the CSTO."

"We are going to terrorize some rooks!" Adam yelled. I laughed watching Adam flex his muscles like some kind of tough guy — he was the nicest guy ever. I had a feeling the job of cadet squadron training officer might terrorize him more than he would terrorize the recruits.

"I'm going to choose the best rook flight wake-up song *ever!*" exclaimed Richie.

"Congratulations, guys," I said.

"Oh yeah? How about you as Aide-de-Camp Armstrong," Richie said, shaking his head.

"Yeah! You little shit," Adam piped in.

"I *know*. Trust me, no one is more surprised than me."

"The key to success, Armstrong-style," Richie joked, "is to get into so much trouble that you meet the commandant, almost get kicked out, and end up working for him in one of the plummest jobs in the wing." He added, "Oh, did I mention that he created the job for her?"

"I doubt that!" I said. It was true that the cadet aide-de-camp bar position was brand new starting next year. It may have existed in the past, but not within recent memory. General Pratt had a full-time regular-force captain as his official ADC.

That night we went to Bill and Alfie's pub for celebratory drinks. While we waited for the others to arrive, Richie and I were rehashing the fall term bar slate.

"So, I'm curious. What do you think about Penny Miller being the only woman to get four bars?" Richie said, taking a sip of his beer.

"She's always been lucky?"

"Cut the crap."

"How prestigious is it to manage the yearbook?" I laughed.

"Four bars are four bars. She got the nod from the establishment."

"I guess, as far as they were giving the nod. None of the senior leadership roles in the wing went to women," I said. With a start that made Richie jump, I slapped myself on the side of the head. "Whoa! You just made me realize! She's a poster child. Truth. Duty. Valour."

"*Don't get caught,*" he chimed in.

"Exactly. *Don't cause trouble.* Pretend that everything is fine. Don't complain. Don't be a threat. Work hard. Stay under the radar. She played the game. She kept quiet, didn't speak out, didn't draw attention to herself. She was rewarded for that. It's a totally different set of rules than for you guys."

"She is the opposite of you. You pushed back, spoke up, played basketball with the boys. It's not like you wanted to be controversial — you just couldn't help it," he said, laughing.

"How am I so controversial?"

"Well ... let's just say that I've seen the history book on the suffragettes openly displayed on your bookshelf."

"I'm not a feminist." In that moment, I believed this to be true.

"I know. Don't worry," he said.

The graduation parade for the Class of 1983, the last class with balls, dragged on into a third hour. There were extensive awards, both academic and military, and lengthy speeches by dignitary guests, reviewing officers, and college administration. Only the presentation of the top awards remained, and then it would finally be over. The LCWB would be outta here.

"The Victor van der Smissen–Ridout Memorial Award," droned the master of ceremonies through the loudspeakers, "is awarded to the graduating cadet deemed to represent the highest moral, intellectual, and physical standards of a cadet at the Royal Military College of Canada. This award is especially prestigious because the recipient is determined by a secret ballot of all cadets.

"This year's Victor van der Smissen–Ridout Award is presented to … Fourth Year Geoff Hampstead of Seven Squadron. Fourth Year Geoff Hampstead has morally demonstrated the depths of his values this year with his public display of personal integrity, intellectually he has achieved academic excellence, and physically he led the RMC hockey team in a victorious season as goalie. Congratulations!"

General Pratt beamed as he shook Geoff's hand for the photo. My knees wobbled in disbelief.

At Jake's graduation ball, I groaned and looked out over the sea of people dressed in black tie — military mess kits, tuxedoes, ball gowns, and scarlet uniforms — for the occasion.

"Let it go," Jake said, and gave me an extra twirl in his arms that lifted my feet slightly off the dance floor. We had reconciled earlier in the spring and I felt more in love with him than ever. "I think you're beautiful. That's all that matters."

"I would give anything to be wearing a ball gown and have my hair done in an updo tonight," I sighed. "But all that matters is that you're happy."

"I'm having a blast," he confirmed, as he squeezed me closer. "Okay, don't look. Geoff and Jane are behind us. I'll turn you. Don't make it obvious that you're looking." He swung me around. "Okay, look now."

Geoff and Jane were dancing together. Jane was stunningly beautiful in a black ball gown, her dark hair rolled into a chignon.

"What the —" I sputtered. Jake squeezed me tighter against him and steered me back into the flow of the dance away from them.

"She quit," Jake said.

"She did? When?"

"Sometime since exams. They're engaged and getting married later in the fall."

"Oh Jesus," I said. "I hope that's what she really wants."

"She seems happy enough to me. They're the prince and princess of the ball."

"They get the happy ending, and next year I'll be living here without you." I sighed into his ear as the music stopped.

"I have news. I was going to wait, but now seems like a good time. My dad's been helping me look and I've landed a job as an engineer with the Urban Transportation Development Corporation, right here in Kingston. They're building a rapid transit system called the SkyTrain for the Vancouver Expo in the summer of 1986. I'm not leaving town!"

I yelped. We kissed in public for the first time. We waltzed off the edge of the dance floor to rejoin his parents.

"I see you've broken the news," said his dad.

I lunged at him and hugged him tight in his chair. "Thank you," I said and kissed his cheek.

At dawn, the end of an era was marked at sunrise on the parade square. I stood bleary eyed beside Jake and his parents on the red bleachers and smiled on command for the traditional graduating class sunrise photo of all the graduates and guests who had stayed up all night at the grad party. The last class with balls experienced their final moment as gentleman cadets. The Royal Military College of Canada was now an entirely coed institution.

The sun rose on a new day at the college.

36

REALITY CHECK

During summer leave back in Abbotsford, my mother and I wore kid gloves with each other, but after prolonged time together, cracks started to show. Even though we had never had another conversation about my abuse since I had initially told her when I was nine, I understood now that my brother Robert had emigrated to Australia to get away from me and the potential consequences, and that my mother still blamed me. I blamed myself, too. But that didn't stop me from being angry with her for all the other stuff.

"Why do you constantly have to call it camp?" I snapped.

"Well, it's confusing. You're still called a cadet, so what do I know?"

"Is it so hard to remember to say RMC? It's just *RMC*. That's it."

"Robert was invited to attend Royal Roads, you know. He even went to Victoria one weekend to visit and they offered him a scholarship. But he decided it wasn't for him. Anyhow, he was getting straight As at UBC until he left. Such a shame he didn't finish."

"Yes, Mom, I know." *I'm on a scholarship, too. Not to mention that I'll be the first person in our family to graduate from university.*

Near the end of the two-week visit, sitting alone with my mother on the back deck having pink lemonade in a moment of cease-fire, I took a risk and told her how excited I was about becoming aide-de-camp to General Pratt.

"Why would he choose you?" she said, swirling the ice cubes in her glass.

"He likes me?" I felt the punch in my gut. Wasn't she pleased that I had distinguished myself and achieved something? I was a pioneer helping to lead women into the new world.

"How did you meet him? Does he even know you?"

"Oh, what's the point?" I said indignantly and stood up.

My mother looked up at me and smiled. Her eyes were icy hard, without a hint of warmth. "Here now, sit down, there's no reason to give up trying to do well," she admonished. "My job as a mother is to make sure you don't get too big for your britches, that's all. No one likes a gloater."

I stood there humiliated. I wanted her approval and she knew it. She was never going to give it.

"Well, congratulations, you're getting an A in motherhood."

"There's no need to be rude about it," she snapped.

"There's no need to get angry about it," I snapped back.

"If anyone's an angry person, it's you," she spat.

"Do you think it's genetic?" I couldn't remember a time when I wasn't aware of my mother's rage. I tossed the remains of my drink on the lawn and went inside.

Jake picked me up at the Ottawa airport. On the way to Kingston, I told him about my fights with my mother. He listened and didn't say much.

"Since you're already in a bad mood, this is probably a good time to take a look at the yearbook — it's on the back seat — and check out Brian Floyd."

I opened the book. "What a slimeball. Even his graduation photo looks evil, like a vampire."

"Read it out loud," Jake said. I started reading and soon came to the offensive part:

> *Always a strict military man who would rather die than be out of step, Brian entered his fourth year in fine style. He seemed to develop a strange fetish about the smell of fish. Some say he could sniff it out from behind closed doors. Brian was team captain of the RMC rugby club and personified all that was clean and courteous about the game. He was a true gentleman in almost every sense of the word except for being a belligerent chauvinist.*

"Sick, eh?" Jake said. "He's fucking proud of being misogynist."

"Fuck him. Let's talk about happy stuff. Tell me more about your new job and the apartment. I can't wait to see it." I tossed the yearbook in the back seat.

Jake's apartment building was a three-storey walk-up built in the 1950s. "Oh my god. This place is adorable," I exclaimed as I stood in the doorway. He had decorated it as a bachelor pad, right down to the coffee table he'd made with a piece of glass set over two large empty wire spools.

He scooped me up and carried me right into the bedroom. "King-sized waterbed inspired by a visit to your sister," he said, dropping me down onto it.

37

TIGERS

Fourth Year. I woke up on the first morning back in my room, directly above the recruit hallway, at 05:30 hours to "Every Breath You Take" by The Police. I held my pillow over my head. It went on forever. It was so loud I could feel the vibration of the speakers. I was going to kill Holbrook. *This is not the best recruit flight song ever, Richie.*

Very quickly, college life returned to its normal frenzied state. The recruits were being terrorized by Richie and Adam, the rest of the wing had returned, and our academic year — the grind of classes, studying, and exams — had begun.

The commandant's garden party took place in the second week of September. The weather was perfect and the garden was in full bloom. Most of the men attending were in uniform, and the women wore elaborate hats and flowing dresses.

My role was simple: be personable, ensure people were having a good time, fill in the gaps by engaging in conversation with anyone who seemed uncomfortable or out of place, and above all else, anticipate any needs that General Pratt might have during the party, including ensuring that his drink was topped up. I couldn't believe my luck and was looking forward to my role as the general's aide-de-camp throughout the coming year.

One evening, I was invited to a family dinner with General and Mrs. Pratt and their two sons, who attended civilian universities, in their home, the commandant's residence. The general handed me a glass of white wine to sip while he finished making dinner with his wife, Martha.

We dined formally, eating rack of lamb and roast vegetables off fine china, using silver flatware, with monogrammed linen napkins in our laps. *This is how I want my home life to be.*

"So, Kate. How do you feel about attending an RCR mess dinner with me in Ottawa next week?" General Pratt asked. The Royal Canadian Regiment is the senior infantry regiment in the Canadian Army, and the general was considered its de facto godfather.

"I would be honoured, sir."

"I think it's time to try and win over some of the strong opponents of lady cadets at the college," he said.

"Yes, sir."

Martha placed her silverware on the edge of her plate. "You are not possibly taking Kate into that den of vipers alone!" Both of her sons laughed.

"She won't be alone. She'll be at the head table with me. Bob Bennett invited me to be the guest speaker. I made my acceptance conditional on bringing one of my ADCs to be hosted personally by him," he said with a grin.

"Howell!" she said. "I thought you liked Kate? Bob is top curmudgeon in the dinosaur league against women cadets."

"Well, then, I'll beg your indulgence to take a run at him with my most valuable asset," he said, looking steadily at me. "Miss Armstrong, if anyone can sway his opinion, it's you. Are you game to give it a shot?"

"Yes, sir, of course. Although, I honestly don't understand what I could possibly say or do to convince him."

"I know General Bennett. I know you. Just be yourself."

"My ceaselessly frustrating self, sir?" I asked.

"If you're talking about nearly being late for parade practice because your haircut took longer than expected, no, don't be that self. Be your charming, witty, somewhat brash self. General Bennett is always quoting the closing lines from Colonel Nicholson's 1973 article 'Where Have All the Tigers Gone?' It reads, 'Please, let us accept, cherish and develop, along with the nice, manageable pussycats, at least a few TIGERS.' I'm going to give him a chance to put his money where his mouth is. You have earned your place as a tiger cub."

The mess dinner took place in Ottawa the following Friday night. I was prepared for a gruff reception, but General Bob Bennett was very charming.

"So, how did you first meet General Pratt?" he asked while the salad course was being served.

"Honestly, sir, I got into so much trouble last year that I was almost kicked out. I met General Pratt one step from the curb," I said, trying to impress him with my forthrightness and not really thinking it through.

"What did you do?" he asked, shifting toward me expectantly. I cringed. "I prefer not to say, sir."

"Well, you must have done something right for him to turn around and make you his ADC," he said, graciously letting me off the hook. "What's been the hardest part about being a female cadet?"

I paused and looked at him for a moment. He raised his eyebrows. "Damn the torpedoes, sir?" I asked.

"Damn the torpedoes." He nodded.

"It's been the attitude of the guys. I've managed to make it through the college curriculum well enough, but the guys have made it really tough. It's like they gave me all the rules, made me train hard for game day, and then benched me for the season."

"Sounds frustrating."

"Kind of. But other than that, it's been good, sir."

He broke into a raucous laugh, loud enough to turn heads. General Pratt looked my way and smiled.

"Still, there must be some advantages to being a woman at RMC?" General Bennett asked.

"Well, I can think of one," I said. "I can spin my skirt around and remove the fraust off the back of my uniform without needing to ask for help like the guys wearing pants."

He laughed again. "Why do I get the feeling that a hundred years from now men will be standing in the kitchen wearing aprons and asking, 'How did we ever let ourselves get in this situation?'"

"Rest easy, sir. We just want to be respected as equals. Women aren't trying to take over, we just want our rightful chance to play alongside the guys."

"I have a feeling we'll see about that," he said.

After the formal dinner, General Bennett and I teamed up as partners in three rounds of crud. Once he had gone home for the evening, I stayed with General Pratt and a band of drunken RCR officers. We played crud late into the night.

The next morning, I arrived at General Pratt's door a few moments before 08:00 hours to let him know that the staff car for our drive back to Kingston had arrived and to collect his luggage. I looked at my watch and knocked on the door at precisely 08:00 hours, as pre-arranged.

"Enter," he called.

I walked in, scanning the room for him, and stopped dead in my tracks. General Pratt stood off to the side, out of view of the hallway, in his underwear.

I shrieked and turned my back. "Oh my god, sir, I'm sorry."

"Come in, and close the door," he said.

"Sir, I'm sorry," I exclaimed. "I'll send the driver up in ten minutes to collect your bags." I rushed out, closed the door, fled to the stairwell, and hid behind the landing door to catch my breath. *Fuck!* Did I make a mistake or had he meant for me to see him in his tighty-whities?

On the drive back to Kingston, General Pratt seemed pleased, chatting about trivial things as if I hadn't just seen him in his underwear. Then his tone became more serious. "General Bennett pulled me aside at the end of the evening and said he was sufficiently impressed by you to give way on his long-held position that women have no place at RMC. Well done, Miss Armstrong."

"Thank you, sir. I was impressed by him, as well." I turned my attention to the bare autumn trees passing by outside the car. The landscape looked brown and dead. I closed my eyes and pretended to sleep.

"Wakey-wakey, Miss Armstrong," said General Pratt, rousing me from a dreamless nap. The staff car was stopped behind his residence back at the college. "I was beginning to take you for dead."

"I'm sorry, sir!"

"Don't worry about it. You're in my good books at the moment."

I jumped out, rushed around the car, opened his door, and saluted as he eased himself out of the seat. I closed the car door and watched him walk away.

38

CHERISHED

Late in November, lounging around in Jake's apartment over weekend morning coffee, I broached the subject of the looming Christmas ball, which was the next Saturday evening. Jake would not commit to attending as my date.

"We've been over this so many times. I don't want to go back to the college so soon," he griped. "And, besides, won't you technically be working that evening as an aide-de-camp?"

"I'm working," I said, "*and* I have to bring a date. It's no fun to attend this stuff without you. It's the last formal function before exam routine and you haven't come out all year."

"I haven't been to a single function?"

"Nothing. Not one."

"Okay, okay," he said. "I'll go." He went into the kitchen. I could hear him toss the dregs of his coffee forcefully into the sink.

"We don't do anything fun anymore," I said. "If I want to see you, I have to come over here."

He popped his head out and scowled at me. "Come on," he said. "Not this again."

Just when I had expected things between us to be better than ever, with Jake working as a civilian engineer in town and my freedom as a fourth year to spend nights in his apartment, we seemed to have lost our gift of playful conversation. I was plagued by doubt and insecurity, which made me short tempered and prone to grumbling about the smallest perceived slight. Something was going wrong, but I was unable to articulate it. And I didn't have time to figure it out. Christmas exams were upon me.

In January, first-term marks were posted. Macroeconomics: 51 percent. I stared at the mark, as cadets jostled me on all sides, trying to read their grades off the list. I was going to lose my bars. I went back to my room and sat in shock.

The summons came before noon.

"Academic restrictions," General Pratt said succinctly.

"Yes, sir." I knew this meant being ineligible for a bar position as a fourth-year. I would be a senior cadet, or s/c, which had the nickname of *slasher*.

"I didn't know you were in such difficulty. How much time do you spend at Mr. Tatham's apartment?"

"Less time than you'd think, sir. It's not that. It's the calculus."

"How the hell did you pass first-year engineering?"

"To be honest, sir, I'm not entirely sure," I said. "The calculus module system definitely saved me and I had help from a tutor."

"What was your rationale for choosing commerce as a major, if you struggle with math?"

"I wanted to study something practical, sir, something with career potential."

"Well, your career potential choice has landed you on academic restrictions. You've lost your aide-de-camp position. This term, you'll be a senior cadet."

Tears welled up in my eyes. "Sir, I'm sorry if I've let you down. I know you stood up for me and gave me this chance."

He shuffled uncomfortably in his chair and waved aside my apology. "Do you have someone to help you this term?"

"Yes, sir. I am going to ask Matthew Coleman."

"Good choice," he said. Matthew was a third year who was studying in the honours economics and commerce program; we were classmates in macro.

"How was your Christmas break?" the general asked.

"To be honest, it was fairly miserable. I was worried about my macro results. Not that my worrying changed anything. And you, sir?" I asked.

"Well," he drawled, "it was delightful. We attended Jane Quigley and Geoff Hampstead's wedding in Oakville."

I grimaced.

General Pratt looked at me with a neutral expression. "Let's part on good terms. Stay the course and put last year behind us. Are we on the same page?"

"Yes, sir," I said.

"I'm sorry to see you go. It's really too bad," he said.

I smiled bleakly. He rose to see me out. When we reached the door, he faced me and took both my hands in his as though we were about to pronounce our wedding vows. A knot of discomfort twisted in my stomach. I flashed to a vision of him in his underwear.

"Martha and I consider you like the daughter we never had," he said. "This doesn't change that. We can remain close."

"Thank you, sir. I would love that. I'm grateful for all you've done for me," I said. He leaned forward and kissed my face, his lips brushing the edge of mine. I pulled back and dropped his hands.

On the way back to the Frigate, I felt devastated that I'd blown my chance to be his ADC for the remainder of the year. I had to make a conscious effort to lift my legs and place one foot in front of the other. *Did he really try to kiss me?* I had a real affection for General Pratt, but not like that. More like for a father. He was so old. He couldn't possibly think that I would ever like him like that. The idea of it confused and repulsed me, coupled with a strange sense of invincibility, like he would look out for me if he *liked* me. The bold part of me wanted to cast the near kiss in this light. But the quieter, scared part of me knew the truth. If he actually tried anything more and crossed the line, I was terrified of what could happen to me. Not from any desire for him, far from it. Rather, my family experience had shown me the catastrophic price to pay for refusing. I had the same sick feeling in my gut thinking about it.

The halls were chaotic as the biannual room shuffle took place. I was staying in the same room this term. I closed my door on the excitement. My military college career had just passed its zenith and everyone was moving on without me. If I failed macro, would that mean my mother had been right about me after all? What else would I do? I had no other plan for my life, and I couldn't come back here.

By mid-February, my tutoring sessions with Matthew Coleman were making the difference. My relationship with Jake continued to be fraught, and I spent more and more time with Matthew. Our friendship quickly grew beyond just being buddies in class and during study hours, expanding to include going to town to run errands together and going out for meals and chumming together at "mandatory fun" events. Looking back now, I see it was an emotional affair. I was still too young to understand that carnal fidelity was not the most powerful aspect of being faithful.

One evening during a study session in my room, as we sat a little too close together, Matthew admitted he had a crush on me. I panicked and quickly reminded him about Jake.

Matthew said, "But he doesn't cherish you, Kate. You deserve better treatment."

The next Saturday, Jake picked me up and as we drove to his place, I was fighting tears the whole way. When he opened the door, I stumbled into his apartment and threw myself on the couch.

"Why are you so upset?" Jake asked, sitting down close to me. "What's happened?"

"I want to be cherished," I sobbed irrationally. I thought back to high school and the only time my dad had ever interfered or given me relationship advice. Gary had stood me up one night, and while I sat in my room waiting for him to show up, Dad had come to talk to me. It was a rare moment, one when I felt he actually cared enough about me to speak up.

"If he treats you like this when he's courting you, imagine how he'll treat you when he takes you for granted," he had said. "It's not good." He seemed to know what he was talking about. I had fought with Gary but never took a stand and was quick to make it all okay. Now, Dad's words made more sense to me.

"Someone told me that I deserve to be cherished." I stared at the floor.

"Was it that Matthew guy?" Jake leapt to his feet and started pacing around the apartment.

"I spend so much time trying to force you to do stuff. It doesn't feel natural anymore."

"What are you talking about?" Jake stood stock-still, looking down at me.

"I don't know what to do."

"Don't do anything. It's almost Valentine's Day. Just sleep on it. You'll feel better if you rest," he said. He crouched down in front of me to make eye contact.

I reached out and stroked his hair.

"I'm sorry. I don't know what's wrong with me. Can you please take me home?"

For the next six weeks, I spent more and more time alone. I broke up with Jake and had a brief relationship with Matthew, but that didn't solve anything. I was a mess and missed Jake and doubted my decision, which made me clingy and insecure and jealous with Matthew. When we broke up, my sense of isolation became acute. It was like nobody noticed that I had disappeared. My mother's voice, her awful teasing game, came back to haunt me. *If only Kate were here, she'd enjoy her last few months at RMC.* In truth, my classmates were just as busy with their own lives as I had been preoccupied with mine. As a senior cadet on academic restrictions, I had no official duties except to study and pass all my courses, so I was one step removed from day-to-day college life. I studied more than ever but struggled to make headway.

One Sunday in the middle of April, well after lights out, someone pounded on my door.

"Who is it?" I asked, disoriented. I had been in a deep sleep.

"Jake," he whispered.

"Hold on," I said. *Shit. I don't want him to see me like this. I look terrible.* I threw on my housecoat and looked in the mirror.

It was only two weeks until final exams. Until now I had refused to see Jake, but I found myself opening the door with a sense of longing. Once he was inside and the door was closed, he turned to face me.

"Oh my god!" I exclaimed. The left side of his face was purple and his eye was swollen half shut.

"I was beaten up and robbed."

"When? Where?" I gestured for him to take a seat, but he continued to stand.

"Friday night, behind the Prince George Hotel," he said. "I was drunk and the guys must have been watching me at the bar. They jumped me on the way to my car. They took my wallet and then knocked me down. One guy kicked me in the face."

"Oh my god, Jake," I said. "Are you okay? Have you been to hospital? You could have a concussion."

"I got checked out. I'm fine — except that I miss you so much." He pulled his left hand out from behind his back and extended a bouquet of pink carnations.

I held his gaze and said nothing as a wave of guilt washed over me. "You could have lost your eye." I took the flowers and filled a mug of water for them.

"Kate, I've been such an idiot. Please, give us another chance. I want to be with you."

"Jake, admit it, we never really recovered from the Floyd and Hampstead disaster," I said. "It changed us."

"I love you. We can fix it. I know we can," he said. "I was going to ask you to marry me on Valentine's Day."

My hand froze over the mug of carnations. *Isn't that what I've always wanted?* "Don't say that. It's not fair. It's just proof to me of how far apart we were. I wanted to break up and you wanted to get married. Why *did* you come here tonight?" I asked.

"I had to see you."

"You mean you had to show me. You wanted me to see your smashed face."

"Maybe."

"You should go. I need to be alone. I need to sleep."

"Any chance of a kiss goodnight?" He leaned toward me, lips puckered on his raw, pulpy face.

"So gross," I said, laughing and averting my face. I couldn't help it.

"*I am not an animal,*" he said. I put my hand squarely on his chest. He leaned into me and I tenderly kissed his hot cheek.

I couldn't know in that moment that this would be the first in a decade-long series of mismatched attempts at getting back together, where one of us would want to try again but we never found ourselves in sync long enough to make it happen.

39

GRADUATION

I passed all my exams. Macroeconomics was my lowest grade: 51 percent. *Professor's fudge. Thank you, Dr. Binhammer.* I felt like an academic idiot. I had three Ds: Macroeconomics, business finance, public finance. I had technically fulfilled the requirements of the four pillars — academics, military leadership, bilingualism, and fitness — necessary to graduate as a cadet from the Royal Military College of Canada, Class of 1984, but I took no pride in it. I had disappointed myself.

A four-year posting to CFB Kingston had come through. I would simply move up the hill on the other side of Fort Henry, live in the officers' quarters, and start working in base supply as a second lieutenant supply officer.

All four women from the Frigate had gone the distance, and we would graduate together. Of the thirty-two women who had started, only twenty-one remained, but this was statistically a much higher success rate than that of our male classmates. In total, our class had started with over five hundred recruits in CMR, Royal Roads, and RMC. Only 229 from that group, including the women, had finished.

Sunday, May 13, 1984. The *Toronto Star* did a cover story on our graduation. Three stories were highlighted on the full-colour headline banner, with photographs, on the front page: one on Lady Diana, "Diana of a Thousand Days Is a Changed Woman"; one on Robert Redford, "A Rare Interview with Robert Redford"; and one on me, "Meet the First Woman Grad of Royal Military College."

During various interviews with the press that week, I didn't say a bad word about the college, and neither did any of the other women cadets. The press clippings had never been honest. We didn't tell anyone the truth. Maybe we couldn't even look at it for ourselves. My boldest comment was in an article published by the *Ottawa Citizen* on May 14, when I commented on missing my chance to train to be a pilot: "I still hope someday I'll be able to. I know I'm capable. I don't think it's fair." It would be another year until the final decision was made to open the pilot classification to women. In the end, my life would go in another direction and I would never apply for pilot. The administration spoke highly of the success of the integration, and we all agreed wholeheartedly that the male cadets had been gracious and supportive, that we had all done it *together*.

Just before graduation weekend, an envelope came in the mail. I didn't recognize the scrawling handwriting or the Ottawa return address, and I opened it with curiosity. I pulled out a folded newspaper article, three pages from the *Ottawa Citizen*. It was the recent interview with Meg and me, including photos. There was a handwritten message in the corner of the margin on the front page, next to a photo of me shining my boots in my room: "Congratulations, I'm proud of you. Bob Bennett."

I was delighted that the "top curmudgeon against women at RMC" from my mess dinner evening in Ottawa had taken the time to cut out the article and send me a supportive note.

Convocation took place on a Friday afternoon, May 18, 1984. My parents had arrived with my sister, Ellen, and my middle brother, Peter. Except for Dad's visit during first year for the father-son mess dinner, none of my family had set foot on the college grounds.

After our degrees were awarded, the celebrations started in earnest. That evening, the sunset ceremony showcased cadet life: Old Eighteen drill team performance, unarmed combat team demonstrations, gymnastics, Highland band and dancers, and various skits roasting staff and professors. At sunset, a bagpiper sounded taps and the college flag was lowered on my military college career. A passing of the colours took place from the fourth-year cadets to the third-year cadets.

My family was seated together in two rows on the red bleachers, Ellen, Peter, and I directly behind our parents. My mother shifted angrily in her seat, complaining about her neighbours. "If he wasn't so tall and her hair wasn't so big, I might be able to see the whole show at once," she grumbled loudly toward the couple in front of her.

Dad patted her knee, but she continued to squirm. Near the end of taps, Ellen leaned forward to gently ask Mom to be quieter. "It's almost over, Mom. Just a few more minutes."

This was met with a middle-finger knuckle in her eye. Ellen gasped and clasped her hand to her face. I leaned in and asked if she was okay. She nodded and motioned for me to quit making a scene, but she continued to hold her eye. The moment the show was over and people stood to disband, Ellen calmly declared, "I need to go to emergency. I think my contact lens is lodged behind my eyeball."

"Are you sure it didn't just pop out?" asked my mother, half-heartedly looking around the benches at my sister's feet.

"I'll take you," I said. I drove my sister's rental car straight to the Kingston General Hospital Emergency Department to have the lens dislodged and then delivered her safely back to her hotel for the night.

Tensions were still high between my mother and Ellen and me the next morning. After the graduation parade, we were loitering in the hallway outside my room, alongside a gathering of classmates and their families doing the same. There was a general atmosphere of celebration, and in the midst of it my mother and my sister started arguing about the previous night.

"I never touched you," declared my mother.

"You poked me in the eye! I had to go to the hospital," Ellen said.

"What a load of nonsense. I never touched you!"

"Please, just be quiet," I said, my face flushed with embarrassment.

Dad scowled worriedly and looked frightened.

My mother shouted, "Don't you dare speak to me that way. You think you're something special, you and all your friends here. You're just a bunch of pompous asses."

I flinched. The crowd around us hushed, a few people staring.

In a flash, Ellen grabbed Mother's arm, dragged her into my room, and closed the door. The crowd became more animated than ever and drifted away from our area. Soon we were nearly alone in the hall.

My mother let out a blood-curdling cry for help. "Gordie! Gordie! Help me! Help me! She's trying to kill me."

I heard the muffled expletives of my sister telling her to calm down. I wanted to die. My father stood transfixed with a frozen look on his face.

283

I stared at him. "Will you do nothing?"

"Why do you girls always have to go out of your way to upset her?" he muttered and stared at the ground.

The next thing that happened was only what could have been predicted to happen.

Nothing.

We pretended nothing had happened and tried to salvage what was left. Just like always. Ellen and my mother emerged from my room and we went out for lunch. That evening, my mother dressed in a teal ball gown and wore a mink stole to my graduation ball.

"Auntie Greta lent it to me." My mother beamed.

"You look lovely, Mom."

We danced until dawn, and then we made our way to the parade square and posed for the Class of 1984 graduation sunrise photo.

I didn't go back to bed that day. I was too excited to sleep. A large room with a loft bedroom was waiting for me in CFB Kingston's officers' quarters, where the next chapter of my life would begin. From my bed, I would look through the two-storey picture windows onto a sloping lawn that led down to the edge of the St. Lawrence River and the Thousand Islands. I had four years of lost sleep to make up.

My RMC clearing-out routine was completed in time to meet my family, who showed up to help me move out of the Frigate. Everyone chipped in. The cars filled quickly. At one point, I saw Mom pick up the vase of dried pink carnations from Jake amongst a few unwrapped delicate items on my desk. I had to resist grabbing them out of her hands to keep them safe.

I dropped the final armload of clothes into the back seat of my graduation present to myself, a brand-new silver two-door

Subaru coupe, and turned to my dad. "Just give me a few moments to say goodbye?"

"For sure, take your time," Dad said, squeezing my shoulder.

I made my way up the fire escape stairs, entered my newly emptied room, closed the door, and sat on the bare mattress. The room was stark — there was nothing left of me there. I looked out at the familiar view of Navy Bay and said a mental goodbye to the harbour. I'd done it. It seemed like a small thing and such a tremendous thing all at once. I felt like I should cry, though I didn't.

In the corner behind my door, I noticed my spider basher. I had kept it with me since recruit term and had killed countless squadron mascots with it. I laughed, grabbed it, and went downstairs to the recruit flight hallway. I stood in front of the headless woman and gave her a silent nod of goodbye. She had helped me make it. *I made it.* I shuddered and pushed through the door to leave my basher stick in the shower room.

On the way out, a streak of pink from the open garbage can caught my eye. I stood and stared into the bin in disbelief. A bouquet of dried pink carnations was haphazardly strewn amongst the paper towels, stalks snapped in half and heads mangled.

I felt such a blast of hatred for my mother that it scared me.

I went directly to my old room and sat on the bed to catch my breath and calm myself. For the first time in my life, I felt that nobody had any right to expect anything of me. I didn't have anything left to prove to anyone. I didn't have to rush anywhere to please anyone, especially not *her.*

The door eased opened and my mother entered. I said nothing as she sat down beside me. I didn't look at her; I didn't want her there.

"So, you're sad to be graduating from camp?" she asked.

"Yes, I suppose I am," I said tersely.

"That's the first time you haven't corrected me when I called it camp."

"That's because my graduation gift to myself is to stop fighting you." I looked over at her pursed lips and narrowed eyes. The whole of our history was written in her pinched face.

"I never should have let you come here. It's ruined you," she said.

"How can you even say that? I'm not ruined. Don't *ever* say that to me again." I moved to get up and she grabbed at my arm, but I eluded her grasp. "You didn't *let me* come here. I made the decision, and I was the one who stuck with it."

"Well, you've definitely changed," she said bitterly.

"Yes, I suppose I have after all." My mother didn't know me. I couldn't make her see me if she didn't see me by now. She didn't want to know me. I didn't want to let her know me.

"Let's go," I said, stepping quickly out the door and leaving my mother behind. She could take her own time coming down the stairs, but I was ahead of her now and I wasn't looking back.

EPILOGUE

Nelson, BC
April 2018

It's late afternoon on a Sunday. Snow is melting off the roof of the woodshed and off the lawn, and last year's green grass is emerging from the edge of the snowdrift under my office window.

I've been enjoying flipping through photo albums and RMC yearbooks. My laughter shocks and delights me — I'm finally on the other side of a journey that started many years ago and felt like a long, cold winter that threatened to never end.

I have been with my husband, Rick, for five years, and am finally in the right relationship. I've married a good man, a bright and kind and supportive partner. I'm watching him hang birdhouses in the trees along the edge of the creek. He built them during the winter months in his workshop using discarded antique doorknobs as perches and reclaimed barnboards for the frames. Despite being in the midst of his own project, he accepts, with his usual generosity of spirit — showing interest and laughing along — my frequent disruptions when I go outside and ask him to listen to this story or look at that photo.

And it hits me. I realize I've been telling myself a lie. It's not true that I wasn't a good cadet and didn't belong at RMC. I was actually well suited to military college life: the antics, the camaraderie, and the skylarks. Under different circumstances, I would have done well academically and even athletically. My future life was a testament to this, scoring grades in the nineties during a three-year program to become a registered professional counsellor while continuing to work full-time at my corporate job, pushing my limits as a whitewater kayaker on the rivers of the Pacific Northwest, skiing off-piste bowls at Whistler, and offshore sailing to the South Pacific during a thirteen-month sabbatical from work. I lean back in my chair and watch Rick on his ladder in the woods. A warm wind blows through my memories and I am not sure if I have ever been so happy. We had a lot of fun at RMC. I can say that now and really feel it. RMC did give me a fabulous start in life and set me up for interesting careers, but I have never been able to reconcile the good with the ugly.

The healing journey started in earnest during the fall of 2014. Unexpectedly, as part of the Class of 1984's thirtieth-reunion weekend, the first thirty-two women had been invited back to participate in the unveiling of a commemorative plaque to acknowledge the historic moment of our entry into RMC, a moment that had lasted four long, difficult years for me and, I'm guessing, for the other twenty women who had graduated alongside me.

The college had changed. The Frigate had been renovated, and my recruit room no longer existed. I had shed the old self of my college days, and the Frigate had done the same. The dining hall had changed, too. The walls on one side were blown out and an entire wing had been added to accommodate the expanded cadet population. The college now boasted twelve squadrons instead of eight, though I took little interest in the new squadron names or their dorms. The present RMC cadets had fobs for entering buildings, and there were electronic monitors for announcements in the dining hall. Cadets wore a mishmash of unrecognizable uniforms, mostly bagged-out looking combats, and they even carried knapsacks. They emailed. Texted. Tweeted.

But one thing seemed to have remained constant. On Friday afternoon I followed the Frigate recruits from the Class of 2018 as they ran the obstacle course. A fourth-year female cadet from my old squadron stood by my side as we cheered the recruits scaling a twenty-foot-high military cargo net.

I asked her, "How are the guys with you?"

"Okay. I'm one of the guys," she said confidently.

"Yeah. I thought I was one of the guys, too."

She turned and faced me. "But weren't you?"

"Not really. I wanted to be. I tried hard. But they never really let me. Not completely. Not in real life after RMC either," I admitted.

"Real life. That's funny."

I tried another tack at my question. "Have you ever had any trouble with the guys?"

"What kind of trouble?" she asked.

"I've been reading in the media about the military rape culture. I've heard quite a few of the cases were reported by female RMC cadets."

"I've never been raped."

"I wasn't either. I know of one person from my time at the college who was raped, but she only told me about it years later."

"I know a few. It's the friends you have to watch out for," she said. Our eyes met.

"What do you mean?"

"It's the friends who rape. You'd think it would be the mean ones or the women haters. They might, too, but the friends are the ones that can destroy a person," she said. My face must have registered my shock. "Yeah. It's not a very nice story. But I've already said too much. I really should keep up."

I watched her run away and thought about regrets: saying too much, not saying anything, the secrets of RMC, the secrets of my family. My mother had died seven years earlier, failing to ever get what she wanted from life, what she thought she needed from me or felt was her due. I'd stood over her deathbed sobbing with regret. We had never figured it out, never connected in a healthy way. My dad died three years after her.

We're taught to expect unconditional love from our parents, but I had always felt like that was what was demanded of me. I felt like I had to earn my place, earn my right to be in the family; I felt like I was being watched and judged and graded. Even after I exposed the reality of my childhood experience to my entire family, I was expected to pretend that what had happened with Robert and my mother hadn't been damaging — that my abuse hadn't scarred me in ways that I am still trying to unravel and heal — and that I was the one with a problem. The shame of what had happened was thrust upon me, like I was causing trouble by asking them to look where they refused to go.

Eventually, I had to concede that my family would never see the situation my way. And I discovered that I couldn't play along in my old role as the scapegoat. I wouldn't do that to myself any longer. I finally walked away, not knowing how to live without family. In time, I've learned to stand not knowing. To thrive in it even. This seemed impossible to imagine in the early painful days, but my sadness and grief didn't kill me, and a new paradigm for family — made of chosen, loyal friends and a loving husband — filled the empty space left within me.

The unveiling ceremony was quiet and dignified and involved only the Class of 1984 with the RMC commandant, Brigadier General Al Meinzinger, and the principal, Dr. Harry Kowal, a classmate from the Class of 1984 and main orchestrator of the plaque, presiding over the presentation. Seventeen women — a handful of whom had not graduated — of the first thirty-two female cadets were in attendance, along with over one hundred of our male classmates. Tea followed immediately afterward. Those of us who had been a part of those first four years and were able, or cared enough, to attend the reunion chatted quietly amongst ourselves. We took photos together in front of the plaque before regrouping outside on the red bleachers to watch the first-year badging ceremony parade.

Nearly three hours later, the commandant gave the final speech to close the parade. He mentioned notable attendees, with special pride and emphasis on the graduating Class of 1979 and their classmate in attendance: the current chief of defence staff, the Canadian Armed Forces' most senior military officer, General Tom Lawson. Lawson would, the following spring, reportedly comment, in response to Madame Marie Deschamp's scathing report on the toxic and sexualized environment of the CAF, that "men are just wired that way." General Meinzinger did not mention the plaque presentation or that our class — and the first women to ever attend RMC — were sitting in the bleachers.

Throughout the reunion weekend, we told stories from our RMC days. A classmate told a story that perhaps best exemplifies the problems the women experienced that none of us were able to talk about, or address, while we were cadets. Referring to the man involved, my classmate called it "his little joke." At the time of the story, she was the most successful female cadet in our year.

"It happened in winter term of fourth year, when I had four bars and was living in Wing HQ in Fort LaSalle. One night, toward the end of study hours, General Pratt showed up at my door. He was wearing dressy casual clothes, with that regimental ascot of his, and seemed quite formal. I felt really uncomfortable, but what can you say when the commandant wants to come into your room?"

"All you can say is 'Yes, sir.'"

She nodded. "Exactly. He came in, closed the door, and then asked me something about uniforms, but I couldn't make any sense of our conversation or what he was doing in my room with the door closed."

"Was he drunk?"

"No, I don't think so," she said.

"Did anything happen?" I asked. "Like anything ... weird?" I flashed back to the sight of him in his tighty-whities.

"He talked to me for about ten minutes," she said. "When the other HQ guys started making noise and gathering in the hall for kye, he went to the door." She paused.

"So what happened?" I asked.

"Well, this is it," she continued angrily. "He said good night, opened the door, looked over at the guys, hitched up his pants, and said loudly to them, 'She was good.' Then he walked away."

"What the fuck? What did the guys do?"

"They just stood there looking extremely embarrassed."

"Did anyone say anything?" I asked.

"No, I just closed the door. And then I cried," she said with tears in her eyes. "How could he do that to me? I had worked so hard and had been a really good cadet. I was getting honours in commerce and doing well in sports. I'd earned four bars. He stole my credibility."

The final kick in the gut came when she received an obscene phone call from General Pratt during the fall after graduation while she was working as a junior officer in her first posting. She never formally reported either incident.

Her story deepened my reflection on my own. *It's time I told the real story*, I said to myself. I was there. I lived it. I had put this off for far too long. Perhaps such a story was too old and not of interest to anyone. Perhaps it shouldn't be told at all. But by *not* telling, I knew I would have done nothing to change things, and I was the one to tell it.

Virginia Woolf wrote the truism that "great bodies of people are never responsible for what they do." Taken in the context of sexism, these bodies are comprised of many individuals whose complicity, or passivity, emboldens others in the cultural systemic discrimination and who could have, or should have, risen up to be the force for change. It's a complicated charge. We all have cultural conditioning to overcome. So far, it remains culturally unnecessary to treat women as equals.

Before my Ex-Cadet Weekend was done, I had to face two fresh experiences of my own along these very lines.

The first experience came in the form of a letter. During the weekend, I paid a friendly visit to Bill Oliver. Bill had been a member of the athletics department staff when I was a cadet; now retired and nearly seventy-five, he was the editor of the weekly college newsletter, *e-Veritas*. When I mentioned my intention of writing about my experience at RMC, he surprised me with an unexpected disclosure.

"There's something I should give you. Something I want you to see. When you were a cadet, you probably don't remember that I went to Staff College. One of my assignments was to prepare a twenty-minute presentation on the history of the decision to admit women into the college. During my research, I found something in the ex-cadet archives that will interest you."

Bill fished in a drawer and pulled out a piece of paper from a file. He pressed a letter written on House of Commons letterhead into my hands.

I scanned the page quickly, conscious of Bill watching me. The letter, dated May 9, 1973, addressed to someone called Swatty, was short and to the point. It was an apology from a

Member of Parliament for comments made about RMC in the government caucus that had upset Swatty. One line jumped out at me: "Please tell the boys that I don't think they need to worry about girls being admitted to the College, and that it really is a tempest in a teapot." The letter was signed by MP George Hees.

"It's an official government letter," I said flatly. I stared at the faded photocopy, which had an old-fashioned receipt stamp in the top right-hand corner. I could hardly process what I had just read. Historically, Hees was known as the guy who had fought in the House of Commons for women to attend RMC. "Who's this Gordon Wotherspoon, or Swatty, guy?" I asked.

"He was an ex-cadet, a past president of the RMC ex-cadet club from 1958 to 1959. Lawyer — Osgoode Hall grad. Second World War hero. Brigadier general. Queen's Council. He was working at Eaton's at that time, trying to save the company. A real character."

"Okay," I said, uncertain what to do next.

"Go ahead, take it, take it," he said, encouraging me with a wave of his hand. "I'll catch up with you later this weekend."

Immediately upon returning to my hotel room, I sat on the edge of my bed, opened my computer in my lap, and clicked on my browser bookmark for Hansard notes for the House of Commons minutes in 1973. I'd been there before.

It didn't take long to review the exchange I had saved between George Hees, Member of Parliament for Prince Edward–Hastings, and the Honourable James Richardson, Minister of Defence. Yes, it was as I remembered it. The official record shows that Hees had argued in the House of Commons *for* the inclusion of women.

The bastard had been speaking out of two sides of his mouth. The George Hees who had *fought for us* was double-dealing. Hees hadn't really wanted women at RMC. He wanted it to look like he did. I set aside my computer, lay back on the feather duvet, flung my arms wide, and let the impact of his letter wash over me. The real George Hees had simply been lobbying for his own career, even apologizing within the alumni community when he met backlash.

"He's just another one of the pricks," I said aloud, staring up at the ceiling of my room. The familiar punch of anger winded me.

The second experience was a lunch date. Davis Jamieson, the cadet squadron training officer from recruit term in 1980, had invited me to meet with him before leaving Kingston. We hadn't seen each other since 1981, when he had graduated.

I admitted the truth. "I was surprised to hear from you. For some reason, I feel kind of nervous."

He cut to the chase. "It's nothing ominous. I wanted to clean up something with you that has bothered me for my whole career. From the moment we laid eyes on you, the recruit flight staff had the impression that you were strong and capable. The natural leader of A Flight, in fact," Davis said.

My throat constricted. "Holbrook was the natural leader."

"No, we saw him as a close second. The first night you arrived we had a meeting to review first impressions of each recruit. We, they, we ..." He stumbled. "That's when it was decided that we needed to break you."

"But why?"

"You were in the first group of women. It wasn't possible for you to be the best. We couldn't let that happen."

"Holy shit. I believed you that no matter how hard I tried, I was this loser who couldn't get it right." I fought the sting of tears in my sinuses.

"That's what we wanted you to believe. The more we did to you, the more you tried, the more troublesome it became to keep you down. You kept going. You gave us a run for our money," he said, chuckling.

I cackled in disbelief. "You had a fucking meeting. So why tell me now?"

"It's haunted me. I guess I finally got the courage. I don't know."

"So, was it you?" I flashed to his foot on my back during push-ups.

"Put it this way: I didn't do anything to stop it, so yes, I was part of it."

Davis gave me an apologetic look. "We dished it hard on you. You kept laughing. You kept trying. I saw a lot of myself in you. You were feisty. I respected you for that."

"Well, thank you for standing in and saying something now. When you've been hazed long enough and consistently enough, small gestures of validation can be a tremendous thrill," I said sarcastically.

He chuckled and exhaled a big sigh. "I should have stood up for you at RMC, for all the women. I feel like I need to apologize for my entire class. We were weak." He paused. "I mean, *weak* doesn't really sum it up. *The bet* sums up my class. Being in trusted positions of leadership and making a bet to see who could fuck the most female subordinates, that's just plain disgusting."

I kept my hands clenched in my lap under the table and didn't say anything.

He went on. "Their attitude was *let's fuck them all.* When that wasn't working out, because most of you weren't co-operating with that plan, they switched gears to punishing you for refusing. It should have been different."

"Yes. It could have been different," I said.

During my drive to the Ottawa airport, I began to understand what had happened back then. They were never going to let me succeed. Women had the appearance of equality, the concept was enshrined in law, but the vast majority of us in the trenches were having a radically different experience: a horrible, deeper expression of struggle based solely on our sex, one part heartbreaking, one part crazy making, and one part infuriating. Now I finally understood that the sooner I became honest with myself, the sooner I could be honest with others. It was time that I learned how to do all the things I had been taught not to do. It was time to start talking and telling my truth. I had needed to fail and falter in order to break myself free of the cultural sleepwalk that had entranced me. It was time for something different and daring.

Now here I stand, years later, laughing and smiling at good memories, my feet on firm ground and snow melting all around me. I finally get it. It was not about trying to change the world. It never had been. It was about changing *my* world. The purpose of delving into the pain of my past wasn't about going back there to fix it — it was about moving on. My scope of influence is right here, right now, right in front of me. I can stop trying to do the impossible and focus on what is possible: letting myself know what I know, feel what I feel, believe what I believe, want what I want, and be who I am.

It's not too late to live the life I would have chosen for myself from the beginning.

ACKNOWLEDGEMENTS

Very special thanks to Elizabeth Philips: my mentor, my editor, and my writing sponsor. This book may never have materialized, if not for her ongoing (and ongoing), loving support, deep caring, wicked sense of humour, and keen intuition about what needed to come out and what was still missing.

I'd like to thank the team at Dundurn Press for believing in my book, all their hard work, and their attentive guidance through each stage of the process, in particular Beth Bruder, Scott Fraser, Rachel Spence, Laura Boyle, Kathryn Bassett, Elham Ali, Heather McLeod, and Jenny McWha, as well as freelance proofreader Ashley Hisson. Special thanks to freelance editor Susan Fitzgerald for her thoughtful and thorough readings.

My gratitude for in-depth writing residency programs, especially Banff Centre and Sage Hill Writing, and for incredible faculty support from Trevor Herriot and Alison Pick, whose influence helped shape my writing experience and my memoir.

To the A Flight of our recruit term, honouring the fact that neither time, nor distance, nor lack of connection can severe the bonds we formed with each other: Andy Travill, Dave Carlson, Jocelyn Dionne, Francis Thatcher, Daniel Beauchamp, Jacques Beaudry, Chris Creber, Elizabeth Dyson, Hugh Ellis, Norm Foss, Roy Keeble, Michel Lacroix, Gilles

Lemieux, Linda Newton, Rick Pitre, Jackie Pothier, Mike Reid, Rob Russell, Paul Rutherford, Paul Schiebel, Kirk Shaw, Eric Strooper, Steve Williams.

And to the remaining women of the First Thirty-Two in recognition that each of us has a story to tell: Kathleen Beeman, Chris Best, Debbie Fowler, Cheryl Debellefeuille, Teresa Murphy, Rebecca Horne, Theresa Hutchings, Jo-Ann MacIsaac, Helen Davies, Brigitte Vachon, Sylvie Bonneau, Sue Raby, Sue Wigg, Dorothy Hector, Suzanne Nadorozny, Lorraine Kuzyk, Kathryn Haunts, Charmaine Bulger, Marie Thomson, Ann-Marie David, Sheila Walters, Brigitte Muehlgassner, Marnie Dunsmore, Julia Walsh, Laura Beare, Marie-Pierre Cloutier, Johanne Durand, and, sadly, in memoriam, Karen Ritchie.

There are others — Heather Haake, Cheri Mortenson-Wiebe, Jacquie Leggatt, Donna and Bill Kutzner, Meredith Aitken, Ingrid Hummelshoj, Catherine MacGregor, Amy Carruthers, Kai Scott, Vita Luthmers, Jen Stew, Sister Monica Guest, Robin MacDonald, Susan Juby, Mary Madsen, Paula Todd, Samantha Haywood, Ann Dowsett-Johnston, Leesa Dean, Bill Oliver, Colin Charette, Jeff Smith, Steven Gable, Harry Kowal, Dean Stewart, Colleen Driscoll, and Annie Strucel — who have all been there when I needed them, and for that I am grateful. Many people, too many to mention, gave love and encouragement, and for that I thank you.

To my constant doggie companions, Cash and Jackson, for your uncanny sixth sense of when I felt sad, for antics designed to make me laugh, and for always knowing when it was time to take me for a walk.

I can never adequately thank my husband, Rick Kutzner, who persuaded me to take the leap and tell my story, and who was always there to catch me. I love you.

Last, but not least of all, gratitude and blessings to the greatest teachers in my life: my family.

MORE GREAT BOOKS FROM DUNDURN

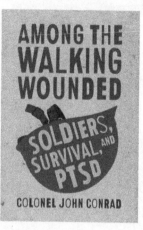

Among the Walking Wounded:
Soldiers, Survival, and PTSD
Colonel John Conrad

In the shadows of army life is a world where friends become monsters, where kindness twists into assault, and where self-loathing and despair become constant companions. Whether you know it by old names like "soldier's heart," "shell shock," or "combat fatigue," post-traumatic stress disorder has left deep and silent wounds throughout history in the ranks of fighting forces.

Among the Walking Wounded tells one veteran's experience of PTSD through an intimate personal account, as visceral as it is blunt. In a courageous story of descent and triumph, it tackles the stigma of PTSD head-on and brings an enduring message of struggle and hope for wounded Canadian veterans. This book is a must-read for anyone who cares about Canadian veterans and the dark war they face long after their combat service is ended.